To Reach Eternity

Edited and with a Biographical Introduction by George Hendrick

Foreword by William Styron

TO REACH Eternity

THE LETTERS OF JAMES JONES

Random House

New York

Grateful acknowledgment is made to Charles Scribner's
Sons for permission to reprint excerpts from *Editor
to Author: The Letters of Maxwell E. Perkins* by John
Hall Wheelock. Copyright 1950 Charles Scribner's Sons.
Copyright renewed 1978 by John Hall Wheelock. Reprinted
with the permission of Charles Scribner's Sons, an imprint
of Macmillan Publishing Company.

Library of Congress Cataloging-in-Publication Data
Jones, James, 1921–1977.
    To reach eternity.

    Includes index.
    1. Jones, James, 1921–1977—Correspondence.
2. Novelists, American—20th century—Correspondence. I. Hendrick, George. II. Title.
PS3560.O49Z48 1989   813'.54 [B] 88-43229
ISBN 0-394-57538-5

Manufactured in the United States of America
98765432
First Edition

BOOK DESIGN BY LILLY LANGOTSKY

FRONTISPIECE: Detail of Company "F," 27th Infantry, Schofield Barracks, Hawaii,
two weeks before Pearl Harbor. Photo by Schofield Studio. Courtesy of Gloria
Jones.

FOR GLORIA JONES

Foreword by William Styron

From Here to Eternity was published in 1951 at a time when I was in the process of completing my own first novel, I remember reading *Eternity* while I was living and writing in a country house in Rockland County, not far from New York City, and as has so often been the case with books that have made a large impression on me, I can recall the actual reading—the mood, the excitement, the surroundings. I remember the couch I lay on while reading, the room and the wallpaper, white curtains stirring and flowing in an indolent breeze, and cars that passed on the road outside. I think that perhaps I read portions of the book in other parts of the house but it is that couch I chiefly recollect, and myself sprawled on it, holding the hefty volume aloft in front of my eyes as I remained more or less transfixed through most of the waking hours of several days, in thrall to the story's power, its immediate narrative authority, its vigorously peopled barracks and barrooms, its gutsy humor, and its immense, harrowing sadness. The book was about the unknown world of the peacetime army. Even if I hadn't myself suffered some of the outrages of military life, I'm sure I would have recognized the book's stunning authenticity, its burly artistry, its sheer richness as life. A sense of permanence attached itself to the pages. This remarkable quality did not arise from Jones's language, for it was quickly apparent that the author was not a stylist, certainly not the stylist of refinement and nuance that we former students of creative writing classes had been led to emulate.

The genial rhythms and carefully wrought sentences that English majors had been encouraged to admire were not on display in *Eternity,* nor was the writing even vaguely experimental; it was so conventional as to be premodern. This was doubtless a blessing. For here was a writer whose urgent, blunt language with its off-key tonalities and hulking emphasis on adverbs wholly matched his subject matter. Jones's wretched outcasts and the narrative voice he had summoned to tell their tale had achieved a near-perfect synthesis. What also made the book a triumph was the characters Jones had fashioned—Prewitt, Warden, Maggio, the officers and their wives, the Honolulu whores, the brig rats, and all the rest. There were none of the wan, tentative effigies that had begun to populate the pages of postwar fiction during its brief span, but human beings of real size and arresting presence, believable and hard to forget. The language may have been coarse-grained but it had Dreiserian force, the people were as alive as those of Dostoevski. One other item, somewhat less significant but historic nonetheless, caught my attention, and this was how it had fallen to Jones to make the final breakthrough in terms of vernacular speech which writers—and readers—had been awaiting for hundreds of years. The dread *f*-word, among several others, so sedulously proscribed by the guardians of decency that even Norman Mailer in his admirable *The Naked and the Dead,* only three years before, had had to fudge the issue with an absurd pseudospelling, was now inscribed on the printed page in the speech pattern of those who normally spoke it. This alone was cause to celebrate, totally aside from the book's incandescent strengths.

It has been said that writers are fiercely jealous of each other. Kurt Vonnegut has observed that most writers display toward one another the edgy mistrust of bears. This may be true, but I do recall that in those years directly following World War II there seemed to be a moratorium on envy, and most of the young writers who were heirs to the Lost Generation developed, for a time at least, a camaraderie, or a reasonable compatibility, as if there were glory enough to go around for all the novelists about to try to fit themselves into Apollonian niches alongside those of the earlier masters. Many of us felt lucky to have survived the war, and the end of the war itself was a convenient point of reckoning, a moment to attempt comparisons. If the Armistice of 1918 had permitted prodigies such as Hemingway, Faulkner, and Fitzgerald to create their collective myth, wouldn't our own war produce a constellation just as passionately committed, as gifted and illustrious? It was a dumb notion (though it often cropped up in book chat), since we had overlooked the inevitable duplicity of history, which would never allow reassembly of those sovereign talents; we would have to settle for the elegant goal of becoming ourselves. But there was tremendous excitement about being a young writer in those days, and of taking part in a shared destiny. When I finished reading *From Here to Eternity* I felt no jealousy at all, only a desire to meet this man, just four years older than myself, who had inflicted on me such emotional turmoil in the act of telling me authentic truths about an underside of American life I barely knew existed. I wanted to talk to the writer who had dealt so eloquently with those lumpen warriors, and who had created scenes that tore at the guts. And then there was that face on the dust jacket, the same face that had glowered at me from bookstore displays and magazine covers and newspaper articles. Was there ever such a face, with its Beethovenesque brow and lantern jaw and stepped-upon-looking nose—a forbidding face until one realized that it only *seemed* to glower, since the eyes really projected a skeptical humor that softened the initial impression of rage. Although, as I later discovered, Jim Jones contained plenty of good clean American rage.

When I first met Jim, during the fall of that year, *Lie Down in Darkness* had recently been published, and we were both subjected to a considerable amount of not unpleasant lionization. Jim was a superlion; his book, after these many months, was still riding high on the best-seller lists. He had achieved that Nirvana which, if I may tell a secret, all writers privately cherish—critical acclaim *and* popular success. My book, on a much more modest level, had also done well critically and commercially, and in fact there was a period of several months during 1951 when still another first novel destined for some durability shared the best-seller list with Jim's and mine—*The Catcher in the Rye*. But Jim's celebrity status was extraordinary, and the nimbus of stardom that attended his presence as we tripped together from party to party around Manhattan was testimony to the appeal of those unforgettable looks but also to something deeper: the work itself, the power of a novel to stir the imagination of countless people as few books had in years. Moving about at night with Jim was like keeping company with a Roman emperor. Indeed I may have been a little envious, but the man had such raw magnetism and took such uncomplicated pleasure in his role as the midwestern hick who was now the cynosure of Big Town attention that I couldn't help being tickled by the commotion he caused, and his glory; he'd certainly earned it. It was a period when whiskey—great quantities of it—was the substance of choice. We did a prodigious amount of drinking, and there were always flocks of girls around, but I soon noticed that the hedonistic whirl had a way of winding down, usually late at night, when Jim, who had seemingly depthless stamina, would head for a secluded corner of a bar and begin speaking about books, about writers and writing. And we'd often talk long after the booze had been shut off and the morning light seeped through the windows.

Jim was serious about fiction in a way that now seems a little old-fashioned and ingenuous, with the novel for him in magisterial reign. He saw it as sacred mission, as icon, as Grail. Like so many American writers of distinction, Jim had not been granted the benison of a formal education, but like these dropouts he had done a vast amount of impassioned and eclectic reading; thus while there were gaps in his literary background that college boys like me had filled (the whole long curriculum of English and American poetry, for instance), he had absorbed an impressive amount of writing for a man whose schoolhouse had been at home or in a barracks. He had been, and still was, a hungry reader, and it was fascinating in those dawn sessions to hear this fellow built like a welterweight boxer (which he had occasionally been) speak in his gravelly drill sergeant's voice about a few of his more recherché loves—Virginia Woolf was one, I recall, Edith Wharton another. I didn't agree with Jim much of the time but I usually found that his tastes and his judgments were, on their own terms, gracefully discriminating and astute. He had stubborn prejudices, though—a blind spot, I thought, about Hemingway. He grudgingly allowed that Hemingway had possessed lyric power in his early stories, but most of his later work he deemed phony to the core. It filled him with that rage I mentioned, and I would watch in wonder as his face darkened with a scowl as grim as Caliban's, and he'd denounce Papa for a despicable fraud and poseur.

It sounded like overkill. Was this some irrational competitive obsession, I wondered, the insecure epigone putting down the master? But I soon realized that in analyzing his judgments about Hemingway I had to set purely literary considerations aside and understand that a fierce and by no means aimless, or envy-inspired, indignation energized Jim's view. Basically, it had to do with men at war. For Jim had been to war, he had been wounded on Guadalcanal, had seen men die, had been sickened and traumatized by the experience. Hemingway had been to war too, and had been wounded, but despite the gloss of misery and disenchantment that overlaid his work, Jim maintained, he was at heart a war lover, a macho contriver of romantic effects, and to all but the gullible and wishful the lie showed glaringly through the fabric of his books and in his life. He therefore had committed the artist's chief sin by betraying the truth. Jim's opinion of Hemingway, justifiable in its harshness or not, was less significant than what it revealed about his own view of existence, which at its most penetrating—as in *From Here to Eternity* and later in *The Pistol* and *The Thin Red Line*—was always seen through the soldier's eye, in a hallucination where the circumstances of military life cause men to behave mostly like beasts and where human dignity, while welcome and often redemptive, is not the general rule. Jones was among the best anatomists of warfare in our time, and in his bleak, extremely professional vision he continued to insist that war was a congenital and chronic illness from which we would never be fully delivered. War rarely ennobled men and usually degraded them; cowardice and heroism were both cel- luloid figments, generally interchangeable, and such grandeur as could be salvaged from the mess lay at best in pathos: in the haplessness of men's mental and physical suffering. Living or dying in war had nothing to do with valor, it had to do with luck. Jim had endured very nearly the worst; he had seen death face to face. At least partially as a result of this he was quite secure in his masculinity and better able than anyone else I've known to detect musclebound pretense, empty bravado. It's fortunate that he did not live to witness Rambo, or our high- level infatuation with military violence. It would have brought out the assassin in him.

I went to Europe soon after this and was married, and Jim and I were not in close contact for several years. When we got together again, in New York during the waning 1950s, he too was married, and it was his turn to shove off for Europe, where he settled in Paris, and where he and Gloria remained for the better part of the rest of his life. We saw each other on his frequent trips to the United States, but my visits to Paris were even more frequent during the next fifteen years or so, and it is Paris, nearly always Paris, where I locate Jim when I conjure him up in memory. Year in and year out—sometimes with my wife, Rose, sometimes alone—I came to roost in the Joneses' marvelous lodgings overlooking the Seine, often freeloading (à l'anglaise, observed Gloria, who took a dim view of the British) so long that I acquired the status of a semipermanent guest. My clearest and still most splendid image is that of the huge vaulted living room and the ceiling-high doors that gave out onto the river with its hypnotic, incessant flow of barge traffic moving eastward past the stately ecclesiastic rump of Notre Dame. The room was lined with books, and an entire wall was dominated by the nearly one hundred thickly hulking, drably bound volumes of the official United States government history of the Civil War. The very thought of shipping that library across the

Atlantic was numbing. What Jim sometimes called Our Great Fraternal Massacre was his enduring preoccupation, and he had an immense store of knowledge about its politics, strategies, and battles. Somehow in the lofty room the dour Victorian tomes didn't really obtrude, yet they were a vaguely spectral presence and always reminded me how exquisitely *American* Jim was destined to remain during years in Paris. War and its surreal lunacy would be his central obsession to the end, and would also be that aspect of human experience he wrote best about.

Into this beautiful room with its flood of pastel Parisian light, with its sound of Dave Brubeck or Brahms, there would come during the sixties and early seventies a throng of admirable and infamous characters, ordinary and glamorous and weird people—writers and painters and movie stars, starving Algerian poets, drug addicts, Ivy League scholars, junketing United States senators, thieves, jockeys, restaurateurs, big names from the American media (fidgety and morose in their sudden vacuum of anonymity), tycoons and paupers. It was said that even a couple of Japanese tourists made their confused way there, en route to the Louvre. No domicile ever attracted such a steady stream of visitors, no hosts ever extended uncomplainingly so much largess to the deserving and the worthless alike. It was not a rowdy place—Jim was too soldierly to fail to maintain reasonable decorum—but like the Abbey of Thélème of Rabelais, in which visitors were politely bidden to do what they liked, guests in the house at 10, Quai d'Orléans were phenomenally relaxed, sometimes to the extent of causing the Joneses to be victimized by the very waifs they had befriended. A great deal of antique silver disappeared over the years, and someone quite close to Jim once told me they reckoned he had lost tens of thousands of dollars in bad debts to smooth white-collar panhandlers. If generosity can be a benign form of pathology, Jim and Gloria were afflicted by it, and their trustingness extended to their most disreputable servants, who were constantly ripping them off. One, an insolent Pakistani houseman whom Gloria had longed to fire but had hesitated to do so out of tenderheartedness, brought her finally to her senses when she glimpsed him one evening across the floor of a tony nightclub, bewigged and stunningly garbed in one of her newly bought Dior gowns. Episodes like that were commonplace *chez* Jones in the tumultuous sixties.

There were literary journalists of that period who enjoyed pointing to a certain decadence in the Joneses' life-style and wrote reproachful monographs about the way that Jim and Gloria (now parents of two children) comported themselves: dinners at Maxime's, after-dinner with the fat squabs at hangouts like Castel's, vacations in Deauville and Biarritz, yachting in Greece, the races at Longchamps, the oiled and pampered sloth of Americans in moneyed exile. Much the same had been written about Fitzgerald and Hemingway. The tortured puritanism that causes Americans to mistrust their serious artists and writers, and regards it as appropriate when they are underpaid, evokes even greater mistrust when they are paid rather well and, to boot, hobnob with the Europeans. Material success is still not easily forgiven in a country that ignored Poe and abandoned Melville. There was also the complaint that in moving to France for such a long sojourn Jim Jones had cut off his roots, thus depriving himself of the rich fodder of American experience necessary to produce worthwhile work. But this would seem to be a hollow objection, quite aside from the kind of judgmental chauvinism it expresses. Most writers have stored up, by their mid-twenties, the emotional and intellectual baggage that will supply the needs of their future work, and the various environments into which they settle, while obviously not negligible as sources of material and stimulation, don't really count for all that much. Jim wrote some exceedingly inferior work during his Paris years. *Go to the Widow-Maker*, which dealt mainly with underwater adventure—a chaotic novel of immeasurable length, filled with plywood characters, implausible dialogue, and thick wedges of plain atrocious writing—spun me into despondency when I read it. There were, to be sure, some spectacular underwater scenes and mo-

ments of descriptive power almost like the Jones of *Eternity*.
But in general the work was a disappointment, lacking both
grace and cohesion.

Among the distressing things about it was its coming in the
wake of *The Thin Red Line*, a novel of major dimensions whose
rigorous integrity and disciplined art allowed Jim once again
to exploit the military world he knew so well. Telling the story
of GIs in combat in the Pacific, it is squarely in the gritty,
no-holds-barred tradition of American realism, a genre that
even in 1962, when the book was published, would have seemed
oafishly out-of-date had it not been for Jim's mastery of the
narrative and his grasp of the sun-baked milieu of bloody island
warfare, which exerted such a compelling hold on the reader
that he seemed to breathe new life into the form. Romain Gary
had commented about the book: "It is essentially an epic love
poem about the human predicament and like all great books it
leaves one with a feeling of wonder and hope." The rhapsodic
note is really not all that overblown; upon rereading, *The Thin
Red Line* stands up remarkably well, one of the best novels
written about American fighting men in combat. Comparing
it, however, with *Go to the Widow-Maker* produced a depressing sense of retrogression and loss. It was like watching a
superb diver who, after producing a triple somersault of cham-
pionship caliber, leaps from the board again and splatters himself all over an empty pool. Jim's nettled response to my
hesitantly negative criticism, set down in one of his letters in
this volume, makes me glad that I never expressed my real
feelings or my actual chagrin; he might have wanted to strangle
me.

But it is important to point out that although *Go to the
Widow-Maker* was written in Paris, so was *The Thin Red Line*.
This would strongly suggest that the iniquitous life that Jim
Jones had reputedly led in Paris, the years of complacent and
unengaged exile, bore little relation to his work, and that if he
had stayed at home, the motivations that impelled him in a
particular literary direction, and that shaped his creative com-

mitments, would probably have remained much the same. Jim loved the good life. He would have richly enjoyed himself anywhere and would have, as always, worked like hell. But a common failing of many writers is that they often choose their themes and address their subject matter as poorly as they often choose wives or houses. What is really significant is that while a book like *Go to the Widow-Maker* represents one of those misshapen artifacts that virtually every good writer, in the sad and lonely misguidedness of his calling, comes up with sooner or later, *The Thin Red Line* is a brilliant example of what happens when a novelist summons strength from the deepest wellsprings of his inspiration. In this book, along with *From Here to Eternity* and *Whistle*—a work of many powerful scenes that suffered from the fact that he was dying as he tried, unsuccessfully, to finish it—Jim obeyed his better instincts by attending to that forlorn figure whom in all the world he cared for most and understood better than any other writer alive: the common foot soldier, the grungy enlisted man.

Romain Gary wasn't too far off. There was a certain grandeur in Jones's vision of the soldier. Other writers had written of outcasts in a way that had rendered one godforsaken group or another into archetypes of suffering—Dickens's underworld, Zola's whores, Jean Genet's thieves, Steinbeck's migrant workers, Agee's white Southern sharecroppers, Richard Wright's black Southern immigrants, on and on—the list is honorable and long. Jones's soldiers were at the end of an ancestral line of fictional characters who are misfits, the misbegotten who always get the short end of the stick. But they never dissolved into a social or political blur. The individuality that he gave to his people, and the stature he endowed them with, came, I believe, from a clear-eyed view of their humanness, which included their ugliness or meanness. Sympathetic as he was to his enlisted men, he never lowered himself to the temptations of an agitprop that would limn them as mere victims. Many of his soldiers were creeps, others were outright swine, and there were enough good guys among the officers to be consonant with reality. At least part of the reason he was able to pull all this off so successfully, without illusions or sentimentality, was his sense of history, along with his familiarity with the chronicles of war that were embedded in world literature. He had read Thucydides early, and he once commented to me that no one could write well about warfare without him. He'd also linked his own emotions with those of Tolstoy's peasant soldiers, and could recite a substantial amount of *Henry V,* whose yeoman-warriors were right up his alley. But the shades of the departed with whom he most closely identified were the martyrs of the American Civil War. That pitiless and aching slaughter, which included some of his forebears, haunted him throughout his life and provided one of the chief goads to his imagination. To be a Civil War buff was not to be an admirer of the technology of battle, although campaign strategy fascinated him; it was to try to plumb the mystery and the folly of war itself.

In 1962, during one of his visits to America, I traveled with Jim to Washington. Among other things, an influential official with whom I was friendly and who was on President Kennedy's staff had invited the two of us to take a special tour of the White House. Oddly, for such a well-traveled person, Jim had never been to Washington, and the trip offered him a chance to visit the nearby battlefields. He had never seen any of the Civil War encampments. Jim went out to Antietam, in Maryland, after which we planned to go to the Lincoln Memorial before driving over to the White House. When he met me at our hotel, just after the Antietam visit, Jim was exceptionally somber. Something at the battlefield had resonated in a special troubling way within him; he seemed abstracted and out-of-sorts. It had been, he told me finally, a part of the battleground called the Bloody Lane that had so affected him when he'd seen it. He'd read so much about the sector and the engagement and had always wondered how the terrain would appear when he viewed it firsthand. A rather innocuous-looking place now, he said, a mere declivity in the landscape, sheltered by a few trees.

But there, almost exactly a century before, some of the most horrible carnage in the history of warfare had taken place, thousands of men on both sides dead within a few hours. The awful shambles was serene now, but the ghosts were still there, swarming; it had shaken him up.

Soon after this, at the Lincoln Memorial, I realized that the cavernous vault with its hushed and austere shadows, its soft footfalls and requiem whispers, might not have been the best place to take a man in such a delicate mood. Jim's face was set like a slab, his expression murky and aggrieved, as we stood on the marble reading the Gettysburg Address engraved against one lofty wall, slowly scanning those words of supreme magnanimity and conciliation and brotherhood dreamed by the fellow Illinoisian whom Jim had venerated, as almost everyone does, for transcendental reasons that needed not to be analyzed or explained in such a sacred hall. I suppose I was expecting the conventional response from Jim, the pious hum. But his reaction, soft-spoken, was loaded with savage bitterness, and for an instant it was hard to absorb. "It's just beautiful bullshit," he blurted. "They all died in vain. They all died in vain. And they always will!" His eyes were moist with fury and grief; we left abruptly, and it required some minutes of emotional readjustment before the storm had blown over and he regained his composure, apologizing quickly, then returning with good cheer and jokes to more normal concerns.

Many years went by before I happened to reflect on that day, and to consider this: that in the secret cellars of the White House, in whose corridors we were soon being shepherded around pleasantly, the ancient mischief was newly germinating. There were doubtless all sorts of precursory activities taking place which someday would confirm Jim's fierce prophecy: heavy cable traffic to Saigon, directives beefing up advisory and support groups, ominous memos on Diem and the Nhus, orders to units of the Green Berets. The shadow of Antietam, and of all those other blind upheavals, was falling on our own times. James Jones would be the last to be surprised.

CONTENTS

Biographical Introduction

James Ramon Jones was born on November 6, 1921, in Robinson, a small town in east-central Illinois. Oil was discovered on the Jones family farm, making Jones's grandfather wealthy. He moved into Robinson, studied law, and became a prominent member of the community. He lived in a southern-style mansion in this midwestern town with a southern air about it. He was a difficult, tempermental, sometimes violent man who insisted that his sons become professional men. James Jones's father, Dr. Ramon Jones, chose dentistry and set up a practice in Robinson. In 1908 he married Ada Blessing, a beautiful woman intent on maintaining the social position of the Joneses. Their first child, George W., called Jeff, was born in 1910, and Mary Ann, the third child, in 1925.

The depression which began in 1929 saw the end of the good life for the entire family. Grandfather Jones had invested heavily in Insull stock, and his fortune disappeared. Dr. Jones ruined his dental practice with his excessive drinking, and Mrs. Jones, a diabetic and grossly overweight, had lost her youthful beauty. She had also turned from her Presbyterian faith to Christian Science. In the biographical sketch Jones prepared for *Twentieth Century Authors,* he wrote of growing up "in an atmosphere of hot emotions and boiling recriminations covered with a thin but resilient skin of gentility."

When Jones was a junior in high school, Dr. Jones lost the family home, and the Joneses were forced to move to rented quarters. Jones saw first hand that social position was ephemeral. He speculated that this experience may have given him "a talent for seeing beneath the surface of lives and various social prestiges; certainly it gave me the desire to."

He had an active life during his childhood. He wrote his aunt Molly Haish on November 23, 1932, soon after his eleventh birthday: "I carry papers in the morning and then go out to school to work on my lessons. After school I play football till it's dark." He did not try to become a member of the football or basketball teams in high school, however, and did not develop his athletic abilities fully until he was an adult.

By the time he was graduated from high school in 1939 he had read a great deal, although unsystematically, and he had done well in his English courses when he was a freshman and junior. He was interested in literature and had discussed story ideas with his brother, Jeff, but there is no indication that he envisioned himself as a professional writer. There was no money for college, and Dr. Jones, who had served in World War I "and remembered it sentimentally," recommended that his son join the Army. With no other prospects before him, Jones agreed. First, though, he went to Findlay, Ohio, to visit Jeff and his wife and small son. There he took a construction job for the summer, but then he left Findlay and went on the bum. The war was beginning in Europe, and perhaps influenced by Ernest Hemingway's service with the Italian Army in World War I, he decided he could get into the fight sooner under a foreign flag. He hitchhiked to Canada and tried to join the Canadian Army but was turned down. He then returned to Robinson, and on November 10, 1939, he enlisted in the Army Air Corps.

Writing to his brother from Fort Slocum, New York, just weeks after he had entered the Air Corps, Jones vividly described the caste system in the military, his sexual frustrations and the lack of female companionship, his prowess as a gambler, the lure of a weekend spree, the promise of a leave to be spent with a supposedly well-to-do friend who could get him a date with the daughter of a Wall Street broker then in prison, and his confinement in the "clap" ward for observation. He

sketched the outline of a romantic but gritty novel, using details from military life and from his exploits the summer before
his enlistment. He was soon sent to Hawaii. He was dissatisfied
with the support services open to him—his poor eyesight
meant that he could not qualify as a pilot—and he transferred
to the Infantry, where he became both observer and participant
in that unique society of the prewar American Army.

Early in his military service he discovered the novels of
Thomas Wolfe, immediately recognized the similarity of their
lives, and decided he would become a writer himself. He sent
out stories and poems to popular magazines, but all these early
attempts to publish were unsuccessful. He was unsure of his
writing abilities and felt the need to find an "authority" to
verify his artistic talent.

The Jones family misfortunes intensified in the 1940s: Mrs.
Jones died in 1941 of congestive heart failure and complications
from her diabetes, and Dr. Jones committed suicide the following year. Jones himself was disillusioned by Army life, was
consistently unlucky or unsuccessful in love, and after the
attack on Pearl Harbor was afraid that he would be killed in
the war, his desire to be a writer unfulfilled.

Jones's worst fears almost came to be. On Guadalcanal he
killed a Japanese soldier in hand-to-hand combat, an incident
that haunted him for years; he was wounded in action, reinjured his weak ankle (originally injured when he was playing
football in Hawaii), and was finally evacuated to Kennedy
General Hospital in Memphis, Tennessee. After an operation
he recovered slowly but was given passes to go into Memphis,
then a booming wartime city, where he used booze and women
unsuccessfully to soothe his unsettled psychological state.

In six years of his early manhood Jones experienced the
events he reshaped into four of his best novels: *From Here to
Eternity, The Pistol, The Thin Red Line,* and *Whistle.* Using
many of the same characters—though he changed their names
from novel to novel—he depicted the peacetime Army, wartime in Hawaii, battles in the South Pacific, and wounded

veterans attempting to recover from their experiences. These four novels, taken together, are a remarkable achievement; they were, however, far in the future, and Jones had to undergo a long and painful apprenticeship before he became a successful novelist.

In November 1943 Jones was declared fit for duty. He had expected to be discharged from the Army; instead, he was reassigned to a new base in Kentucky. He went AWOL and returned to Robinson. He stayed with his uncle Charles and aunt Sadie Jones but did not tell them he was not on official leave. Jones was drinking heavily and in great psychological distress.

His aunt Sadie sought help for her nephew from an unconventional woman in the community, Lowney Handy. Lowney's father was the sheriff in the nearby town of Marshall. She had married Harry Handy, an engineering graduate of the University of Illinois, a member of a prominent family, and eventually the superintendent of the Ohio Oil Refinery in Robinson. The marriage had not been a success. Lowney told various stories to explain that failure. She reported that she contracted gonorrhea from Harry and, because of the operation she underwent during treatment, was unable to bear children. Whatever the truth of that story, the Handys did not have children, and though they continued to live in the same house, they went their own ways. Lowney had turned to mothering "misfits"—unmarried pregnant girls, troubled servicemen, ex-prisoners. She was forty years old when she met Jones for the first time, and he was seventeen years her junior. She was not beautiful, but she had a magnetic personality, used bawdy language, and had interests considered strange in Robinson: Theosophy, Oriental religions, and strong beliefs in irregular medical theories, such as fasting and the efficacy of enemas.

Lowney wrote fiction herself, and though she was never successful in publishing her stories, she recognized Jones's potential as a writer and was immediately interested in helping him. She became the authority he needed—someone who believed in his creative talent, believed that he would become a successful novelist. They soon became lovers.

Jones returned to his Army post, but he was a recalcitrant soldier and went AWOL two more times. He was finally confined to the psychiatric ward of the base hospital before being honorably discharged. He then moved into the home of Harry and Lowney Handy and continued work on a novel, *They Shall Inherit the Laughter,* which he had begun while he was still in the Army. He felt the need for additional education, went to New York City, enrolled in New York University, and, while studying there, submitted his novel to Maxwell Perkins at Scribner's. Perkins immediately became to Jones another "authority." Perkins recommended a complete revision of the manuscript; but he was encouraging, and Jones returned to Robinson to work with Lowney on the changes. Perkins was not satisfied with the revised version, but he found merit in Jones's proposal to do a novel about the peacetime Army. Jones then put *Laughter* aside and set to work on *From Here to Eternity.* He spent years of intense work on the novel.

Perkins died before *Eternity* was completed, but Jones found another authority at Scribner's, Burroughs Mitchell, who was to edit most of Jones's major works. Some of Jones's most probing letters are those to Perkins and Mitchell. He discussed the plots for his fiction, his artistic problems, and his personal views on literary matters and on fellow writers.

When *Eternity* was published in 1951, its reviews were as remarkable as its sales. The *New York Times* reviewer wrote: "This block-buster of a book . . . is raw and brutal and angry. . . . A mature achievement of impressive stature." The *Los Angeles Times* noted: "James Jones has written a tremendously compelling and compassionate story. The scope covers the full range of the human condition, man's fate and man's hope. It is a tribute to human dignity."

Jones enjoyed his new celebrity status, and he slowly and painfully moved away from Lowney's influence. He met Norman Mailer, William Styron, and other writers in New York; his relationship with Mailer was not without its difficulties, but his friendship with those novelists gave him new artistic perspectives. Lowney was jealous of his new associations, and her possessiveness helped bring about their final break. Jones still felt greatly indebted to Lowney, however, and he helped her with a long-held dream: founding a colony for writers. Her Colony was established in Marshall, Illinois, on the farm owned by Harry's mother, and Jones used his earnings from *Eternity* to subsidize it. The Colony received widespread publicity, partly because of Jones's fame and partly because of Lowney's method of teaching writing. She believed that young writers should begin by copying the works of authors she chose from her approved list, which included Ernest Hemingway, Thomas Wolfe, and Dashiell Hammett. Lowney controlled the diet, the recreation, and even the sexual lives of the Colonists. She was the warden of the almost-prison, and several of the inmates did write successful novels.

Jones was spending most of his time struggling with his next novel, *Some Came Running,* an ambitious naturalistic study. It, too, took years to complete. After it was finished, Jones went to New York to confer with his editors. He had become increasingly estranged from Lowney and chafed under her attempts to control him. He wanted a different life, a different companion. While he was in New York, he met the beautiful, high-spirited Gloria Mosolino, and they were married a few weeks after they met. He did not reveal to Gloria the exact nature of his relationship with Lowney.

Some Came Running was savaged by the critics. "If you like bad grammar," Edmund Fuller wrote in the *Chicago Sunday Tribune,* "it is there, as much in the narrative as in the dialogue. If you like the grossest promiscuity, the most callous adultery, aggressive vulgarity, shoddy and befuddled philosophy, 'Some Came Running' is your book." Fuller's comments were typical of the 1958 reviews, but Jones consistently defended the artistic merit of his second published novel, as several of the letters in this collection will show.

He and Gloria returned to Illinois and lived in the bachelor house Jones had built at great expense near the Colony grounds. After a few weeks the jealous Lowney attacked Gloria, and while Gloria was not injured, the frightened Joneses left Illinois, never to return. It was during their flight from Marshall that Gloria first learned that Lowney had been Jones's mistress. Though both Joneses were under great stress during those first days after they left Illinois, they did save their marriage. They first settled in New York, where he wrote *The Pistol*, and then in Paris, where they lived from 1958 to 1974. Gloria gave Jones a stable home life he had never had before. He was an attentive father and spent much time with their two children, Kaylie and Jamie. An outgoing, fun-filled person, Gloria also helped him develop a satisfying social life, something sadly missing during his Army career and in the long years he spent writing in eastern Illinois.

In Paris he completed work on one of his greatest achievements, *The Thin Red Line.* He drew on his European experiences in two critically misunderstood novels, *The Merry Month of May* and *A Touch of Danger.* Another novel, *Go to the Widow-Maker,* dealt, perhaps too obviously, with Jones-Lowney-Harry-Gloria, but it exorcised Lowney forever from his life. That novel was attacked by critics much as *Some Came Running* had been, but his collection of short stories, *The Ice-Cream Headache,* received good notices. Despite the unfavorable critical reviews of many of his books, they were popular successes.

In 1974 the Joneses decided to return to the United States; he was suffering from congestive heart failure and wanted to be in his native country again, and he and Gloria wanted their children to attend American schools. Besides, living in Paris had become increasingly expensive. He taught for a year at Florida International University in Miami, and then they settled in a renovated farmhouse in Sagaponack, on Long Island, New York. During the last years of his life Jones completed some of his most impressive work: *Viet Journal, WW II,* and *Whistle.* In his last months he was in and out of hospitals frequently, but he doggedly kept working on *Whistle*, dictating the final section from his hospital bed just days before his death on May 9, 1977.

During his life Jones was charged by some critics with selling out for commercial success, with having "a commonplace mind," "an antiquated approach to fiction," and a slovenly style. On the other hand, recent evaluations have agreed with James Giles, who wrote in *James Jones* that the war trilogy (*From Here to Eternity*, *The Thin Red Line*, and *Whistle*) "is our most important fictional treatment of U.S. involvement in World War II." Even Jones's novels which were most attacked when they were first published—*Some Came Running* and *Go to the Widow-Maker*—are being favorably reevaluated. Willie Morris in *James Jones: A Friendship* and George Garrett in *James Jones* have pointed out the artistic virtues of Jones's critically maligned works. The reassessment of Jones is sure to continue, but Garrett's conclusion is pertinent and likely to be repeated in various ways in the years to come: "Boy and man, Jones never lost his energetic interest, his continual curiosity, the freshness of his vision. It was these qualities, coupled with the rigor of his integrity, which defined the character of his lifework." Jones's letters give us insight into his life and artistic vision and the exercise of his talent. He stated frankly and clearly his driving ambition in a letter to his brother in 1942: "I would like to leave books behind me to let people know that I have lived. I'd like to think that people would read them avidly, as I have read so many and would feel the sadness and frustration and joy and love I tried to put in them, that people would think about that guy James Jones and wish they had known the guy who could write like that." Jones's goal as a writer was clear: He wanted to have a permanent place in American letters. "I write," he told a *Newsweek* interviewer, "to reach eternity."

GEORGE HENDRICK

Editorial Matters

James Jones wrote long novels, he wrote long letters, and he wrote hundreds of letters. In order to include as many letters as possible, some have been edited to eliminate repetition and irrelevant material. In every case, I have noted omissions by the use of ellipses. Jones himself almost never used ellipses, and when they occur in the letters, they indicate that words, a sentence, or a paragraph or paragraphs have been omitted. In a few cases, names of living people have been replaced with ellipses. Jones wrote a huge number of business letters, but I have excluded all of these from this collection.

In his early letters Jones consistently misspelled such words as *received, sergeant, liquor, volunteer,* and *disciple.* I have silently corrected those spellings and also typographical errors. Punctuation has been silently omitted or added in order to aid the reader. I have, however, maintained his nonstandard spellings such as *enuf, thot, nite, rite, biografy.* At one period of his life, when he was writing *Some Came Running,* Jones consciously omitted apostrophes, and I have followed his style. He was not consistent in his use of titles: At times he put the titles of short stories in quotation marks and at other times he used all caps. Titles of novels were sometimes underscored, sometimes not, or sometimes all in caps. I have italicized book, magazine, newspaper, and movie titles, and placed titles of short stories in quotes. Moreover, Jones's signature to letters has been italicized.

Jones's letters are to be found in only a few depositories. I have, at the end of each letter, indicated where the letter is to located, using the following code:

Boston University Library	B
Houghton Library, Harvard University	H
Fales Library, Elmer Holmes Bobst Library,	
New York University	N
University of Oregon Library	O
Princeton University Library	P
Archives, Sangamon State University	S
Harry Ransom Humanities Research Center,	
University of Texas at Austin	T
Beinecke Library, Yale University	Y

I have also used the following abbreviations to give information about letters:

Autograph letter signed	ALS
Autograph letter (not signed)	AL
Typed letter signed	TLS
Typed letter (not signed)	TL
Carbon copy	C

Thus P/TL/C would indicate the letter is at Princeton, that it was typed, and that it was a carbon.

I have, whenever possible, used the ribbon copies of letters (Jones usually typed his letters), but in many cases I have had to use carbons. My comparison of ribbon and carbon copies of the same letter indicates that he almost always transferred his corrections to the carbon copy.

I have not wanted to overburden the text with identifications. Well-known people, places, and events are not identified, but the not-so-obvious are.

To provide continuity, I have supplied some headnotes, a few of which are extensive, to give information not found in letters. For biographical details used in the headnotes and footnotes I am especially indebted to Gloria Jones, who has patiently answered my many questions, and to Frank

MacShane's *Into Eternity: The Life of James Jones,* Willie Morris's *James Jones: A Friendship,* James R. Giles's *James Jones,* George Garrett's *James Jones,* Burroughs Mitchell's *The Education of an Editor,* J. Michael Lennon's "Glimpses: James Jones, 1921–1977" in the summer 1987 issue (no. 103) of *The Paris Review,* Hilary Mills's *Mailer: A Biography,* and Peter Manso's *Mailer: His Life and Times.* I am also greatly indebted to Lucy Kroll and Robert Loomis for their professional advice and to Willene and Sarah Hendrick for their help.

Librarians at Boston University; the Houghton Library, Harvard University; the Fales Library, Elmer Holmes Bobst Library, New York University; University of Oregon; Sangamon State University; Harry Ransom Humanities Research Center, University of Texas at Austin; the Beinecke Library, Yale University; the University of Illinois at Urbana-Champaign; Princeton Univeristy; and Pan American University were helpful in innumerable ways.

The following gave me permission to quote from materials under their supervision: Mugar Memorial Library, Boston University; the Houghton Library, Harvard University; the Estate of James Jones; Kenneth Spencer Research Library, University of Kansas; Fales Library, New York University; Special Collections, University of Oregon Library; Princeton University Library; the Archives, Sangamon State University; Charles Scribner's Sons; Harry Ransom Humanities Research Center, the University of Texas at Austin; Collection of American Literature, Beinecke Rare Book and Manuscript Library, Yale University.

The Army Years,

1939-1944

*A*fter he enlisted, Jones kept in touch with his older brother, who had studied journalism at Northwestern and was interested in writing. These early letters to Jeff Jones were long and detailed, in many ways exercises of a young man with ambitions to become a writer.

TO JEFF JONES

[FORT SLOCUM, NEW YORK]
THURSDAY NITE [CA. EARLY DECEMBER]
1939

Dear Jeff:

I received your letter yesterday while I was working in the Post Exchange. I'm terribly sorry if I offended you by only sending a card, but you spoiled me during my stay in Findlay: I got so used to typing my letters that now, when I try to write them, by the time I get one sentence written, I forget what I'm going to say in the next one. Besides that, my hand writing is so atrocious that it is next to impossible to read. Last nite I tried to print one. Having only 3/4 of a page written at the end of an hour, I quit and went to the show. I guess you'll just have to bear with me.

I think the idea of writing once a week is bully. The only ones I really miss are you & Dave [Jeff's son]. So if I can keep in touch with you and follow Davy's exploits by proxy, I'll really enjoy it. (I'm still waiting for that picture of him in his playsuit. Will you send it?) There are so many things I've filed away in my memory to tell you that I don't know where to start. I got a good laugh out of your inquiry as to my getting any stuff here! Fort Slocum is built on an island off the city of

New Rochelle. I've been in quarantine up to now, and the only females I've seen have been at least 100 yds. off, on the other side of the parade-ground, with the exception of the theatre. There the officers' children, who are the only girls on the island, sit in the balcony. We common herd sit in the "pit" as the rabble did in Shakespeare's day also. We are not allowed to associate with the officers' children at all. I was told of a fella who was running around with an officer's daughter here about a year ago, and he laid her. She had a baby, and he is still serving his year in the guardhouse. When he gets out, he'll get a D.D. [dishonorable discharge]. Then he'll have to marry her. Another boy was walking down a walk and a little girl skating past him fell down. He picked her up. The girl thanked him, but the sergeant who saw him got him a month in the "little red schoolhouse."

You ask how I like the Army. Well it isn't so bad. The food here is terrible. As an example, on Thanksgiving we had for breakfast: a small sample box of cereal; a half-pint of milk (the only milk we get all day); a small slab of butter (no seconds); and a stomach-turning dish rather aptly described by the sol-dier's word for it: shit on a shingle. It is composed of a rubbery piece of toast covered with a thick gravy composed of the leavings of yesterday's dinner. If I didn't have my dice I don't know what I'd do. Dad gave me three bucks when I left Robinson. By the time I reached Rantoul, it had swelled to $7. After four days at Chanute Field, I left for New York with $18, not counting what I'd spent, which was quite a bit. Since then my bankroll has never been less than $6 and as high as $27. With that money I haven't needed to draw any canteen checks, so my pay will be that much higher. Also, I can buy my meals at the Post Restaurant, when the food is too rotten to stomach. I can engage in the sports at the Y.M.C.A. building where in spite of their undoubted self-sacrifice for the soldier's soul, one has to pay to do *anything*.

For a week I was interned in the hospital. There was some-thing wrong with my kidneys. I'll tell you all about it farther down. The point is, while I was there I ran [my] wad up from $12 to $23. We had to have something to do, so we started a black-jack game, for nickels. Naturally, the stakes kept getting higher. By the time I left, I had just about broke everybody in my ward. There was a sergeant in the same ward with a cold. Usually, non-commissioned officers don't associate with us casuals. But there in the hospital his stripes didn't count so much. He sat in our black-jack game, and during the week he and I got quite chummy. The result was I've been invited to go on a binge with him and a couple of his buddies this week end. We ought to have a lot of fun. We'll go into New York and raise bloody hell.

About my being in the hospital: While at Rantoul, I began to notice a discharge from my peter. When I'd take a leak, it would burn like hell. I was afraid I'd caught gonorrhea. I waited until I got here, so that if I had, no one I knew would find out about it. The second day I was here I went on sick call and got examined. They took a microscopic test of the discharge and my urine. They couldn't find any gonorrhea germs, but as the symptoms were the same, I was put under observation. While under observation I had a chance to observe the men who had the "clap" as it is called in the army, and it gave me a good idea for our book. I don't know whether I can explain it or not. It hinges on the attitude those guys in the clap ward have toward themselves and the disease. It's all a big joke to them. They stand around a long sink and treat themselves with solutions. They laugh about it and make wise-cracks about themselves. While I was being examined, I didn't know whether or not I had it or not. I was so humiliated and ashamed at the aspect of being in that ward with those guys.

Here is the idea for the plot. Take just as you figured it from the start. Have Bob go out on the bum like we agreed. While on the road Bob realizes that he will never be content to be a bum. He gets a job on a steel gang building a sky scraper in, say, Denver. He works there three weeks. During that time he sees three men fall to their deaths. He decides that he can't have a future in this either. Eventually his turn will come and he'll slip. He quits and goes on the bum again. To try to find himself a place in this world of the money-mad, he gets a job as apprentice brick layer. After seeing more men die, he quits the job, too. In desperation he joins the army, hoping to make it his profession. His sensitive nature can't stand being herded around like cattle; treated like scum; being ridden by the noncoms. He serves his enlistment and goes out on the bum again. After trying to get settled, with less luck than before, he finally enlists again. During his second enlistment, he contracts gonorrhea from a girl he uses to try and forget his remorse. He is interned in the hospital at his post. He can't understand the attitude of the chaps who are in the "clap" ward with him. They joke and laugh about it as if it were just a cold. He is terribly ashamed of his position. He considers himself unclean. The body that he had always been so proud of, and that he had reveled in the beauty of, is rotten now, to the core. Finally, in shame and mortification, he jumps thru the window next [to] his bed in the "clap" ward. The fall that he had quit so many jobs on account of finally came about voluntarily. He welcomed it as a relief, a refuge, and rest.

That will give you some idea of what I think of the army. I, who am better bred than any of these moronic sergeants, am ordered around by them as if I were a robot, constructed to do their bidding. But I can see their point of view. Nine out of every ten men in this army have no more brains than a three year old. The only way they can learn the manual and the drill commands is by constant repetitions. It is pounded into their skulls until it is enveloped by the subconscious mind. The tenth man cannot be excepted. He must be treated the same as the others, even if in time he becomes like them.

But things are not all bad. My bunkmate (we sleep one over the other) is a chap named Hill. His father had quite a bit of money when he died. He lives in Montclair, N.J., a suburb of New York. He has invited [me] to spend a weekend leave with him at his mother's house in the country. He has promised to get me a date with Madaline Whitney, daughter of the Whitney recently convicted of embezzlement.[1] The family is still very well to do. There will be plenty of good liquor and women at "Frauensee" (I don't know what the name means). He joined the Air Corps to try and get into Randolph Field. There is another lad named Harrison, who is going to Hawaii like us, whom I run around with. He is a fine chap. He and I were talking the other day, and he told me he was going to save half of his pay each month, and at the end of his enlistment, take a trip around the world, on the bum. I fell in with his plan right away, as you might imagine. We're both going to Hickam Field, so we'll be able to keep in touch with each other. We'll come home first and then meet and start for California. From there ship out on a steamer to wherever it takes us.

I won the [P]ing-[P]ong tournament held for the Casuals (those who are here temporarily). I'm working in the Post Exchange heaving beer kegs and cases of pop. I get all the stuff I want to eat while I'm working. Also, it ought to make a man of me.

Write me soon and tell me what you think of my plot. If I can get hold of a typewriter, I'll write you all the details of army life, and also that stuff about the "clap" ward. If you can, I wish you'd send my chessmen and the book about chess that is there, also. Don't forget to send Dave's picture in that playsuit of his.

Give my love to Sally [Jeff's wife] and kiss Dave for me. You don't know how much I miss him.

Jim.

---

[1]According to *Who Was Who in America*, Richard Whitney's daughters were named Nancy and Alice. Perhaps Hill or Jones misremembered Ms. Whitney's name or Hill was exaggerating his social position, but it is not now possible to determine the facts in this matter. In *From Here to Eternity* Robert E. Lee Prewitt had an affair with a society girl who gave him the clap. The cure in the GU Clinic was painful, "with lots of long-handled barbs and cutters."

P.S. *Remember once a week.* If you only knew what a task it is for me to write like this.

P.P.S. Have you read *The Way of a Transgressor* by Negley Farson?[2]

Y/ALS

---

[2] The title of this long-forgotten book would suggest it is a religious novel, but it is in fact an account of the adventures of a foreign correspondent.

James Jones stayed at Fort Slocum only a few weeks, and on December 18, 1939, he sailed to Hawaii by way of the Panama Canal and California, where he received a five-day pass and visited his mother's sister, Molly Haish, in Los Angeles. On his way back to Fort Mason, from which the troopship would sail on to Hawaii, he met a girl who asked him to visit her. "I'll keep in touch with her," he wrote Jeff on February 1, 1940, "and if she isn't married by the time I get back to the States, I'll look her up." Perhaps because it was expected of him, perhaps because he had a romantic imagination, in the months to follow Jones was to allude often to his amatory exploits. He wrote his aunt Molly in an undated letter soon after his arrival in Hawaii about a Chinese girl he met: "I know she loves me. Her eyes shine so when I kiss her. Her hair is as black as her eyes, if possible. It has a soft fragrance that makes my heart pound in my ears like a native drum." This passage has an air of fantasy about it.

His military life was far from any romantic view he may originally have had of it. His eyesight was poor, and he would never be able to qualify as a pilot. The Air Corps support units were not held in high repute and were badly treated. It was during this particularly unhappy time of his life, while he was at Hickam Field, that he made a discovery that was to be a turning point in his life. As he recounted it in Twentieth Century Authors: *"I stumbled upon the works of Thomas Wolfe, and his home life seemed so similar to my own, his feelings about himself so similar to mine about myself, that I realized I had been a writer all my life without knowing it or having written."*

In September 1940 he transferred to the Infantry, a branch of military service he considered more manly than the Air Corps. He went through basic training again and was stationed at Schofield Barracks, which he was to describe graphically in From Here to Eternity.

His duties in the guardroom and then as a waiter in the officers' club were not demanding, and he had time for his writing. He began to send stories and poems to popular magazines. All his submissions were rejected, but he worked with determination at his writing, which helped mitigate his loneliness.

He seldom wrote to his parents. On March 3, 1941, his father sent him an airmail letter informing him of his mother's death; on the outside of the envelope his father wrote: "Bad news, Jim." In that letter Jones learned that his mother had died of complications from congestive heart failure and diabetes.

Jones's reaction to this death—going on a three-day drunk and refusing to expose his feelings directly—should be viewed in light of the difficulties between mother and son. Mrs. Jones was ill equipped to cope with poverty or with an introspective child, and she made life difficult for her younger son and for her alcoholic husband. She tried to express some of her feelings about her life in a letter to her son written on January 28, 1940: "Dad is feeling that long spell of drinking. He is having to build his business all over. I get scared sometimes, no home, and when that's gone [Dr. Jones's practice] I wonder. I try to use my [Christian] science but I get scared anyway."

In the letter announcing her death, Dr. Jones wrote: "She missed your letters dreadfully, and enjoyed them immensely whenever she did get one." This letter and Jeff's letter about the death of their mother, asserting that Mrs. Jones loved Jim more than her other two children must have distressed Jones.

Unable to write about his feelings for his mother, Jones turned to a discussion of Thomas Wolfe, whose mother was, in different ways, as difficult as Mrs. Jones and was turned into a memorable character in Wolfe's fiction. The mother figure is carefully excluded in Jones's paean to Wolfe.

In this letter Jones mentioned for the first time his need to find an "authority" to tell him he had promise as a writer. He was later to discover such authorities in Lowney Handy and Maxwell Perkins.

TO JEFF JONES

[HAWAII]
MONDAY [APRIL] THE 7TH [1941]

Dear Jeff,

I wrote to Dad about a week ago. Apparently, he wrote to you before he received my letter. I tried to explain the way I felt—without much success, I'm afraid—and tried to help him, what little I was able. It's hard as hell to try to write a letter of that sort, especially when you've been away so long without any contact except writing. I felt so futile and helpless about it, that the only relief I got, and which kept me from going off my nut, was the taking of a three day pass, going to Honolulu, where I was alone, where no one knew me or bothered me, and staying stinko for the three days. After I got back, I was disgusted and ashamed of myself, but I felt a whole lot better mentally, altho I was a helluva lot worse physically. If it's all the same to you, I'd rather just drop the subject and not refer to it in future letters.

I'm sorry I haven't written you for so long. Now that I'm a clerk in the orderly room, I've been spending all my spare time in there, writing. I have full access to the place, and it's a good place to write: no one can come in and bother me, and I can stay there all night, if I choose.

I'm really serious about this writing thing. What time I haven't been writing, I've been reading: Thomas Wolfe, if you know who he is. His writing is mostly built about the central character of a writer, himself. Altho it's fiction, it deals with his life and experiences. In my opinion, little as it's worth, he is the greatest writer that has lived, Shakespeare included. He is a genius. That is the only way to describe him. And in reading of his childhood, his youth, and his struggles to get out of him the things he wanted to say, I can find an almost exact parallel with myself. Of course details are different, but the general trend is practically the same.

Now don't misunderstand me. I'm not stating I'm a genius, altho I'd like to think I was for it would give me confidence I need; even if I did rank as a genius in the eighth grade, according to the Stanford Achievement Tests.

I, too, like Wolfe, have felt myself different from other kids, especially while I was in high school: I never seemed to mix with the other kids; I didn't think at all like they did; I never ran around with the gang of boys that were the elite of the campus, nor did I run around with the gang that envied them and disliked them, and ganged together in a sort of mutual protection, because they were excluded from the select group: I did feel hurt about it, and I wasn't able to understand it; but I don't think I was little about it. I fell into the habit of going with myself, and expressing my "radical" thoughts to no one. Even at home they didn't see things the way I did. Don't think I'm a victim of an inferiority complex or an aesthete, who is always complaining he is misunderstood, because I'm not. I don't feel sorry for myself. I've gotten so that I like my own company. I can understand me better than anyone I know.

Anyway, it seems I've always felt a hunger and unrest that nothing could satisfy. I couldn't understand what it was. It was like an idea for a story you have in the back of your head that you can't quite grasp. You know it's there, but it keeps receding before your grasp like a mist. Do you remember when I fell so hard for that girl in Findlay? (If you don't remember her name, then I won't say it for the thing is forgotten and in the past now.) We had even talked about getting married. But something, some vague wisp of dissatisfaction kept sifting thru my mind. I didn't know what it was then. I think I do now: It's that desire to write, to be famous and adored, to be known and talked about by people I've never seen. Yet, that's not all it is. It's more than that. I—well, I don't want to go melodramatic on you. I'm afraid you'll laugh at me. Here's the way I wrote in one of the things I wrote a while back: "But since he had been in the army, he had come to understand his un-graspable longing and his phantasmal and belly-shrinking dissatisfaction: there were such things he wanted to be, to do, to write: He wanted to be the voice that shrieked out the agony of frustration and lostness and despair and loneliness, that all men feel, yet cannot understand; the voice that rolled forth the booming, intoxicating laughter of men's joy; the voice that richly purred men's love of good hot food and spicy strong drink; men's love of thick, moist, pungent tobacco smoke on a full belly; men's love of woman: voluptuous, throaty voiced, silken-thighed, and sensual."

I suppose that sounds an awful lot like Wolfe, but if it does, it's exactly the way I feel. You know, there's really nobody that I can talk to with[out] being afraid of being laughed at, not even you. Right now I'm afraid you'll laugh when you read this; or worse, feel sorry for me and pity me, because I'm a idealistic, romantic kid, who doesn't know what in hell he's talking about. In fact, this is the first time I've ever come anywhere near telling you what I thought.

Which brings me to another subject, one I hope you'll say nothing about to anyone, not Sally, Dad, and least of all, the one involved, if you should ever run across her in rambling thru the metropolis (Robinson, I mean): I'm very strongly afraid the old cynic has fallen again.

I doubt if you remember. . . . Probably you never met her. She was in my class in high school. Very smart: Editor of the N 'n E [*Notes 'n Everything,* a school publication], 4 A student, et al. I had a few dates with her in high, but never succeeded in kissing her, a fact which made me mark her off my list quickly, altho I did have a lot of fun with her. Well, she asked Tink [Mary Ann Jones] two or three times to ask me to write her, after I got here. Tink mentioned it a couple of times and one day down at Hickam, when I had nothing to do, I wrote her a little letter and inclosed a copy of that poem about the soldier I sent to you (that was after I had gotten the corrected copy back from you). It was a pretty raw thing to do, especially in a first letter, what with its knocking women in general and all; but I was feeling low and wanted to shock hell out of somebody. Well, I got an answer pretty quickly. She liked it and wanted to know if that was the way I really felt. From that [inauspicious] beginning our correspondence was founded. I've sent her copies of my stories, poems, and of the sketches and descriptions I've been writing ever since I got out of the hospital.[1] I've written her exactly as I feel, mincing no words, speaking the truth exactly as I felt it. I've written her my ambitions, hopes, fears, just everything, I guess.

As far as I'm able to discern, I am in love with her. I don't think I really knew it until I got her last letter.

You see, she is engaged to marry some guy in Robinson. I've known about it since her first letter. In her next to last letter, she told me they planned on getting the bowline twisted in June; and proceeded to ask me whether or not we should continue writing—now. It seems her OAO [one and only] got very jealous, and that he suspected her of corresponding with me. She didn't know whether she should write to me, when he felt that way. She was afraid of messing things up. She didn't love me, but she did enjoy writing me, and hearing from me.

Well, the outcome was, that I wrote her a very strong letter. (I'll send you a copy of it sometime, if you like, for that's the only way I could describe the thing.) I told her that I'd never had anyone I'd been able to write to like I could her, and suggested he censor all letters, among other things. I also got pretty frank about the marriage business. The matter of fact way she talked about marrying him got under my skin: she talked just as if she were going on a picnic, or out to buy a new dress.

Well, she met me word for word, phrase for phrase. I guess it was when I got that letter that I realized I was in love with her. I wouldn't let her know it for the world. In the first place, it would destroy the frankness that exists between us; and in

[1]Jones had an appendectomy. See his letter to Irwin Shaw, April 11, 1964, for an anecdote concerning a prostitute's comment on the appendectomy scar.

the second place, I know she loves this other guy (at least, I think I know), and I can't stand to be pitied, laughed at, or felt sorry for by anyone.

In this last letter, she said that . . . , the guy, had decided to volunteer for his year in the army, and that she wanted me to write to her some more. She thinks my stories are great, and that I have a great future as a writer. I'd like to think she's right. But I'm no [William] Saroyan. I'm working in the dark all the time. Whenever I do write something, that black, forbidding doubt is in me, making me wonder if I'm just some damned egotistical fool, or if I really have that spark of genius it takes to be a really great author like Wolfe. If I only had some way of knowing. If only some authority that knew would tell [me] I was good and had promise, then I'd be all right, but as it is, I'm always full of that fear that maybe I'm not any good. Sometimes I get so damned low I feel like blowing my brains out. That's no shit, it's the straight dope.

I've rewritten the story about the guard and am going to send it to *Esquire*. I doubt if any magazine but *Esquire* would publish a story like that with the national situation as it is.

I'm sleepy as hell, and am going to quit. We go out in the field for a week in the morning. Get up at 4:30.

Love to Sally and Dave,
Jim

I'd sure like to see the little devil right now.

Y/TLS

The next months were difficult ones for Jones. He was part of a corrupt, caste-ridden military life which paradoxically, because of its regimentation and male bonding, provided him some security. As a common soldier he was treated as a pariah, which blighted his social and sexual life. He had almost no money, and like most of the "dogfaces," he was forced to frequent the whorehouses or, as he remarked, take care of himself.

Jones's duties as assistant company clerk allowed him time to go on with his writing, though he was still not successful in placing any of it. His life in the peacetime army was ended on December 7, 1941. He wrote in WW II *a vivid account of that day.*

At Schofield Barracks in the infantry quadrangles, those of us who were up were at breakfast. On Sunday mornings in those days there was a bonus ration of a half-pint of milk, to go with your eggs or pancakes and syrup, also Sunday specials. Most of us were more concerned with getting and holding onto our half-pints of milk than with listening to the explosions that began rumbling up toward us from Wheeler Field two miles away. "They doing some blasting?" some old-timer said through a mouthful of pancakes. It was not until the first low-flying fighter came skidding, whammering low overhead with his MGs going that we ran outside, still clutching our half-pints of milk to keep them from being stolen, aware with a sudden sense of awe that we were seeing and acting in a genuine moment of history.

As we stood outside in the street huddled back against the day-room wall, another fighter with the red suns on its wings came up the boulevard, preceded by two lines of holes that kept popping up eighty yards in front on the asphalt. As he came abreast of us, he gave us a typically toothy grin and waved, and I shall never forget his face behind the goggles. A white silk scarf streamed out behind his neck and he wore a white ribbon around his helmet just above the goggles, with a red spot in the center of his forehead. I would learn later that this ribbon was a hachimaki, *the headband worn by medieval samurai when going into battle, usually with some religious slogan of Shinto or Emperor worship inked on it.*

Jones spent much of the rest of the day carrying messages for "distraught" officers.

There was fear that Japanese troops would invade the Hawaiian Islands, and Jones's company was sent to guard a stretch of beach east of Honolulu. He was there for months. This desolate spot was used as the background for his story "The Way It Is" and for the short novel The Pistol. *It was during those uncertain days soon after the beginning of the war that his father committed suicide.*

Perhaps it is coincidence, but the first paragraph of this controlled yet emotional letter Jones wrote to his brother after learning of his father's suicide contains the key words in the titles of Jones's first and last published novels: eternity *and* whistle. *In his imagination, Jones re-creates Dr. Jones's thoughts just before the "blackness hit him." Jones later used this insight in creating the mental states of Bloom in* From Here to Eternity *and Landers and Strange in* Whistle *just before they took their own lives.*

TO JEFF JONES

[HAWAII]

MARCH 22, 1942

Brother Jeff,

Your letter came this afternoon. When I opened it, the last sentence in the first paragraph seemed to leap out from the paper before my eyes in letters a foot high. I didn't say anything to anybody. I folded the letter up, stuck it in my pocket, turned on my heel, and walked away from the Orderly Room. I went down to my tent, sat down on my bunk, and lit a cigarette. Then I took the letter out of my pocket and opened it up and read it. Then I folded it, stuck it back in the envelope, and just sat there on my bed, smoking. Sometimes the air is awfully clear here. You can look off to sea and see the soft, warm, raggedy roof of clouds stretching on and on and on. It almost seems as if you can look right on into eternity. The wind was blowing and the sun shone thru the leaves and dappled all the ground with light and shadow. Last nite I was down on the beach over the hill, standing on the sand at the water's edge, watching the sunset. A crab ran up a couple of feet in front of me and stopped there, and I stepped on it and smashed it in the sand for I do not like them. The sea rolled up and covered up the crab and my footprint. When it rolled back in its ceaseless motion, the sharp outlines of my foot-print were gone, and the crab was completely covered. Then the sea rolled up again and back again. In a little while there was no mark upon the sand at all and the crab was nowhere to be seen. The sea rolled on, timeless in its vastness, and did not seem to care that a crab had been killed here. I thot to myself, that life is like the sea, brutal and relentless. It can't go back. It can't stand still. Therefore it must go forward. It plays the percentage. It is governed by a law of Nature. What does it matter, if some little crab or human being is smashed upon the rocks? It can't be bothered. It can't go back. It can't stand still. Therefore it must go forward, and woe be unto those who think they may defeat it. For life, just like the sea, has never lost a battle yet. Perhaps it has been thwarted for a time, but it always comes back in the last quarter to score again, for the game has no final whistle. It ends only when you quit or cannot fight some more.

I have been expecting Dad to do that for quite a while. I don't know why, call it a premonition if you will, but it didn't surprise me to hear that he had killed himself. I was talking to him one time up at the office and he told me then, "Well, Jeeper, if the time ever comes, when I'm sucked clear under the muck up to my ears, and I know that the net profit isn't worth the cost, I wouldn't hesitate to kill myself. When a man can't see anything to gain in putting up with living, which at best, is a pretty dismal affair, the thing for him to do is get out. And don't ever let anybody tell you it takes more guts to go on living than to kill yourself, because it doesn't; and those who say it does say so because they know in their hearts that they'd never have the guts." I'm rather proud he went out that way, instead of hanging on and hanging on, wanting to be out, but held back because of his fear of death.

Sure, he was weak. But that was no fault of his. He was not the kind of a man to be tied down in a place like Robinson, where the split-tongued sluts and carrion crows like to pick and tear and spit on everything above them to satisfy their egos.

I don't know if my insurance policy has reached there yet. It is supposed to be sent to Tink. It's for ten thousand and now I guess you are the guardian of it. I also sent my boxing sweater to Tink. You might check up on it, if you move away from Robinson before it gets there. I'm glad Tink is going up to Findlay with you and Sally. She's had to shoulder all the grief that was mine before I left. But I'll be coming back some day, and we'll all sit down in the kitchen with some coffee and pie and maybe a [C]oke or two and hash over all the things that happened and perhaps just sit there, glad to be together again, and look at each other and know that we've got a bond, we three, that a lot of people wouldn't even understand.

You'll probably get a letter sometime soon from a girl. . . . She lives in California. I met her in LA, when I was on furlough there. I've been writing to her ever since. She wrote to me and asked that I send her the address of my folks (which is you, now) so that if anything happened to me, she would be able to find out. We figure we might get married some day, if things turn out rite. I've explained to her that after the war, if I'm still around, that I'm going back to school and that I'm going to be writing for a while before I get any breaks, but she says she doesn't care. She'll wait. I don't know. If she doesn't I guess I'll just add another wrinkle. And go on writing.

I'm enclosing a poem I sent, correction, am going to send (provided I can get it thru the red tape) to *Collier's*. They probably won't take it, so I'll send it to someone else. I don't know any mags that publish poetry. And anyway fiction is my first love.

It's 0430, which is 4:30 ayem. I've already overstayed my shift at the telephone a half hour. So I think I'll cut her off.

Tell Dave I want him to write me as soon as he gets that big. And I can't think of anything I'd rather have than the honor of being the one you named the new one after.

So long, Jeff. I <u>will</u> take keer a maself.

Jim

PS It just struck me that first and last Dad was a dreamer. After Mother died last March, he lost his only touch with reality.[1] In that last split-second before the blackness hit him, he probably grinned and told himself what a Goddam fool he was.[2] But then, without Mother, maybe he didn't give a damn, anyway.

Jeeper

Y/TLS

---

[1] In *Viet Journal,* Jones gave a slightly different interpretation of his father's death:

> In January of 1942 my father went around to the nearest recruiting station and tried to volunteer for a commission in the Infantry, as a lieutenant. He was 56 at the time, a known alcoholic, a mediocre vet of World War I, and a failure at his profession of dentist. The Army turned him down. Cold. They didn't even want him as a dentist. He wrote me a rather despairing letter about it. I read it, wondered how he could imagine the Army would want him for anything. At the time I was on a beach position in Honolulu, a corporal of Infantry myself. Before that spring was out, my father was to commit suicide by shooting himself in the head. Later I would speculate often whether that turndown by the Army had not been such a slap in the fact that it helped awaken him to what he was, what he had become, and he could not stand to face it. I loved my father, and I hated to see it end like that. He deserved a better fate.

[2] Jones was deeply affected by his father's death, and he later wrote several dramatic scenes about suicide:

> After Bloom in *Eternity* pulled the trigger, he tried to yell: "I dint mean it! I take it back! I was only kiddin! I was just showin off!"
>
> Landers in *Whistle* deliberately killed himself by stepping into the path of a car driven by a beautiful woman. Landers had lost touch with reality, as Dr. Jones had.
>
> Strange, in *Whistle*, could not stand the thought of more war, could not stand to see more bloodshed, and jumped into the cold waters of the Atlantic.

Mary Ann Jones, then seventeen, found the body of her father when she went by his office after school on March 11, 1942. "Dr. Jones," the Robinson Daily News *reported on March 12, 1942, "was apparently seated in a rocking chair in the back room of his office when he fired the automatic into the back of his head. The first shell misfired, and was ejected, being found lying in front of the chair on the floor." The suicide had far-reaching effects on Mary Ann. She went to live with her brother Jeff and his family for a time and then aimlessly roamed around the country, working at odd jobs. She eventually joined Lowney's Colony and was working on a novel at the time of her death.*

Jones had been given permission to enroll as a part-time student at the University of Hawaii; the initial excitement following the attack upon Pearl Harbor had abated, and Jones had several months of relative quiet.

TO MARY ANN JONES

[HAWAII]
MAY 20, 1942

Sister Tinkus,

I am enclosing the warrant I received for making corporal. You can hang it on the wall in the front room beside my picture, after I am blew up with bombs and stuff. You can show it to your children and tell them their Uncle Jim was a corporal and got killed in the war of '42, the one before the one their Daddy got killed in. They can show it to their grandchildren, your grandchildren rather, their children, and tell them that is their Uncle Jim, who was a corporal and got killed in the war of '42, the one before the one their granddad got killed in, which was the one before the one their Daddy got killed in. And so on ad infinitum. I guess that's the way it will be. Those of us who are so foolish to think that eventually mankind will rise above wars are nuts anyway, when we believe what we write will have an effect on them and help to see their error.

I sort of wish that I could have made it before the folks died. I think they would have liked it—liked it because they would have believed that it's in a way a success. Of course, they would have been wrong, but as long as they did not know that, it would not have made any difference, would it?

I wish you would tell Jeff that the poems I sent him are not supposed to be blank verse. They are free verse.

I have everything arranged to go to the summer session at the University of Hawaii. No doubt something will turn up to prevent it, but at present it seems to appear that I will get to go. It is fixed so that one day a week I will get off to go to the University. I shall go to the two classes I will be taking and while there will get data on the other two classes for that week, which I shall miss. It will be hard, but I think I will be able to make it, because I will be studying things I want to study. My chosen courses are English I and a special course: Philosophies of Life.

There is not much else to write. We are continuing in the same corrupt, ignorant, monotonous rut that I have been in since joining the army. We must suffer the same indignities, the same favoritism, the same graft and red tape. The sooner the Jap comes, the better it will suit me. I think I will enjoy jabbing my bayonet into a man's belly and watching the agony on his face. Just on general principles. I am sick and weary of everything I can think of. In answer to Jeff's question about the liquor, I do not believe that I will ever reach the place where I will drink from habit. Altho at present I take every opportunity of becoming soused that offers itself, because it's so nice to sit in a whirl and not have to be thinking. Thinking is something that is better not. What? It is much better to eat, drink, and be merry for we will be dead or out of the army up to our ears in a depression that will make any we have had look like the prosperity that has always been dodging around corners. Personally I think it is a far, far better thing than we have ever done to be disciples of Bacchus rather than of Christ.

Goodbye now, and tell Davy to start learning how to shoot a rifle.

Jim

P.S.—I wish I was a dog. Dogs just eat and sleep an[d] bark.
. . . .

s/TLS

At the University of Hawaii Jones enrolled in a course in compo-
sition taught by Dr. Laura Schwartz and a course in American
literature given by Dr. Carl Stroven. For both professors he wrote
highly charged papers filled with rhetoric much akin to Wolfe's.
Drs. Schwartz and Stroven recognized his abilities and encouraged
him to continue his writing. On campus he met several girls with
whom he tried to form romantic entanglements, but he was not
successful. He was like a stock character in the movies: the confidant
of a beautiful woman but not her lover.

His university life was short-lived; his company received orders
to ship out on December 6, 1942. It was a time of uncertainty, and
Jones wrote in an undated manuscript: "I might be dead in a
month, which would mean that I would never learn how to say and
never get said those things which proved I had once existed some-
where." In a little over two weeks Jones arrived on Guadalcanal,
where bloody battles had been and were to be fought. The conditions
on that island were terrible, and the troops suffered from malaria,
dengue fever, and other tropical diseases and, of course, from fear.
The fighting was fierce, and each soldier had learned, he noted
eloquently in WW II, *"that his name is already written down in*
the rolls of the already dead."

Three events that were to change his life irrevocably occurred on
Guadalcanal: He killed a Japanese soldier, he was wounded, and
he reinjured his ankle.

He did not mention the killing in his letters; but he later told
friends about it, and he gave a vivid account of it in The Thin
Red Line. *In the fictionalized account the character Bead went into*
the jungle to defecate, and while he was squatting down, a starved
and dirty Japanese soldier came charging at him with his bayonet.
The two fought on the muddy floor of the jungle, and Bead,
younger and stronger, was able to claw at his enemy's face. "Bead
heard a high keening scream and thought it was the Japanese
begging for mercy until finally he slowly became aware that the
Japanese man was now unconscious. Then he realized it was him-
self making that animal scream. He could not, however, stop it."
Bead seized the bayonet and plunged it into the chest of the Japanese

soldier. Bead lost his sense of time, and when he finally came to, one
hand was resting "in a friendly way" on the knee of the dead
soldier. Bead "had an obscure feeling that if he did not look at the
corpse of the man he had killed or touch it, he would not be held
responsible."

Jones's wounding and the aftermath, including his views on
luck, are described in the following two letters.

TO JEFF JONES

[GUADALCANAL]
JANUARY 28, 1943

Dear Jeff

I'm writing this more or less to set your mind at ease concerning me. I've inquired around here as to what a guy is able to write, and—as per usual—I've found that there's not a helluva lot to say that won't be censored.

It's apparently OK for me to tell you that I've been wounded and have just been released from a Base Hospital in the South Pacific. I'll elaborate that statement before moving on to something else. I wasn't hit very badly—a piece of shrapnel went thru my helmet and cut a nice little hole in the back of my head. It didn't fracture the skull and is healed up nicely now. I don't know what happened to my helmet; the shell landed close to me and when I came to, the helmet was gone. The concussion together with the fragment that hit me must have broken the chinstrap and torn it off my head. It also blew my glasses off my face. I never saw them again, either, but I imagine they are smashed to hell. If I hadn't been lying in a hole I'd dug with my hands and helmet, that shell would probably have finished me off. The hole was only six or eight inches deep, but that makes an awful lot of difference, and it looked like a canyon. I'm not much good without glasses; it bothers you a lot to know you can't see well and that any minute some sniper you should have seen but couldn't is liable to cut you down. The glasses don't help a lot either; you have to keep wiping sweat off of them every five minutes, and after a couple of days you don't have any rags or handkerchiefs clean enuf to wipe them without leaving them badly smeared. That surprised me quite a bit, because before I hadn't thot wearing glasses would make much difference. But it does, a helluva lot: the knowledge that you can't see well bothers the shit out of you—especially when you can't make more than one misstep. I learned a lot of other things, too.

I found that reading books about other people fighting wars is adventurous, but when you are doing the fighting, it's a helluva lot different. When you read a book like *All Quiet* [*on the Western Front* by Erich Maria Remarque] you understand what the hero is going thru and sympathize with him. Even when he gets killed at the end of the book you sympathize, and in sympathizing, you feel a sadness you enjoy. But all that time while you are putting yourself into the hero's place you still have the knowledge that after the hero dies you still will be around to feel sad about it. When at any second you may die, there is no adventure; all you want is to get the fighting over with. You don't spend any time in consoling yourself that if you die, you will be dying for your country and Liberty and Democracy and Freedom, because after you are dead, there is no such thing as Liberty or Democracy or Freedom. It's impossible to look at things thru the viewpoint of the group rather than your individual eyes. The group means nothing to you if you cannot remain a part of it. But in spite of all this, you keep on fighting because you know that there is nothing else for you to do.

I also learned that in spite of all the training you get and precautions you take to keep yourself alive, it's largely a matter of luck that decided whether or not you get killed. It doesn't make any difference who you are, how tough you are, how nice a guy you might be, or how much you may know, if you happen to be at a certain spot at a certain time, you get it. I've seen guys [move] out of one hole to a better one and get it the next minute, whereas if they'd stayed still they wouldn't have been touched. I've seen guys decide to stay in a hole instead of moving and get it. I've seen guys move and watch the hole they were in get blown up a minute later. And I've seen guys stay and watch the place to which they had intended to move get blown up. It's all luck.

The guys who are fighting now will have less of a chance of being alive when the war is over than the guys who haven't started fighting yet. Of course, some of us will live thru it, but that doesn't help one guy any, because if he doesn't live thru it, what happens to the rest doesn't make any difference. I've sort of got a hunch that I'm not going to make it. Partially that comes from having seen how much luck has to do with it and because from now on until the war ends I'll probably be in and out of action all the time. Then, part of it comes from being hit. Until you get hit, there's a sort of egotism in your subconscious mind that, even while your conscious mind is tearing itself apart with fear and anxiety, gives you confidence in the fact that this might happen to other guys but not to you; you can't conceive yourself getting hit. After you've been hit, you lose that confidence. The more fights you go thru without being hit, the stronger it gets. But once you're hit, you realize as an individual you'll have to be God damned lucky to get out alive.

I'm going to ask you something. If I do get killed, and I honestly don't see how I can help it, I want you to write that book we were thinking about when I enlisted. If I get it, it's a cinch I won't be able to do it, and it would make me feel a whole lot better to know that if not my name and hand, at least, the thot of me would be passed on and not forgotten entirely. You know, sort of put into the book the promise that I had and the things I might have written so at least the knowledge of talent wasted won't be lost. This girl, Peggy, I told you about told me once that the day after my last pass, Dr. Schwartz, during her lecture to Peggy's class, said something about how much talent would be lost without anyone having guessed it existed because of this war. Peggy told me that she thot Schwartz had me in mind when she said that. If I get it, no one will ever know to what heights I might have gone as a writer. Maybe if you wrote about the promise that was there, all wouldn't be lost.

Give my love to Sally and the boys and to Tink. You might tell Dave if I ever get the Purple Heart I got coming, I'll send it to him. It probably wouldn't bring six bits in a hock shop.

Jim

Y/TLS

TO JEFF JONES

[GUADALCANAL]
FEB 19, 1943

Dear Jeff,

I got two of your letters yesterday evening. The ones dated Jan 25th & 30th. I think I could have done a much better job had I tried to answer them then, but there wasn't enough daylite left; I was in a mood to write then more than now. I sat on an old log till dark there by myself with the letters. Every once in a while I'd pick one of them up & reread it. Then I'd just sit & watch the dying sun & let the thots of what life would be like for us after the war flood my brain. It's the first time since I got hit that I've done that. I thot for a while I could keep the thot of the future out of my head. I can't. I thot I could live in the present from one day to the next without hoping for anything, without expecting anything. I can't, even tho I'd like to. I did for a while, but I guess that was the reaction from being hit. Eventually, if we go in a few more times & I live thru it, that temporary reaction will become more or less permanent. I guess the human psyche, like the human physique, will stand only so much without an attempt at defense. I don't want to hope or plan even now, but I can't help it. The reason I don't want to is because it makes me sad as hell—unpleasantly sad. That's a diff[er]ent sadness than the one I feel about soldiers as a whole. I can turn the latter on & off like a water spigot, & it's a pleasant sadness because it's impersonal & all twisted up with my wanting to write about people. But this new sadness is wholly personal & connected with the fact that I probably won't get to write about people or anything else, & so it hurts like hell, this new sadness; that's why I want to avoid it. It's hard to talk about that; it's too personal for any body who doesn't know what I'm like inside to understand. Maybe that's why I'm telling you; I have no <u>real</u> friends here—or anywhere, for that matter, except you & the Eng profs at the University.

I imagine my last letter to you (the one while I was in the hospital) hurt you quite a bit—provided you understood it (which I doubt because of your so evident desire to get in despite Sally & the kids).[1] If that desire was strong enuf, it would keep you from understanding what & how I wrote. I don't think anyone is capable of understanding it, unless they've had the drama & romance of popular opinion stripped from war by being in it. Even press correspondents can't see it that way, after being on the front. All of us felt as you do until we got up on the line. Anyway, I wanted to tell you that most of the bitterness is gone, replaced by that sadness. I still don't expect to come out, but I'm not so bitter about it now. But that doesn't change the fact that logically I can't see how I'll come out. I still wish I'd lost an eye or a foot. That wouldn't leave you helpless, but you'd be unfit to fight any more.

I had a letter from Laura [Schwartz] a while back, & she said she'd gotten a letter from you the same day she got mine. She also said she'd looked up Findlay C. & that it was a Sectarian school, "run by the Churches of God of North America," & had an extremely small library. She said both she & Stroven

---

[1] Jones thought it would be a mistake for Jeff to leave civilian life for a position with the Red Cross. Jeff did not take his younger brother's advice.

think college would help me a lot at this stage of the game, but that a Sectarian school is worse than none. I agree with them. I want no asinine religious scruples cramping me. Religion is all rite in its place, I guess, altho I think it's a shame that people should need it to keep them human; but I don't need it or believe it or want anything to do with it. Its attempts to hush & hide moral issues [are] disgusting to me. I think the church does as much harm as good, if not more. Stroven is to quit teaching in June & give all his time to running the Library. I hate that, but I think he'd take time to work with me if I ever came back there. All of them believe in my ability & want to see me make good. What would you say to my going back there? I'd rather go there, I think. It's going into a known quantity, one that won't be lacking. With my allotment & oil checks [royalties from an oil well on family property] & a little help from you I could make it easily. I could get a room to myself, free, for only watering & mowing the lawn, if I had to. I know, because I had one lined up when they turned my furlough down in '41. Or maybe I could stay with "Mom" White, altho I'd rather not if I could get some place where I'd be left entirely alone. She tries to mother me & is a fiend on health foods & church. She's a swell old gal, but she'd get on my nerves if I had to stay there. I even imagine I could stay with Stroven if I wanted to. Summers, of course, I'd be in Findlay. Work there, if necessary, & write the rest of the time. Will there be a cot & a coffee-maker in the cabin? You & I will shoot some pool or [P]ing-[P]ong in that basement playroom in the evening & maybe go down to Dietze's for a [C]oke. Every now & then I'll go up to Toledo or Cleveland on a bat & stay for a week & get gloriously drunk & whore around. Just to take off the edge I'll get from writing all the time. Then, after I get out of school, I'll move in permanently. I ought to have a good, long MS ready to go to Scribner's or Harper's by then. Of course, I'll come home for a while, 2 or 3 months, before I go back to Hawaii to school. You know how to play chess, don't you? If you don't, learn before I get back & we'll have some good games. Jesus Christ! That's a wonderful picture, isn't it? It makes my belly cramp up & gives me a ticklish feeling in my balls just to think about it. I've been in the army so long, it's hard for me to believe that I'll ever be able to do those things.

. . . .

I had to laugh at your complimenting my brilliancy of mind. It's no good to me unless proven. If I'd made a name, I'd probably be an officer with a good job in Washington like Steinbeck or Saroyan, but no fame, no pull or payoff. I was just born 5 years too late. I may be a potential great writer, but it does me no good here—rather it works the other way.

Keep writing as much & as often as you can. A letter is a Godsend here. And I think Air-Mail gets here quicker than V-Mail. And it hold[s] more words.

Give my love to Sally & the kids.

Jim

Y/ALS

"On the third day of a fight for a complex of hills called 'The Galloping Horse,'" Jones wrote in WW II, *"I was wounded in the head through no volition of my own. . . ."* He spent a week in a hospital on Guadalcanal. After his release he returned to duty, reinjured his ankle, and was again hospitalized on Guadalcanal. Evacuated to the United States, he spent months in an army hospital. He did not write letters about his reactions to that bloody battle but instead composed a long poem, "The Hill They Call the Horse." The undated poem is included here as an important biographical document. Years later many of the incidents alluded to in "The Hill They Call the Horse" were reworked into The Thin Red Line.

THE HILL THEY CALL THE HORSE

A POEM
by
JAMES JONES

I am in a hospital, and it is the middle of the night.
I cannot sleep.
My body lies relaxed, inert upon a mattress,
Soft yielding mattress, bandaged up with clean starched sheets.
A pillow, smooth and cool, in which my head is buried.
I lie in comfort—but it is very strange.
My body is not used to comfort. It has forgotten.
I must reteach it.
This must be the reason for my wretched wakefulness?
Perhaps. It may be so.

I lie thus—and keep on lying.
That which is me stands apart—a me that is not me—
And feels my teeth grate in their grinding
And feels my ears reach out—
With every nerve and fiber in them—
Listening—listening—straining for the Sound.

My brain is slavering and drooling spittle
Like a great hound straining at its leash

Eager to be off into the thick and slimy darkness.
The leash of frantic will is slender.
It snaps. I do not care.
The hound is off, baying to its echoes.
My brain has broken loose and left me.
It rushes forward eagerly into Time To Come.

I am standing, lonely in the writhing blood of dawn,
Atop a hill—I know this hill.
I have stood before—because far off the sea,
Like a basin underneath a leaking pipe,
Like a vampire underneath a leaking throat,
Yawns wide its maw to catch the bloody drippings of the
    dawn.
I have stood before—because all about me,
Over earth, on trees, into thirsty dust,
(I can feel it on my hands; it's sticky on my face).
Dawn's jugular pours.
And yet I am a stranger here; I do not know this place.
I am of the tortured past (the so-conveniently forgotten past),
And in this present of the future the past is out of place.
This future present is of death, of silence,
And of the deathlike memory of life
That is no longer life but deathless death.
For, you see, I am standing on The Horse, brought back
By some mad joke of laughing demons,
Brought back in fear and loathing and against my will.
(I can already feel it, that remembered blade of terror,
Stark and black, sawing dully at my belly.)
Because memory will not let me lose it,
I am standing on the blasting, cursing, gasping Horse of Then
That is the dead, decayed, and sleepless Horse of Now.

Everything is quiet now.
The awesome still I do not know is heavy and opaque.
It drips from the trees and rolls slowly, like thick syrup,
Into crumbling foxholes.
It is the stillness of forgotten hate and of reluctant memory.
Yes, everything is quiet now, but the evidence is here:
Crumbling holes half-filled with stagnant rain;

A twisted bit of steel that might have been a helmet;
A bayonet crusted deep with tropic rust still sticking upright
    in the earth;
Half-buried rifle barrel, stock long since rotted into
    nothingness;
One place the gleaming baldness of a skull
With splintered teeth.
Its empty sockets stare at me reproachfully:
I have disturbed its sleep.

And my fear crawls up and chokes me.
This is why I came!
This is the force of madness that took me by the hand
And would not let me cringe! Why me! Why me!
Dumbly with cloven tongue I stand in the bloody dawn
Atop The Horse.
I would run: My legs laugh in my face.
For across the crest they come
In solitary line
As I last saw them:
Dried mud ground into their green fatigues, gritty to the
    touch;
Helmets, those who have them, rusty, caked with mud;
Sweat streaming down faces twisted with the agony of fear
    and tension.
They pass by me with stumbling tread,
And each looks at me reproachfully and sadly:
They died; I lived. They resent my luck.
They cannot see that I am not the lucky one.
As they pass I see them as I saw them last:
George Creel—
A little string of brains hanging down between his eyes;
Joe Donnicci—
His eyes big behind his glasses and a gaping hole where once
    had been his ear;
Young Shelley—
Balls shot away and holding in his guts that pooch out
    between his fingers;

Hannon—
Stumbling along, face gone below the eyes;
Big Kraus—
No marks, no blood, just dead with hard-set lips and
    unbelieving eyes;
Set Lecchessi—
Belly ripped wide open, still gasping: "Help me. Help me.
    Can'tcha see? I'm gonna die!"
The line goes on—for there are many.
Red Johanssen—
Both legs gone and spouting fountains while he drags himself
    across the ground.
The line goes on—for there are many more.
There is the boy (I never knew his name)
Who was lying wounded on a litter,
Glad he had been wounded,
And believing he was safe at last
When a sniper blew his brains out
And filled the litter with a pool of blood.
The line goes on—
I see it in the distance, climbing,
Groping blindly up that hill,
That hill they call The Horse.
Then my unseen chains release me,
And I am away—through swirling wisps of madness and of
    pain.
I am back inside my body with its straining antenna of fear.
I am safe—at least for now,
But I cannot relax:
I know I must go back some day—provided that I live.
I must see this place in stillness—when the jungle has
    reclaimed it.
Or I shall never rest.
I cannot sleep tonight. . . . . Perhaps a pill.

Y/T

Jones's injured ankle was operated upon at a naval base hospital in the New Hebrides, and he was then returned to the United States by hospital ship. After a short stay at Letterman General Hospital in San Francisco, he was transferred to Kennedy General Hospital in Memphis, Tennessee. After his ankle improved, he was given passes to go into town, and he often took a suite at the Peabody Hotel, where he enjoyed the sexual freedom of this booming wartime city. "It was a wild time then," Jones wrote; he drank heavily and began to pick fights in the local bars. His ankle still bothered him, and the review board at the hospital told him him that he was unfit "for full Infantry duty." He wrote the Reverend Dr. Marshall Wingfield on March 6, 1951, that the review board asked him if he wanted a discharge or reassignment "to Limited Duty on a job of training new men." He elected limited duty, but when his papers came through, he was "assigned back to full Infantry duty—and with the Yankee Division (Nat'l Guard) then at Camp Campbell preparing to leave for Europe, and the D Day everybody knew was coming. I was also somewhat bitter about this."

Jones requested a furlough to visit the remnants of his family in Robinson, Illinois, but it was denied. He was distressed about the treatment he received from the army, and in November 1943 he went AWOL and took a train to Robinson, where his uncle Charles and aunt Sadie Jones now lived in the family mansion. Jones was often drunk, and his actions greatly concerned his uncle and aunt. Sadie took him to meet Lowney Handy, an unconventional woman in Robinson who spent much of her time helping people in trouble.

A. B. C. Whipple in a long article "James Jones and His Angel," read by millions in the May 7, 1951, issue of Life, *spoke of Jones's emotional state just before he met Lowney: ". . . he was a whimpering neurotic. It was like a case of shellshock, complicated by all the long list of disappointments he had had since his earliest childhood." Though "whimpering neurotic" is overly dramatic and not precisely accurate, Jones was psychologically scarred. Sadie told Lowney, who was an unpublished writer, "He thinks he wants to write."*

Lowney gave Whipple and Life *readers an account of their first*

*meeting: "You should have seen him then. He swaggered; he wore
dark glasses; he even asked me to read his poetry aloud. He had
obviously come over for a free drink. Then he saw my books.
. . . Jim got out of his chair and began to take out the books. He
flipped through them and plopped them back as if he were gulping
down what they had in them."* Lowney in that last sentence was
characterizing Jim's reading in terms used by Thomas Wolfe in
describing Eugene's devouring the contents of books at Harvard.
Was Lowney aware then that she would play a role in the life of
James Jones similar to that of Aline Bernstein in Wolfe's life?
Lowney, as was Aline Bernstein, was old enough to be the mother
of the troubled aspiring writer. She and Aline Bernstein both maintained their lives with their husbands as they each took a young
lover, whom they began to support emotionally and financially.

Jones returned to Lowney's house the next day, November 8, 1943.
He wrote in his diary that he spent the day in bed with her, that
she liked his writing, and that *"she subjected herself to me; she made
herself my disciple in everything from writing to love."* In view
of Lowney's domineering personality, it is difficult to believe she
was not acting when she declared herself subservient to him. Jones
did not at that time feel guilty about cuckolding Harry and wrote
in his diary that Harry understood.

The Whipple story in Life did not mention that Jones and
Lowney began an affair. Whipple's narrative continued: *"A few
days later he was back, and this time Harry was there. The three
talked on and on. After Jim left that evening, the Handys made
the decision they have stuck by ever since. They decided to take Jim
into their household. Before they could invite him, he had written
them a note asking if he could come and live with them."*

Whipple did not know or did not report a great deal of the truth
about Jones and his Angel: that the Handy marriage had failed
many years ago, that Lowney privately charged that Harry had
affairs with other women and that he drove over to Terre Haute
to visit the whores there, and that Lowney was Jones's mistress.

Jones could hardly come live with them at the time of their
invitation to him. He was still in the Army, and he was AWOL.

At the end of two weeks Jones reported to Camp Campbell. He wrote Dr. Wingfield that he "was not busted and court-martialed" because of the intervention of a warrant officer who marked his "papers with a two-week delay in route." In From Here to Eternity, *Jones has Warden protecting Prewitt the same way. Jones was then sent on maneuvers that lasted four weeks. He was still angry about being returned to active duty, and he had continued pain in his ankle. Again he went AWOL. When he returned to duty, he was reduced in rank to private and reassigned to the quartermaster gas and supply company, which had in it a large number of misfits. He was working on a novel he called* They Shall Inherit the Laughter, *fictionalizing Lowney and Harry Handy, Uncle Charley and Aunt Sadie Jones, prominent members of the Robinson social set, himself, and other veterans. The novel was about an AWOL soldier in his hometown while the war was still going on. The hero was a hell raiser, as Jones was at that time.*

Jones was particularly antagonistic toward his uncle Charley Jones, a prominent attorney in Robinson. A conservative, practical man, he did not believe that his nephew could support himself as a writer, and he refused to give Jones financial help for the months or years it would take to learn the craft. Uncle Charley also disapproved of Lowney Handy and her unconventional ways and worried that townspeople would gossip about the relationship of the middle-aged woman and his young nephew. Uncle Charley allowed his troublesome nephew to be thrown in jail, and he took action to see that Jones was not transferred to a base nearer Robinson and Lowney.

TO CHARLES JONES

[CAMP CAMPBELL, KENTUCKY]
JANUARY 26, 1944

Dear Uncle Charley,

I can remember back when I was a small child that my grandfather used to say to me: "Jimbodder, I'm always for

you—good or bad; but I'd rather be for you good than bad."
I didn't really understand that thing he used to say to me until
a long time after he was dead—until after both my parents
were dead also. But even tho I couldn't understand what he
would say to me, it always made me feel good inside, safe
like—just as it made me feel good when Dad used to tell me
that if I ever did anything bad, if I'd get to him and tell him
about it before anyone else did, he'd back me to the limit. Once
I pushed a boy thru a large plate window of a store. It was
directly across the street from the bowling alley, and the first
thing I did was make tracks for the bowling alley to see if Dad
was there. He was, and I told him about it. Even tho he was
half-tight, he got right up and went back across the street with
me and took the whole thing on his shoulders and got it
straightened out. I'll never forget that. It's a fine thing for a boy
to have someone who is rather like a rock to his small intellect,
someone who will always be there when needed—no matter
how deep the feeling of guilt. I had that feeling of Dad—even
tho he was one of the village drunks. I think it was somewhat
the same thing with both Granddad and Dad: they felt that I
was a part of them, that I was a Jones, if you want to be
snobbish about it, and that, while we might disagree within
ourselves, we would present a united front to the world and
stick together. I remember you telling me something of the
same line one of the times when I was at your home. At the
time I took it to mean what Dad and Granddad had meant. I
have only just found out—positively, that is—that I had entirely misunderstood you. What you meant by telling me to be
proud of being a Jones was not that the Joneses were aligned
against the world, but that the Joneses had a "face" to keep up
for the world to see.

A couple of days ago, working in the Orderly Room as I am
(I told you that, remember?), I was given a letter to file. Natur-
ally, I read the thing. It was a letter from you to Captain
Dunham requesting that any request by me for transfer to
George Field be refused. Captain Dunham, God bless his con-
scientious soul, had dutifully sent the letter forward to my

present outfit, which only helps prove to me the opinion I had already formed of Captain Dunham. (I had told you of that opinion, remember?) The CO [Commanding Officer] I have here is a pretty swell guy: he did not hide the letter from me and clandestinely keep it filed in some secret place. He put it with the other stuff to file and said nothing at all about it. Apparently it did not rate that much of his attention. The exact opposite of what Captain Dunham would have done with it.

It made me rather sick to read it. In reading it, I recalled several other things that I had not allowed myself to interpret correctly: the fact that you tried deliberately to humiliate me by having the night cop toss me in the clink is one of them. I suspected that at the time but refused to believe that that was why you did it; I could not believe that you would try to break me thru fear or humiliation, which is only a little brother of fear, try to break me to doing as you wish and think is right. I have told you that your and my opinions of what is right and what is wrong differ. Apparently that holds true in almost everything, because I cannot, by any scheme of thinking, believe that it is <u>right</u> for you to have me tossed in the jug to humiliate me or for you to write that letter that you wrote trying to screw me in the transfer. Another thing I happened to find out in the course of a conversation was that you told Harry Jones that you didn't know that the night cop put me in jail until the next morning—which is almost a lie, isn't it?

The attempt to humiliate me by having me thrown in jail was foiled by me: I made it a deliberate point to tell everyone I saw about my being thrown in jail and also pointed out to them, in case their obtuse thinking didn't catch it, what a damned good joke it was on me. I also told them all about your telling the night-cop to put me in. I think that foiled it— everyone is of the opinion I enjoyed it I think. Unwittingly, I have foiled the plan to make me look like a child with the letter, because the idea of asking for a transfer to George Field was entirely out of my brain—I know too much of the army to even hope that it might be approved unless I had pull from the other side, which item you also took of.

I know that I have allegedly done several things that <u>you</u> do not think were in keeping with the Jones name and the burden of keeping it unsmirched. I, too, am proud of the name of Jones—but I am proud of the name in the same way I am proud of Dad's committing suicide. Altho you do not seem to realize it, I am of age and am accountable only to my own conscience (and of course the law) as to what is right and wrong. None of my beliefs are in accordance with yours—I can see that much more clearly now than I did before. But that is not nearly enuf reason to change them. I am not under your jurisdiction, being legally an adult. Neither have you in the least part tried to understand my beliefs—altho I sweated blood in a self-conscious agony when attempting several times to explain them to you. You shut your mind to them. I shall not bother to try to tell you about them any more.

   . . . .

Respectfully,

т/тl/с

At Thanksgiving 1943 Jones went AWOL for the second time. He went to Robinson for three days, and when he went back to Camp Campbell, he told Dr. Wingfield that he was "busted to private" and "became latrine orderly."

He was soon transferred to a new quartermaster gasoline supply company, along with over a hundred "physical misfits." He was still at Camp Campbell. In this unit he was assigned to the orderly room and was soon promoted to sergeant. The officer he worked with, who was Jewish, was relieved of his command, and the officer who replaced him was a disciplinarian. Jones wrote Dr. Wingfield:

> *I got drunk one night on 3.2 beer in the PX, and I did not see any point in any of it, I felt outraged for our Jewish Lt who was on the s---list at the 2nd Army Hq, I felt degraded at having to answer the beefy Capt's damn phone, I knew we were shortly going to Europe and I felt I had done all they could expect of one man, let somebody else do it, and I felt in my bones that I had used all my luck up, that if I went to Europe I wouldnt be coming back. I caught the bus at midnight, aware I was leaving for good, though I didnt know where or how or what would come of it, and didnt much care, and left the Post, and looked back from the bus and watched the lights fade away. At the risk of seeming sentimental, I will say I loved the Post I was leaving, all of it. I also hated it.*

He did not stay with the Handys this time, for he was afraid he would get them in trouble. Instead, he told Dr. Wingfield, he lived in the home of a country sheriff. In the following letter he tells a slightly different story to Jeff, but he does so, I believe, because he thinks his letter will be read by military authorities.

TO JEFF JONES

Dear Jeff:

I suppose you've already had a letter about my being AWOL. So it won't be a surprise to you to know I'm in jail. I'm in the psychiatric ward in the station hosp. If you write, write the letter to my old address of the 842d.

When I got back & had the customary interview with my C.O., I was sent here for mental observation & treatment.

What happened was very simple: I had stood the army as long as I could. You know about *They Shall Inherit.* For weeks I'd been trying to work on it after hours. All during the day, when I had work at clerking, ideas, sentences, whole paragraphs would pop into my head—& I wasn't able to write them down. At nite I'd sit for hours trying to write & I couldn't. The atmosphere in the army isn't conducive to writing—you should know that. I'd write page after page and tear it up and throw it away. So I went over the hill. It was a force completely beyond my control. I could no more help what I did than I could help urinating if my bladder was full. I had to get that stuff out of me. If the same thing happens again, I'll have to do the same thing.

I went to Indianapolis—contrary to what you thot. I stayed with some artist friends whom you don't know. I wouldn't tell you anyway, because they probably censor the mail here, & I don't want them to get into trouble. They don't care about laws any more than I do. An artist is beyond laws.

. . . .

Lowney had a letter from my C.O. (which made me believe you probably got one, too). She didn't know I was gone, but when she got the letter she started calling around & found me. She said she half-suspected that [I] was where I was. She came over to Indianapolis & got me & talked me into coming back.

I had intended to stay until I finished the book or else got caught.

I talked to one of the psychiatrists here & to a Red Cross Social Worker. The Red Cross is writing to you & to Dr. Brooks, who, being the family doctor, should, they think, know something about my childhood—altho, in my opinion, nobody knows a goddam thing about my childhood except me, because I never talked about the way I felt mentally.

I told them everything I could: that I am a genius (altho they probably won't believe that); that if they attempt to send me overseas again I'll commit suicide; that if I don't get out of the army I'll either go mad or turn into a criminal—which is just next door to an artist anyway; that all I want to do is write, and that nobody and no thing means anything to me except writing. I don't know whether they believe me or not; I'm afraid they'll [think] I've cooked up a story. I told them that I could live with you, if I'm discharged, that you would take care of me & all I'd have to do would be write. I told them how I hate the army, that the army has done nothing but screw me, whether consciously or unconsciously. I just can't stand it any more; I've reached the saturation point. If I hadn't been overseas, if I hadn't done all a man could be expected to do, it might be different. If my ankle were a wound instead of an operation as it is, I would have requested a discharge. More than once I've seriously considered sticking my leg under a train here. It'd be worth the loss of a foot to get out so I could have some peace and write. I just can't take it any more.

If they decide to send me back to duty, I don't know what I'll do. It'll either be go over the hill for good or go crazy. One's about as bad as the other.

I'd rather you wouldn't mention Lowney in your letter to the Red Cross. She had nothing at all to do with my going over the hill, & I don't want her to get in trouble. If it wasn't for her I'd still be gone.

Love to Sally & the kids,
Jim

Y/ALS

The Apprentice Years,

1945-1950

Jones told Dr. Wingfield that "it was through the intervention of Mrs. Handy who talked to my Capt that I was allowed to see the psychiatrists at the hosp." Jones's case was investigated thoroughly while he was in the psychiatric ward, for the military authorities wanted to make certain that he was not malingering. The psychiatrists had more than one diagnosis but eventually decided upon "psychoneurosis." The Army authorities concluded that his "psychoneurosis" had not been present when he enlisted, had not been his own fault, and that he could be discharged "for disability in line of duty and not due to his own misconduct." Jones was honorably discharged on July 6, 1944.

Before he returned to Robinson, he made a literary pilgrimage to Asheville, North Carolina, where Thomas Wolfe had been born. Back in his own hometown, Jones moved in with Lowney and Harry. Uncle Charley and the conventional members of Robinson society were scandalized by the conduct of the two: They were together all day while Harry was at work; they sunbathed on the front lawn for all to see; they were totally indiscreet.

Jones went on working on They Shall Inherit the Laughter; *but he knew that he needed more education, and he applied to and was admitted to New York University, where Thomas Wolfe had taught for several years. He registered for the spring 1945 term at NYU and found an agent, Maxwell Aley, to whom he showed a draft of the novel and several of his stories. Aley advised extensive revisions of the novel, and Jones worked at improving his text while he was taking classes at NYU.*

Jones was not altogether pleased with Aley as an agent, and he took direct action to try to place his novel. A. Scott Berg in Max Perkins: Editor of Genius *gives an account of Jones's approach to Perkins, the Scribner's editor who worked with Fitzgerald, Hemingway, and Wolfe. Without an appointment, Jones came to Perkins's office, manuscript in hand, and asked to see the editor. The* secretary said that Perkins was not in, and she asked Jones to leave his novel, which would be read. He refused. The secretary went into Perkins's office and came back to report that he had returned by way of a back entrance and would see the visitor. Only later did Jones learn there was no rear door to the editor's office.

Jones and Perkins talked about the war and about Jones's novel, and finally they adjourned to the Ritz Bar. Perkins did not read the novel but assigned it to two other editors, who were not enthusiastic. Perkins, however, had been impressed with Jones and went through the novel himself. He then wrote Maxwell Aley, "It is a serious attempt to do a big piece of work and the author has the temperament and the emotional projection of a writer." He went on to say, "We do not feel however that They Shall Inherit the Laughter quite comes off as a novel, nor does it turn out to be anything for which we could make you an offer."

Jones left New York at the end of the spring term and returned to Robinson and the Handy home. Lowney was convinced he was going to be a major writer, and Harry provided much needed financial support. Jones turned to more revisions of the novel, and in the fall he went to Florida, where he worked part time on a fishing boat and where he completed the revisions. He then wrote to Perkins asking if Scribner's would consider the manuscript again.

TO MAXWELL PERKINS

MARATHON, FLA.
NOVEMBER 20, 1945

Dear Mr Perkins,

I am writing you in reference to my mss, "They Shall Inherit the Laughter," which you did me the honor of reading in January of this year. I have just completed a new, finished draft of the book, which has entailed my rewriting most individual chapters at least several times and occasionally more often than that. I am now preparing to go over it again, copy-

ing it up in mss form and making what smoothing and finishing changes I will find necessary. I expect to have the completed mss done within a month or five weeks from date.

If you are interested in seeing it again, please write to me at
the above address. Since having talked to you and having seen
the letter you wrote Mr Aley in reference to the mss, I am
writing you first to see if your firm would like to see it before
I attempt to contact anyone else.

I am no longer with Mr Aley, with whom I signed a contract
shortly after I first submitted the book to you. By a mutual
agreement we have dropped the association, and I am now
handling the thing entirely by myself. Mr Aley was kind
enough to give me the letters of both yourself and Mr Wheelock[1] and to report some of your comments to me verbally.
One of the chief complaints with the mss you saw was that it
"lacked resolution," I think Mr Aley said. While I did not
understand that criticism at the time, I think I do now, and I
am grateful the book was not published as it was. I think I have
given it resolution now, among other things, and I also feel that
in searching for resolution for the book, I also found a great
deal of resolution for myself.

The book itself is greatly changed in structure, although it
follows more or less the original timeplan and the original
characters. But then this tell[s] you little or nothing, and to
bluntly put down in a sentence just what those changes are, for
me at least, detracts from their subtlety and meaning.

I am offering it to you now first, partially because I still have
a soft spot for the character Tom Wolfe drew from you, but
mainly because I feel I owe you a debt of gratitude for not
publishing the book as it was when I submitted it.

I will wait to hear from you before I start trying [to] contact
anyone else.

Sincerely,

s/AL/C

---

[1]John Hall Wheelock, a poet, was an editor at Scribner's.

Perkins responded on November 27, 1945, that he would indeed read the manuscript again. Jones thought he would finish revising about January 1, 1946. Perkins expressed personal interest in his concluding sentence: "I have often wondered how things were going with you." Jones read and reread Perkins's letters—they were like sacred texts—and in Some Came Running *he had the courtly Bob French, the most sympathetic character in the novel, say to Dave, Jones's persona, "Weve been wondering what had happened to you."*

Jones took time out to write a "fan" letter to Upton Sinclair.

TO UPTON SINCLAIR

MARATHON, FLA.
DEC 5, 45

Dear Mr. Sinclair,

Enclosed you will find two dollars for two copies of *The Book of Life*. I stumbled upon a digest of it in a current magazine of psychic research, and I think there is a lot I could learn from it.

I have read several of your recent books on Lanny Budd, and they seem to be dealing with a number of puzzling problems with which I also am beset, principally the problem of society, and of Socialism. I am almost entirely ignorant of the platform and aims of Socialism, and the allusions to it in your books have both whetted my appetite and impressed me with my own ignorance. I wonder if you would send with the above books a bibliography of your own works dealing with Socialism, and also the names and authors of some other books that go into the subject at length.

. . . .

I am 24, out of the army a year, just completing the third draft of my first novel—fascinating words! I've been lucky enough (or unlucky enough) to get a contract with one of the better known agents in New York and by him was introduced around among that literary and publishing group. From that disillusioning association I found it much better to work alone without benefit of aid, broke the contract and got the hell out of New York before I could be transformed into a Faith Baldwin.

I have heard the story of the trouble you had getting *The Jungle* published, and it seems similar—though greater—to my experience with the "You can't do that!" prevalent in New York. From my reading I've come to the conclusion that your attitude toward literature, art, society, and life in general (and the problems of life in general) seems to be the most down-to-earth, commonsensical, and unbiased one I've found. I would like to have access to some of the knowledge that went into the creating and maintaining of that attitude. There are a number of those problems which are constantly on my mind, and for which I am trying to find an answer, not only for myself but for my characters.

This is my first effort at a "fan" letter, and I can assure you it would not have been written if I had not at least thought I found between the lines of your work the kind of character worth writing to.

Sincerely,

y/TL/C

Jones's aunt Molly Haish (his mother's sister) was one of his favorite relatives. During his childhood she always sent presents at Christmastime, and he had visited her in California just after he enlisted. In the following letter he makes one of his early mentions of his interest in Oriental religions and the occult. He was reading Paul Brunton (1898–1981), author of A Search in Secret India, A Hermit in the Himalayas, *and many other books.*

Jones was never a true believer in Theosophy/occultism as Lowney was, but he was drawn to the theory of reincarnation and a belief in the oversoul, ideas much in the American grain in the middle of the nineteenth century, for they are to be found in the works of Emerson, Thoreau, Whitman, and other Transcendentalists. In Jones's novel Some Came Running, *the occult beliefs were propounded by Bob French, father of Gwen French, a character remarkably similar to Lowney Handy. Bob French was given some of Harry's characteristics, but the Oriental religious beliefs in actuality were Lowney's, not Harry's.*

TO MOLLY HAISH

[MARATHON, FLORIDA]
DEC. 13, [1945]

Dear Aunt Molly,

Am answering your last letter. I expect to be here for at least another month, so if you send a package I'll get it. How about some of those Tollhouse cookies, the ones with the drops of chocolate in them, whatever they are called? Don't you send me any money unless you are absolutely sure you have no need of it, because I'm making out fairly well. Maybe I'll be able to send you some in a year or so.

I've been doing a little commercial fishing both in the Gulf and in the Atlantic, when I run short of dough. I go out with a man who lives next door who owns a 34 ft launch. It's fascinating, and a good break now and then from writing too hard. I made $20 one night, and that's only ½ of the net profit. But then again, I made 2.50 another night. . . .

Don't you worry about my getting more education. When I finish this book, I'm going back to school, probably Duke University. And you needn't fear any backslide on my part because my whole life is planned, a constant progression from learning one thing (and writing a book about it) to learning another. . . . Lately, I've been intensely interested [in] socialism. And by the way, Upton Sinclair is from your neck of the woods. When you answer, tell me what you think of him. He must have made some news in Calif. since you've been out there. You probably studied his platform for governor. I've been reading his books, and he's got a lot on the ball from what I can see.

I've also been doing a lot of looking into religion. Bought myself a grand $14 Bible which has everything including even a history of the books of the Bible and how and by whom they were written. As you probably remember from my old letters, I was pretty fanatically anti-religious. It took me a long time to overcome the antipathy to religion that the churches of Robinson, Ill. had instilled in me. But now I've learned that if a man can disregard and forget the churches, that there's a tremendous amount of knowledge in the Bible. I've also been reading a man named Paul Brunton, who spent a great many years in India, studying their religion. He's studied the ancient Egyptian and Greek "Initiate" religions. He's written a number of fine books on religion, and it's good points of truth.

   . . . .

I've been thinking a lot lately about the Xmas presents you used to send us kids in Robinson. You'll probably get a good laugh out of it. You remember the little gadgets you used to stick in? We never could figure out what they were. Hollywood was so far advanced that all of those you used to send us were completely strange. You sent me a Yoyo once, and nobody in town knew what it was or how to work it. By the time Yoyos got around to Robinson, I'd lost it. . . .

Love,
Jim

T/TLS

Jones was not able to keep his January 1, 1946, deadline for completing revisions on his novel They Shall Inherit the Laughter, *and he wrote Perkins a letter of explanation. Perkins responded on January 7, 1946, in a fatherly fashion: Since writing is not an exact science, the time it takes cannot be calculated. He advised Jones to send the entire manuscript once it was retyped.*

Jones sent the revised manuscript to Perkins on January 17, 1946.

TO MAXWELL PERKINS

TALLAHASSEE, FLORIDA
FEBRUARY 10, 1946

Dear Mr Perkins,

Since the notification of the receipt of my mss, dated Jan 22, I've had no other word from you. I realize the time necessary to study a mss, etc.; a number of people have to read it, then discuss it, then make suggested changes or perhaps a heightening of a certain scene. All that takes time and a lot of it. Last Jan I know you had the thing over a month before returning it. But I guess that besides being a moralist by nature, I am also naturally impatient. [A] number of things, possibilities of rejection, etc., certain things in the book that I thot wonderful a while back seem lousy now. You know how it is, I imagine, a song you've heard many times before.

But I have a number of plans I'm champing to get into action, and all of them hinge on this book: whether it is accepted or rejected, whether you will consider that it needs more work (personally, I'm sure it doesn't, but it's just possible my judgment may be biased), and of course the money angle, how large an advance and how soon. I'm stony broke right now. Extended rests and vacations seem to be impossible for one of my personality. I'm sitting here, living on my brother's faith right now, and what should be rest has only become jitterishness. I suppose you're used to being drafted as a father confessor.

I have been making unintelligible notes on more than one future novel. I'm all ready to start in on one now, but I can't work here in the midst of kids, and I can't reasonably free my mind to concentrate it on this new idea when the possibility exists that I may have to do more work on this one. And of course, dough: the underlying theme, heard at regularly recurring intervals. The book I have in mind was originally a pure combat novel. After seeing the movie of *A Walk in the Sun,* and reading several reviews of the book, I decided that someone should write a real combat novel, telling the complete truth, or as near the complete truth as a writer can ever approach. Also at intervals I've made notes on a certain type of character which I encountered first in the army and later in some civilians, and which I was for a period one of them myself. I've wanted to use that character as a protagonist in a novel; the depth and wealth of material on that kind of person [are] endless and will make fine writing. At the same time I want to inject the true reason why a man becomes like that: social forces which bottleneck and dam up his natural energies rather than giving them a channel in which their tremendous powers of energy and work may be useful. The type of man I have in mind is somewhat similar to Capt. Flagg and Sgt. Quirt in *What Price Glory.* But that play was to my mind exaggerated, and in being so lost a great deal of its power. Flagg and Quirt are archetypes, to me, rather than real living persons, so that a reader had no way to understand or associate them with his own personal life. I want to avoid that mistake.

In addition, I have always wanted to do a novel on the peacetime army, something I don't remember having seen. Do you think such a novel, combining these three plans, would be badly received now? I'm quite capable of writing it now, but it may be that the reading public is getting fed up with army and war—altho for their own protection, they should never be so. I wanted to ask your advice on that point.

I'm quoting a paragraph of notes to give some idea of what I want this protagonist to be: (Stewart is an old friend in the army, Wendson is a former 1st/Sgt of mine. I would use both in the same company.) "Draw Stewart's life in army, his intense personal pride, his six months on stockade rockpile rather than admit he was wrong and accept company punishment when he felt he was right in his actions. The small man standing on the edge of the ocean shaking his fist, the magnificent gesture, both Wendson and Stewart completely fearless (unloved men, yet forced to prove to themselves that they can get along without love, because they have never had honesty or love, insist that they neither miss them or want them). Almost a criminal, almost an artist, but not either—and so adopting the ideals of the Great Adventurer, the Soldier of Fortune, accepting on the surface the Soldier of Fortune role, but wise enough underneath to realize that such an archetype cannot exist in reality, consequently a wit (bitter, sardonic) and yet so subtle that it passes as simple humor to all but one man in a thousand. A man with the energy and conviction to lead, a man to have a following because he is so sure of himself that other men immediately are willing to follow what he says."

I've decided that this probably won't make much sense to you, but it calls up innumerable incidents and manifestations to my mind. But mainly, I want to know if there will be a market for this book if I write it now. I'll do better writing it while the army is still fresh in my mind.

But if not, I've another idea which is noted in considerable detail, using the idea [of] the character of the perfect citizen, as our society wants and expects a man to be, a man who has fulfilled all the obligations asked him by society, but who has not received the rewards society promises to such a man, as no honest person ever has, I think. A man of upper middle class with a fine family, a good job, but who has never been able to own his own home or get any money ahead. The villain of course is society. And under this exterior of the perfect citizen, respected and admired, runs the sense of his own dissatisfaction and unhappiness. As a side plot in this one, I intend to use a negro family who works for the perfect citizen, a completely tragic story, picked up from bits I've learned and from negroes I've known while living here in the south.

There are several more ideas I've made notes on, but what I want to know first is the fate of the book you have now. I've learned from the Vets Adm that they do not provide glasses unless the injury is Service Connected. Mine isn't, so I must pay for getting my eyes fixed up myself. I'll have to have the money to do that before I can think about going back to work on the next book. I'm getting more and more restless here every day and I want to get on with my work. If there's anything you can do to speed up this thing without discommoding yourself too greatly, I'd appreciate it immensely.

The army novel I mentioned can be written and completed in six months I think, what with the advantage of all I've learned in writing the first one. Another plan I have is to buy myself a jeep from the army and make a trip around to the various strikes, hang around in dungarees and pick up what I can learn. Besides the material for fiction I'll gain, I've considered as a result of that trip a non-fiction book of reflections on what I observe, something in the line of Dos Passos' *Rosinante*. So you can understand why I hate to waste any more time here when there are so many things I need to be about.

I'll wait here till I hear from you in answer to this letter. If in your answer you have no information about what's to be done with *They Shall Inherit* (or an advance check, I hope), I'm going to forgo the jeep and start out on the bum. I'll take, among other things, your letters, because it's very likely I'll run into trouble in Georgia or Tenn. so if you happen to get a wire from some jerkwater town in the wilds, think nothing of it. It would be much better if I had the jeep and a backlog, but as I said, I guess I'm just naturally impatient, and I've been on the bum before.

Somehow or other, I'm quite positive that you will want to take the book, altho I worry about it considerably at times. The only thing is the time, and I have much to do and see. Eventually, I intend to get an education, but not now.

When I take off from here, I intend to go first to Detroit. When I leave there, I'll go to an address in Illinois, and so I'll send you that address where I can be reached before I leave here. All this provided, of course, that you can't give me any info on the disposition of the book when you answer this. I fervently hope you'll be able to include an advance check, because that would settle all my problems.

Awaiting your reply, I remain,

Respectfully,

s/TL/C

Perkins responded by telegram on February 15, 1946: "Would you consider payment five hundred now for option on Stewart novel and setting aside INHERIT LAUGHTER for reasons I'll write? Some further payment to be made after we read say first fifty thousand words. Wish to cooperate but have more faith in second novel and have further revisions to propose for LAUGHTER." The "Stewart novel" was to be published as From Here to Eternity.

Jones had found another authority who believed in him. Lowney had been telling him forcefully and dogmatically that he had great abilities as a writer, and now the best-known editor in the United States had faith in his potential. Jones wired his acceptance on February 17:

PROPOSITION ACCEPTED. PLACING MYSELF IN YOUR HANDS AND AWAITING LETTER HERE. WIRE FIVE HUNDRED DOLLARS ANY TIME TO 202 WEST MULBERRY ROBINSON ILLINOIS.

Perkins wrote Jones a long, considerate letter on February 19, 1946, giving reasons for not accepting Laughter. *He felt that the public would not be interested in the subject at that time and that the novel would insult military people and civilians. It might be more acceptable in a few years, he said. In addition, the revisions were still not extensive enough. Perkins mentioned a new young man in the office who had read the novel and thought that much more still had to be done to improve it. This unnamed young man was Burroughs Mitchell, who was to edit Jones's major novels.*

Brilliant editor that he was, Perkins knew how to encourage the young man whose first novel had once again been rejected: "As for the book you are now to do, it seemed to us from what you said, that you saw something truly important, and that you were right in your interpretation of the nature of that type of man, and that he had never been portrayed in a way to make him understandable. There is something widely appealing in him, too, and something tragic. I hope therefore, that you will go forward with enthusiasm in the writing."

In a letter dated March 27, 1946, later published in Editor to Author, *Perkins urged Jones to keep a notebook. He suggested that Jones make notes on cards and then classify the notes under key words. "I think," Perkins wrote, "if a writer did that for ten years, all those memories would come back to him . . . and he would have an immense fund to draw upon. One can write nothing unless it is, in some sense, out of one's life—that is, out of oneself." Jones did make some notebook entries following Perkins's suggestion, but he did not do so over a long period of time. Jones did, of course, make notes and character sketches, but he did not classify them as recommended by Perkins.*

TO MAXWELL PERKINS

ROBINSON, ILL.
APRIL 9, 1946

Dear Mr Perkins,

I enjoyed your last letter very much. So much so that I went out first chance I got and bought myself a small looseleaf notebook and filled it with stiff cards. I've already started making notes in it. When I have enough I intend to index them according to a general emotional classification with little index tabs on the edge.[1] Of course, how far I shall get with it is

---

[1] Jones made only a few entries in the notebook. The following one was classified under the heading "Rebellion-Frustration":

How Lowney and I fought over her story in the final copying. And finally she said to hell with it, it doesnt mean that much to me, I'll just not finish it.

And I said, "Thats not true."

And she looked at me and said, "It dont mean a fuck to me."

"Thats a lot of shit," I said. "And you know it."

"All right," she said, as if that meant something, "I'll prove it to you." And got up and walked out.

I wanted to beat my fists against the wall with the frustration IN ME.

something else again. I can recall, as I suppose anyone can, a number of fine ideas that I started in on with great enthusiasm and ended up by deciding maybe they weren't so hot, or else they took too much time and energy, and finally ended by laying them aside. It always irritates me to do that, (I find it very hard to decide which ideas are worth continuing and

---

I lay on the floor with head in my hands, but in the back of my mind was the picture of her coming back and finding me in this obviously tragic position. But she did not come back. I wandered around the room and went outside and came back in and told myself it didnt mean anything to me, it was none of my worry, and finally I went out front, where she was sitting languidly indifferently on the steps smelling two flowers, a purple iris and a white one of some kind, and I knew that she was calculating her attitude for me to see it, just as I had calculated mine before.

I was very angry and piqued because I had to go outside, instead of her having to come inside to me, and thought how it always happens that way, it was always me who had to make the first overtures.

But I told her it was stupid to do that, and reminded her of how I would use to threaten to tear up my writing when I got mad and disgusted or hurt.

"Are you going to finish this story?" I said.

"I really just dont think its worth it, Jim," she said, with an air of great put-upon tiredness, the supreme indifference of worn-outness.

"Then I think I just wont finish my novel," I said.

"Well," she said, "thats up to you, isn't it?"

"Its the same thing," I said. "As your not finishing the story."

Both of us had apparently forgotten all about the original purpose, as she propounded it, the chance of getting $2000. This had become a battle between wills, sort of.

"I mean it," I said. "If you dont finish this story, I wont finish my book. I mean it."

"All right," she said with great exhaustion. "All right. I'll come back in in a little while. Just leave me alone a while. Please, just leave me alone."

I went back inside, but before I went I heard a small plaintive whistle repeated at continuous intervals from somewhere near the high-bush-cranberry, and began looking for it.

"Its a thrush," she said, still with this great tiredness but not nearly so much now because of her great instinct of protection for the thrush. "He's right at your feet. Dont move or you'll scare him."

which aren't) and at the first signs of waning interest I begin to berate myself and usually force myself to go on, lots of times when it isn't worth it. I'm having that problem now with something else.

I've started spending a certain amount of time every day—at least I planned a schedule to that effect, altho it seems I never follow it—in clipping news items from various papers and following up the stories from day to day, for example, the Pauley scandal over which Ickes resigned, and the Lichfield army trials,[2] which I'm particularly interested in. The lack of interest has already hit me: there are so damned many things I started clipping on that I envision waisthigh piles of scrapbooks stacked all around the room, filled with notes and stories of so many things that I'm as bad off as when I started because I'm never able to find them anyway. I'm slowly and painfully working my way thru a kneehigh stack of papers dating back to Jan 1st. (It has occurred to me recently that the waste of paper in the printing and distribution of daily papers must really be prodigious.)

The whole trouble seems to be due to a lack of efficiency on my part, but for the life of me I can't find any way to efficiently encompass all the myriads of things I feel I ought to encompass. Somewhat like Tom Wolfe in the library: so oppressed by the sight of so many books he could never read that he couldn't even bring himself to read what he could because it was comparatively so pitifully small. The trouble with me is my mother was a German, and I seem to be cursed with the German mania for cataloging everything and having it in its little niche. Only trouble is, there aint that many niches.

The idea you wrote me about is the best system for keeping notes I've ever seen, but I am depressed because it isn't perfect.

[2] The brutal treatment of American servicemen in the Lichfield stockade was called by *Time* (September 9, 1946) "the most shocking Army scandal of World War II." Jones did use information from the trial in his stockade section in *From Here to Eternity*.

Already I've made notes that I'm incapable of classifying generally. They're not Fear, tho some have fear in them. And they
aren't Courage. They aren't Sadness, altho they have elements
of sadness, and they aren't Pathos, or Joy, or Bitterness. Yet
almost all of them have two or three of these elements in them.
You see what I mean by German mind? I'd need a Dewey
Decimal System, only I don't know how to read one very well.
And besides, I haven't one.

I think my writing has the same trouble. Not a plethora of
words but a plethora of detail, all of which needs to be there
to get just the right shade of meaning. I'm particularly hipped
on this right now, because I was stuck a couple days ago on
a passage which seemed too long for the overall of the book,
and yet was not too long for the passage.

At present I have about 80 pages of first draft, about 24,000
words I figure, and I have not taken care of one-eighth of what
I outlined as being contained in the first 50,000 words. So there
you are, or rather there I am. Yet all of it is good—or will be
when I've rewritten it five or ten times—and all of it is necessary to the development of the characters as I see them, and to
the scene as it ought to be developed for the reader who had
never been to Hawaii. So far I have only one important scene
that I outlined in the synopsis; the rest is additional. I expected
it to be added to, but not that much.

It'll all come out eventually, I suppose, and yet I sometimes
despair of ever learning technique, so I can just sit down and
write. I have trouble with transition in the middle of chapters.
There is, I am told by ever so many books on it, a technique
to the novel. Yet nobody ever says just what it is, or how to
acquire it. The only plotting I know is to have a man do what
he would do in his life, but that apparently is not enough.
Plotting is supposed to be an improvement on life. I wonder
if there is any direct and systematic way to learn the technique
of the novel.

I have planned the book in three parts: one, from 1930 to Dec
7/41; two, from Dec 7 to Nov/42—a very interesting time in

Hawaii; and three, from Nov/42 (when this Regiment shoves off for the South Pacific) to the death of Prewitt 8 months later on New Georgia. I've made a detailed action synopsis of the peacetime period, conflicts between various characters and what they do to or for each other, which I intended to keep within 50,000 words. At present, I have about 24,000 and have hardly begun to touch the action I laid out for 50,000! Also, I have not made a synopsis of the other two-thirds, intending to get a first draft of this first done before going into them, and now that's beginning to worry me. Perhaps I should have completed a synopsis first, altho I have a vague general plan in mind and a complete list of characters. My characters, particularly the women, and excepting for Prewitt and Warden (the topkick), come into these two's lives and then pass out again. That's the way they do in real life, and if I twist it so that they reappear, it loses its sense of reality, for me anyway. It appears contrived and unlifelike.

How in the name of God I'm going to get in all that I want in, I don't know. Yet it all belongs in.

Tomorrow I begin plugging away again. I who have that cursed German mania for system am never able to satisfy it enough. There is too much of life to be filed away, I guess. Yet you can't do without system at all, because there are so many things to forget. I'm continually making mental notes to get something in in the next sentence, and then leaving it out because I think of something for the sentence after, and then remembering I left something out without being able to remember what. It's all a matter of moderation, as most things in life seem to be, and I suppose someday I will learn technique and an adequate system, or as near to it as one can come.

I have concluded, somewhat hopefully, from your letter that I am in essence a writer, altho it works a little differently with me: Instead of remembering the exact day, sharp and clear, I seem to remember with equal sharpness and clarity, not that day itself, but the way that day should have been for the particular scene I'm writing. In effect, the day, the temperature, all the thousands of little things fit themselves to the scene, the way they should be for that particular scene; no matter what they actually were when the actual drawn from actually took place. I guess, tho, that that is only another way of saying exactly what you said.

Ha! If I could only learn to quit psycho-analyzing myself. Then I could really learn to write.

Since I began writing this letter, I have made a note to cut out the first three chapters entirely (about 15 or 18 pages); they are good writing and give a reader a fine picture of what I'm leading up to, but I guess they are more or less superfluous. So if you can bear with reading these letters, it may do me a lot of good. Perhaps someday I shall even learn to write, who knows? Stranger things have happened. I can write any scene and write it well, but it's the tying them in and the whole general picture that I can't get.

Always my best regards,
James Jones

Would you suggest that I go ahead and make a synopsis of the rest of the book first, and then come back to the actual writing? Or [is] it better to go on as is, and construct the synopsis of the other two parts after I have first drafted the first part?

P/TLS

TO MAXWELL PERKINS

ROBINSON, ILL.
MAY 27, 1946.

Dear Mr Perkins,

You asked me to keep you informed, so here's a report. To date I have 173 pp (14 chap) which I have included under Book I completed, I think, except for final copying and touching up. In addition I have the first two chapters of Book II done in first draft, but which hits pretty close to what I want and won't need much change. In addition to that I've got several segments and scenes which I intend to use later, scenes cut out of Book I when I was rewriting it. So much for the facts.

What I want to know is do I write too much? And if so, how does one go about not writing too much? The obvious abnormality of the length of the other book, from Mr Mitchell's report, is bothering me, and it has been daily becoming more depressing. It's got to the point where it bothers my working. I expect as I have it planned to have five books in all, each probably as long as this first one. I've done a good bit of cutting on the first book in rewriting it. I guess I could go on cutting it. I am reminded of the ancient proverb where the king ordered the scholar to compile the history of man. Finally the guy ended up with: He is born, he suffers, he dies.

I am oppressed with what seems to be the disjointedness and pointlessness of practically all I've written to date. So much so that I have difficulty going ahead. Yet I know everything I have written so far is interesting, readable, and an important facet of the lives I'm trying to show. The ambivalence of it keeps me from sleeping, eating and enjoying myself at all when I'm not working. If I wanted to make inordinate symbols of these characters I could write a short and meaningless novel like [Richard Brooks's] *The Brick Foxhole.* As it is, I find myself muzzled by the necessity of restraint when I want to say something I feel needs to be said. So then I think this doesn't need to be said, because it's taking too much space. Which puts me in a position where I don't know what does need to be explained and said and what doesn't. It's depressing as hell, and I'm beginning to wonder if I can write at all. I'm almost afraid to write anything for fear it will make the book too long.

I don't suppose this tells you a great deal, but I am hoping you can tell me something that will help me. If you like, I can copy up Book I and send it to you. You said that after the first 50,000 words were approved, there was a possibility of further payment. What with the inflation, the rent and board I'm paying, the debts I've had to pay, and the foolish spending of a fair portion, I could sure use another advance. This book, at 250 to the page, will run 37,500, I think, but I also think with the margins you see here, there's probably more than 250 to the page. But mainly, I'm interested in what you can do to help me. Having read of your trouble with Tom Wolfe, I guess you ought to know something about this. Only with me it's not poetic description, certainly. I don't know what it is.

Do you want me to copy this up and sent it? It'll probably take three weeks. Until I hear from you I'll endeavor to struggle on.

Sincerely,
James Jones

P/TLS

Jones wrote many long letters to Maxwell Perkins to give an account of the evolving plot and the motivation of the characters.

TO MAXWELL PERKINS

ROBINSON, ILL.
JUNE 13, 1946

Dear Mr Perkins,

. . . .

I had hoped also to enclose Chapter 15, and possibly 16. I have 15 to 19, inclusive completed in first draft. But when I read fifteen over last night preparatory to copying, I didn't feel it was in good enough shape. Most of these have been worked over several times and I think they show it.

. . . .

Chapter 14 is the end of Book One. Book Two begins with a shift to the viewpoint of Karen Holmes. You are given her view of her husband's company, the Officers' Club (where I worked as a waiter and bartender), and her view of Warden, with whom she is having an affair. She is not able to understand Warden any better than anybody else. She introduces him into the partying life of tourist Waikiki section, through which moves the figure of Jim O'Hayer, the gambler. Warden later has an epic fight with O'Hayer which I've sketched out roughly. There are several scenes in which Karen tries to pry into Warden to find out [what] motivates his life, hoping that there may be some answer to her own unhappiness there. Mostly, she envies him the vitality with which he lives, in spite of the poor position life has seen fit to place him in. Her own life is lacking in vitality.

Warden is warned by Stark about playing around with Holmes's wife, but pays no attention. Stark, as well as Wilson and Henderson, has had an affair with her in Fort Bliss. Choate, using his friendship as a weapon, "tricks" Warden into giving Prewitt a Pfc rating. This is done against the background of Range Season, in which it is found Prewitt is an excellent shot, almost as good as any of the old timer clique. This is done in chapter 16.

Chapter 17 concerns itself mainly with Warden and Karen. The main thing that has drawn Warden to Karen (discounting his desire to cuckold Holmes) is the fact that she is cold, fearless, and doesn't give a damn about anything. When she falls in love with Warden, Karen begins to worry about the chances he takes, and thus no longer has that quality Warden admired in her. It is plain that the affair is going on the rocks, as it inevitably must.

Chapter 18 is short, showing a typical party at the Club through the eyes of Karen. At this party she has a humorous discussion of Warden with her husband's second in command, a callow young man just out of the Point named Culpepper.

Chapter 19 flashes to Warden in a River Street dive. He is trying to seduce a Portagee waitress. Prewitt enters with Andy and Friday, on a bar to bar tour. There is a brawl between Warden and the waitress's boyfriend and his five buddies. Prewitt instinctively helps Warden, who is the underdog, and by this action he is irrevocably forced into an alliance with Warden which he would not have chosen, had he been given a choice. This unthinking aid puts a constraint on their old hatred, so that Fate has apparently seen fit to force the two enemies together. This is a subtle point I was having trouble with getting across when your letter came. Do you see what I want to do with this? One man tries to knife Warden and Prewitt prevents him from it by an act of instinct in the middle of the fight. Neither Prewitt nor Warden can ignore this saving of Warden's life, even if they wanted to, and they do want to.

Later on, the Portagee waitress becomes Warden's mistress, his "shackjob." He discards Karen for this woman.

After the fight, they escape the MPs by climbing through the back window of a whorehouse where Warden is apparently wellknown. While here, Prewitt meets one of the girls with whom he later falls in love. Prewitt wants to marry her, but she refuses on the grounds that since she is a whore he obviously cannot love her. She is working in Hawaii to make enough money to go back to Oregon and live a respectable life and marry a respectable man.

Back at the company, Warden tries to ignore what Prewitt has done for him, and Prewitt tries to ignore it too, but neither can. Warden organizes a group to go down and take over the "Blue Anchor," the place where the fight occurred, and this bar becomes more or less the hangout of the company when in town. Stark nicknames it the "Blue Shanker." But after the company moves in, Warden moves out. Rose, the waitress, quits her job. They shack-up, but nobody sees them. Warden still remains a man alone.

Prewitt later has a fight with Bloom, which has been prepared for in Chapter 14, and whips him. Bloom, disgraced (he feels) by this defeat, falls in with a group of homosexuals in Waikiki, and later is called up in an investigation. Bloom gets off; he was only called as a witness; but he feels himself further disgraced, so much so that he commits suicide in the barracks.

I had intended originally to have Prewitt go on Special Duty at the Officers' Club as a waiter and a bartender. While there he would have a fight with the head waiter, an ex professional fighter, and Prewitt would be whipped, badly. I have about discarded this because of the limitations of space. But I think the fight is important, to show how Prewitt accepts defeat in a fight—or rather doesn't accept it. The fight was to have been the reason for Prewitt's going into the bar and his quitting being a waiter under Porchenick. Later, Porchenick was to have been beaten up so badly in town that he was hospitalized. Hit from behind. Porchenick would not know who did it, but it was obviously Prewitt. I had also planned for Prewitt to meet Karen and discuss Warden with her.

After coming back to the Company from the Club, Prewitt is accosted by Gallowitz, the ignorant Slav, who is drunk and harangues Prewitt for not doing right by Gallowitz's idol, Capt Holmes. Gallowitz draws a knife and Prewitt knocks him around. He is tried and sentenced to six months in the stockade for striking a superior noncom. The irony is that Warden, who would have liked to have put Prewitt in the Stockade, was unable to do it. Actually, Prewitt is railroaded because Holmes fights the self-defense angle because Gallowitz is one of his favorites. But by an even deeper reality, it is Prewitt's inherent personal honor that puts him in these bad positions.

Having known a number of these men, I am convinced that the great majority of real criminals—not petty thieves, but criminals—are what they are because of a high personal integrity and a high personal pride. I told this to Mr. Aley and Lewis Lundeen, the painter (who knew Pretty Boy Floyd—he claimed) at luncheon one day & they laughed at it and thought I was crazy. The same thing that sets an artist out to correct the baseness of his society makes a criminal repudiate his society. This one of the main things I want to show in the character Prewitt. In the Stockade Prewitt is saved from becoming an incorrigible by a man named O'Malley, himself an incorrigible. O'Malley is beaten with pickhandles, his ears torn loose from his head (I _saw_ this same thing, incidentally, when I was in the Prison Ward of the Station Hospital at Camp Campbell, Ky.), and confined in the Black Hole, a pit dug under the stockade with no bunk, no floor, a #10 can for a latrine, bread and water. (I have a strong feeling that most of the men in the recent Alcatraz riot were probably Prewitts; two of them were from Ky., two were Indians from the Cookson Hills in Okla.) But O'Malley committed to a course of perpetual resistance talks Prewitt out of resisting while he is in the Stockade.

(Have you ever read Jack London's *The Star Rover*?)

When Prewitt comes back to the Company, he is of course changed. Surprisingly, he is more like Warden. He applies for, and gets, a job as assistant clerk under Warden, because Mazzioli has been transferred to Regimental Personnel Section, as all the clerks have, in preparation for war. Prewitt finds the Company vastly changed, what with the beginning preparations for war—all manner of technical things.

The relationship between these two men becomes the main event from now till the war begins. Prewitt saves Warden by going to his shackjob to bring him back when Warden is drunk. Warden and Prewitt sit out in the middle of the highway on a beach position, each refusing to leave till the other leaves, and drink themselves into unconsciousness—luckily one of the Company's patrols finds them that time. A number of these incidents occur. There is a sardonic hatred between them that covers a mutual regard.

One of the official changes while Prew is gone is that Holmes gets his majority and moves to Battalion HQ. He takes O'Hayer with him. The next day all his favorites are privates. The new Company Commander is a reserve officer, a Jewish lawyer from Boston. He will remain with the company until he is relieved of his command on Guadalcanal for talking back to the Battalion Commander. Before that time comes Holmes has transferred to another regiment as a Lt Col, taking both his wife and O'Hayer with him and out of the book.

There will be a book devoted to combat on the 'Canal and on New Georgia. Most of the men the reader has met will be killed one way or another.

At the end of the book, Prewitt dies, not heroically in battle, but by getting drunk and falling in the river and drowning. Warden alone of all the old men in the company remains and he muses on the implications in the death of Prewitt and upon the things that are inevitably coming as a result of the war. You see him walking through the jungle, bearded, his helmet in his hand, dirty, half-drunk, but shouting bitterly at the sky that you can kill a lot of us but you can't kill us all. Some of us will live, despite anything you can do.

This is a pretty short résumé of the last part of the book, but I have a host of memories to draw from, and I have not bothered to elaborate a number of scenes dealing with various characters which I nevertheless have sketched out roughly and filed away.

Before your letter came, I had considered dropping the two chapters dealing with Violet Ogure, since they didn't further the plot any and I felt that they took up too much space in between the continuity of events. I would like to have your opinion on keeping them. They are as near an insight into the strange mixture in Hawaii as I think I can ever come, and I think they are good writing. Someday I think there will be some great literature come out of Hawaii, written by the second generation Japanese and Chinese. I met a number of these boys at the U. of H. who would be capable of it.

I'll be gone for two weeks, and I expect to have a renewed zest when I return. Right now I'm pretty well saturated with writing or this letter would have been better than it is. I will be anxious to hear from you.

Ever sincerely yours,
James Jones

P/TLS

TO MAXWELL PERKINS

ROBINSON, ILL
AUGUST 1, 1946

Dear Mr Perkins,

When I am working and doing something wrong or that does not come up to my expectations, I am depressed and irritable, just as you are when you have a bad cold that you do not consider. Something is wrong and I feel it but I can't put my finger on it. That was the way it was.

I think I had begun to put my finger on it before your letter came, and you have hit the nail squarely on the head. The amazing thing to me is that in that poorly constructed 200 pp you could see what I'm driving at. Tho I had started to form a plan to correct its errors, the assurance and advice of a man with your experience and reputation in writing [are] a tremendous lift for me.

I have been reading Remarque's *Arch of Triumph,* studying the economy of words, the technical device of short very active scenes in which the talk itself give most of the explanation. When I went back, at the mention of Katczinsky, to look over *All Quiet,* I could see the immense progress Remarque had made in technique. I intend to study *Arch* and use the technical device he uses in my own book, without, of course, letting his material or method of Ravic's single viewpoint affect me. I think I am still recovering from my New York jaunt and the restrictions it placed upon my writing; I've been struggling too hard to convince the reader that "this is really true, really it is."

Before I'd heard from you I'd already begun to make inroads on the first 200 pp, and after getting your concurrence, I can cut the bands and start ripping it apart. I've been working on short scenes, from two to six pages, all of which deal with the juxtaposition of various characters. I took Warden and O'Hayer and wrote chronological scenes in which they meet, each a step further toward their climax. I did the same thing with Prewitt and Bloom, with Warden and Karen (Holmes's wife). Later, I will fit these scenes together with whatever small changes necessary to make them flow together—so that all of the conflicts move along side by side, with as little superfluous exposition as possible. I don't think it's going to be such a hard thing to cut it and reshape it. It takes me a hellish long time to grasp something, but when I do get it, I've got it for good and I have no more trouble with it.

I'm glad that you think everybody is real as far as they are presented. The whole crux of the trouble was that they were not presented far enough, for 200 pp. I intend to introduce Karen Holmes much earlier as I do it over. Also I need to introduce John Slade near the front, a soldier drawn from myself; and I need to introduce his girlfriend, Betty Temple, sooner. I will also bring Prewitt's second woman, the New

Congress whore, in much sooner. Then these three male characters will each have his female counterpart, and the resulting conflicts that go with them. That will in part take care of the women readers, but more important it will make their lives move more truthfully as they should.

You are perfectly right about really good officers, and I shall have several of them before I'm done; I have them in my mind but I needn't bother you with them now; you can't know them yet of course. And I also want to show sympathy for Holmes before I'm through, show that he is more the victim of circumstances than of anything lacking in his potentiality. He's a very pathetic character in many ways. One of the notes I made in my cardboard notebook you suggested I keep was that it ought to be a universal requirement of all writing, as ironbound a requirement as a plot, that every character should be handled with sympathetic understanding—even the worst son of a bitch—because it is in him. This is no Tolstoyan moralistic principle, it is a truth of life that too many people overlook. If Irwin Shaw had made his character of Michael's wife in "Girls in Their Summer Dresses" sympathetic, he would have had a much greater story there. Not meaning Shaw, I can't stand a writer who uses his work to get rid of his personal prejudices.

I'm very, very thankful that there is a man in the publishing business who can see what you are driving at when you tell him, even though you tell him very badly, he is still able to pick out the kernel and see what you mean. I've had some very disheartening experiences with publishing, and I'm damned glad you are there at Scribner's and that I came to you.

I'm going to keep in mind that I don't need to explain too much. That will be as valuable to me as was the advice of Hemingway to stop when you're going good.

It sure is good to know that there is someone whose opinion you can trust who believes in what you're working at. And that you back it up with the advance helps not only my finances, which need it, but also my morale.

The check wasn't in the letter. I don't know whether you

meant to enclose it in the letter or send it to the bank as you did before.

You will hear from me later.

Ever sincerely yours,
James Jones

p/TLS

TO MAXWELL PERKINS

ROBINSON, ILL.

OCTOBER 21, 1946.

Dear Mr Perkins,

I did not feel like working tonight and I figured you were about due for some kind of word. I did about 2500 words of very good stuff this afternoon and am still so enthused over it that I am reluctant to plunge in again. However, after I finish this letter I think I shall feel more like it.

(Incidentally, that bit of advice you gave me about quitting while I'm hot has proved invaluable. I hope someday to be able to thank Hemingway for it also. It strikes me that I must appear as rather set against Hemingway to you. I certainly am not. I think he is a fine writer, but to date I have discovered only two writers whom I can take all the way, or at least nearly so; and those are Scott Fitzgerald and Tom Wolfe. I think Hemingway is confused on lots of things, just as I think the *Fountainhead* was confused; but I also think both are magnificently right in many things.)

After your last letter I started in to rewrite that first 200 pp. To date I am just emerging through the last scenes of it and a number of scattered scenes Id written before I got your letter. As I worked along, I saw things Id missed of course, and so much you have not seen has been added while I was cutting the other. I followed the original scene plot up until I got through the episode with Violet before adding anything new.

And at that point I had cut 82 pp to 43 pp. After that it becomes too involved to explain in a letter, for I've added scenes and cut whole sequences. I've done some rigorous cutting, let me tell you.

Perhaps it isn't much to show for three months' work, but several personal problems requiring time and thought got in my way and I did not work as much as I wanted to. However, I've acquired a good deal of material for future use.

What amazes me still is that you could see through all the strained bungling boring exposition the underlying worth. I shall never get over that. Had I been the editor I've have thrown it all out.

I wrote quite a number of scenes while waiting for your answer and opinion, and I discovered that they too suffered from the same fault as the other. Also, I could see gaps opening up in the plan I had had, so that I figured it would better to begin again and get the first satisfactory before going ahead. Now, I am just emerging through that anguish and I feel like a man who comes out of a dark narrow alley into a well-lighted thoroughfare. Until the day before yesterday, it had been three months since I wrote a fresh scene in first draft and it was a wonderful experience to find I could still do it, and that it, as writing, had improved thru the rework of the other. I am beginning to spread my wings again, and I feel very satisfied with the job of rewriting what you've seen—which is the reason for this ungodly letter.

I have evolved a plan (due directly, I think, to learning how to manipulate my first checking account) by which I keep a running account of chapters, the scenes in them, and the number of pages in each scene. Thus I can refer to my account instead of having to thumb through scores of pages, if I want to know what happened to certain characters as such and such a place. In addition I have separate lists titled by characters in which I list each scene concerning that character consecutively and also the proposed scenes for that character along with notes of how I want to write it. So I take these and by them map out ahead the final draft, interlacing the scenes between various characters. Wonderful, isn't it? If I fail as a writer, I can always become a bookkeeper.

I have always been bothered because I couldn't remember details of time, place, etc. and I used to find myself either surrounded by reams of written pages, or else rewriting the same thing three or four times. This helps somewhat to alleviate that. To date I have finished 21 scenes totaling 129 pp which covers 4½ chapters. The longest, on Violet, is 15 pp, but there is only one, where before there were two chapters. Of course, there are scenes within scenes and when I set myself a prospective number of pages for any one scene I always overrun it, but at least I dont overrun it as much as I did.

I am ashamed to take up your time like this. I only wanted to let you know I was not dead and had not become so desperate as to reenlist.

I bought a Viking portable Tom Wolfe the other day and read a few scenes. I read through *Story of a Novel.* After that I got out your letters and read them through. Then I drank a couple of bottles of beer and sat around pinching myself on my left elbow. I was high as a kite, and not from beer. Also, I realized I have come one hell of a long way since 1940 and the days at Hickam Field when I read the *Angel* and decided I was so much like this guy Wolfe that I was going to be a writer myself. My semester at the University of Hawaii I copied Wolfe's style [so] much that even the teachers were curious. I find even now that if I read his fiction I tend to fall back into the Wolfeian flow of prose, which is why I don't read him. Someday, after I finish this book and revise "Laughter" and have both published, I shall sit down and gorge myself on him. I certainly wish I could have known him.

. . . .

Also by the way, I have found a title for this book. *From Here to Eternity.* Taken from the "Whiffenpoof" song, of Yale drinking fame. It goes: "We are little black sheep who have gone astray, baa . . . baa . . . baa. Gentlemen songsters out on a spree, damned from here to eternity. God have mercy on such as we. Baa, etc."[1] Maybe it's maudlin, but so am I. I get chills every time I sing it, even when sober.

I wont take up any more of your time. I'll keep you informed as to how I make out along.

ever sincerely yours,
James Jones

P/TLS

TO MAXWELL PERKINS

ROBINSON, ILL.

OCTOBER 30, 1946

Dear Mr. Perkins,

. . . .

I wrote to thank you for the book [Roger Burlingame's *Of Making Many Books: A Hundred Years of Reading, Writing and Publishing*]. Not only because I am so interested in the world it portrays, which I have never seen, but because it suddenly makes it appear as if I am, or might be anyway, a writer after all. Ive read of many of the Scribner people in Tom Wolfe and wanted to know them and more about them. And this puts me closer to them and to the world of publishing and of writers. Really, I cant thank you enough.

Despite the above harangue, I can see much progress in my stuff. Some of it is really wonderful. I am learning gradually what to leave out. To me it seems largely a matter of emotion projected, even the thought must be basically emotion in fiction, or else it becomes essay. It can be done just as well in general action or in specific action, according to the immediate needs. I did one little scene yesterday on advertising I am

[1] The title is actually from "Gentlemen-Rankers" in Kipling's *Barrack-room Ballads*.

tremendously enthused over. Prewitt sits in the dayroom and looks at the ads in a slick mag. He doesn't bother with the lovey-gooey stories at all. He is broke and has not had money enough for a woman for months and I show how the ads excite him sexually to a point of madness. There is absolutely no moral ground in the scene; I dont say the ads are immoral, or just missing pornography. I just show how they affect Prewitt (finally make him angry), and it is shocking. Even pleasantly shocking (to me), and it does not touch at all the moral grounds of such ads. I think it's a unique approach that will startle "our cottonwool citizens" as London says.

Do other people write you long letters like this and use you for a mental cathartic? I suppose they do from the book, but I never can quite get over a guilty feeling. I assuage myself by convincing myself they are readable.

But my God! "the lone art." Burlingame sure hit that one at six o'clock.

It is a very hard thing to realize that I am in process of becoming one of the Olympians of whom he writes so casually.

Dont bother to answer this.

Ever sincerely yours,

s/TL/C

Jones was never a food faddist as Lowney was; but he did experiment with his diet, and at times he fasted. There is no indication in other letters about the nature of his illness.

TO JEFF JONES

[ROBINSON, ILLINOIS]
[DECEMBER 1946]

Dear Jeff,

. . . .

[S]ince Ive been sick lately, I wanted to find out why. Been reading a book called *Initis,* which is written by an Indian M.D. who practiced in England. His theory [is] that most sickness is a direct development of eating too much. Im experimenting with myself in diet. Only liquid for breakfast (coffee and orange juice); my only solid food at noon followed by a three hour siesta (in Mexico and India both the siesta is centuries old; funny aint it?); then perhaps a glass of milk only in the evening and coffee again. I only began it a few days ago, but am feeling better already. No doubt you will laugh, as usual. You, my brother, have a peculiar habit of laughing at everything that either frightens you or else seems to require more energy to attempt than you think you can afford. You are not different from the rest of the Western world who know so little, and yet can convince themselves of their superiority enough to sneer and laugh at the Gandhis. So that also does not bother me. But for a long time I have noticed references to diet in the works of white men. One was Upton Sinclair in *Book of Life,* but up until now I have told myself they were crackpots without giving them a fair shake. Rather than go into detail about *Initis* here (its the writer's name for the intermediary stage between dyspepsia and a multitude of diseases which derive from it). Im enclosing nine pages from his book which I copied on the typewriter. I had a hard time understanding it, a hard time forcing my interest and concentration upon it because it seemed so silly—so I sat down and typed it word for word to get myself below the surface of the words. If you really want to understand it, you can do the same. Anyway read it carefully.

You see, I really have at last renounced society. It not only is completely wrong (save for one salvation: the good heart that exists in every man), but it even begins from wrong premises. I used to accept its premises and try to argue its logic and its conclusions. You see the difference. Actually, what I wanted to do was to come around in back in a roundabout way and enter back into the fold of society, to be accepted by its standards on my own sayso. I wanted the results without having to pay the price. It makes me laugh to think of the "Whiffen-poof Song," after reading Kipling's poem. Kipling's poem is in itself the bleating of the Black Sheep who wants to be admitted back into the fold, an orgiastic bout of self-pity. Yet for Yale freshmen, Yale Freshmen, mind you, to bleat about being Black Sheep is so ridiculous that it makes me sick to my stomach. The soldiers had some justification; but Yale freshmen, with everything handed to them on a silver platter by rich parents—I dont guess I need to elaborate. . . .

I used to tell you about all the women I'd slept with, how I slept with . . . with . . . , and that each taught me a little toward becoming a writer. Did I ever tell you about the Portagee gal I had in Honolula? shacked up with her? Ive told most everybody else at some time or other. It like the others was a lie. It was an attempt to make a hero out of myself. It was a very swashbuckling picture, romantic, heart-stirring; pretty, but untrue and in being untrue creating a false conception of a soldier, adventurer. I think it always thrilled you, made you want in some way to play that role yourself. There is no answer in playing roles. There is no answer in the Magnificent Gesture, only pathos; and pathos is no answer. I no longer want to myself or want other people to feel sorry for me. Do you? Dont you write these terribly heart-stirring letters up here, thinking: "God what an abused character I am, how I suffer, how terribly life has treated me, how Jim must weep when he sees what straits Im in"? Ask it to yourself, honestly; you needn't say it to anybody else if youre ashamed of it. But listen: Remember down in Georgia when I went out with . . . and came back to the cabin and told you Id slept with her? Then later told you, truthfully, that I had not slept with her? And you asked me why? I think I said I didnt know. I know now. And it was a simple self-pity, and self-heroism. I was lying to myself, kidding myself into playing a role I thought pretty and enviable. But why do we want, or need, people to envy us? The envy you put in somebody else's mind always come back to your own. And the envy you feel is just as chimerical as the envy you have created in them. Why should a man who disdains the dishonesty of society also hunger for the same dishonest approbation he disdains? Thats not only illogical, its plain crazy. The truth of what happened with . . . is not nearly so pleasant as the fictitious role. After I came home that night I went out and jacked-off, took care of myself, building up in my mind a picture of a romantic non-existent me sleeping with. . . . And that was the same thing I did all the time I was in Hawaii—all those women I used to write you about sleeping with I didnt. I took care of myself instead. No very pleasant or heroic picture, is it? Yet it is invariably the <u>true</u> picture that lies behind any such self-dramatization, self-deception, self-lies. And the more and greater the lies, the more unpleasant the true picture—and consequently the more we lie to ourselves trying to hide the <u>true</u> picture. That will be the picture of Slade in the novel.[1] If the people around here dislike me now, theyll cross the street to keep away from me after this book comes out. Yet underneath it will be the spark that will someday come out on top, because Slade will in the end refuse to accept either his own or anybody else's false picture as a pattern for life. Which Prewitt will not, and why Prewitt will

---

[1] In the finished version of *Eternity*, Slade's role is diminished.

die. I could go on indefinitely, pointing it up with illustrations, yet it is all here above for you to see. . . .

Merry Xmas and all that shit.

s/TL/C

TO MAXWELL PERKINS

ROBINSON, ILL.
MARCH 16, 1947

Dear Mr. Perkins,

. . . .

The truth is things arent going so well. I had thought the damn thing would be finished by now. I think I'm getting so I'm almost afraid of it, which is something that never happened to me before. (Maybe it did; I think maybe it happened in the Keys when I was working on "Laughter" and now I've forgotten it because it's past.) I have a fear of failing that I never used to have. I think it's because I've never actually published anything. I guess it's silly, but I keep feeling I should have published something by now.

I dont need to tell you: writing is my life, if I couldnt write I dont know where the hell I'd be. But writing without publishing is like eating without swallowing.

I'm having troubles I never had before. "Laughter" was largely autobiographical and I had a readymade plot and characters who followed it; all I had to do was heighten it and use my imagination. But here I have nothing to go on except certain people I knew in the army and what made them tick. There is no plot at all except what I create. I'm not even a character in the book myself, except in so far as I am every character. What I have to draw from is 5 1/2 years experience in the army. There was little or no dramatic intensification in the lives of the people I'm writing about now. From what I can gather in reading, this is a problem that every "young writer" has to face eventually, that makes it better I guess, but I still have it to face, because the thing these people were did not come to the surface materially in external events, except now and then haphazardly.

I've done a lot of reading on it, although most of it hasnt helped me much. About the best help I got was from Tom Uzzell's *Technique of the Novel*, altho if I did everything like he said I wouldnt have to write, Id be enough of a mastermind to just take the world over tomorrow and run it right. Also I bought Ellen Glasgow's *A Certain Measure* and am trying to get hold of Edith Wharton's *The Writing of Fiction* which you folks published.

What has actually happened to me is I rewrote what I first sent you two different times, completely, cutting a lot and adding many more scenes, a great many of them written before you saw the first part. There is much you have not seen, so much I dont know where to start to tell you about or to ask your help. The help I need is in the plotting, in the discovering of *external events* which will display the undercurrents I'm working with, and I guess I have to do that alone. The lonely art, that's good all right.

Both times I rewrote it after reaching a certain point I found myself at a complete dead end. I couldnt go on. I had so much to get [in] I should have got in sooner I was stuck. After two such experiences I decided the thing was to start with the germ and figure it out in advance from there, giving each person his proper place and part in the connection he has with either Prew or Warden, the two main people. I've been doing that, and it is tough sledding, and at the same time I've been reworking the first part with this in mind. (I worry often because it isnt going faster, it isnt going near as fast as "Laughter." If I knew how to ask for help and what to ask for I'd sure do it, but I dont know what to ask for. Maybe you could help me by suggesting reading, or something.)

I have access to a copy of Fitzgerald's unfinished *Last Tycoon,* the edition you put out in '41, and it has helped me a lot just to study the way he worked, much more than if the novel had been completed, altho I cant say exactly how. Maybe the fact that he had spent three years on the book to date without getting it finished is what helps me. I dont know.

At present I have Book One nearly finished, I think. I have two or three new scenes to write up in it yet that I'm working on—at the same time working ahead in trying to plot it. At present I've divided it thus: (I figure Book One at close to 25,000 words, and plan the other four to be near the same.)

Book One—"the transfer"
Book Two—"the company"
Book Three—"the women"
Book Four—"the stockade"
Book Five—"the reenlistment blues"

Of course the subjects overlap, but it more or less follows the time sequence. At present the time sequence runs from April '41 to December '41, and the climax ties in with the event and emotional turmoil of Pearl Harbor. I have had to abandon the major wartime Hawaii part for a later book. I cant do it justice here. The same holds true with the combat part. And the way I see it, these are not of the same pattern with the earlier part. e.g., Prew's time in the Stockade, if he just came out, went on with the Company, it lost meaning. The same holds true of Warden's affair with Karen (which is to be the real love story of the book), if he just left her and went on, the meaning was gone.

(You see I'm working with entirely invented stuff. In real life Prew did go to the Stockade, but he came out and went on to the 'Canal with us. In real life I dont think Warden ever met Karen, let alone had an affair with her because he came to the outfit some time after Holmes and his wife moved on.)

I've figured it out I can do the same thing, and do it better (about Prew and what I wrote you) by, instead of having him die in the river on the 'Canal, having him desert before Pearl.

He deserts because he kills a man ("he has to do it"). The man is the S/Sgt in charge of the prisoners in the Stockade, along with the Capt over him (who comes from Harlan), is a disciplinarian. (This is drawn from my own experiences in Camp Campbell, Ky., in the lockup ward in the hospital.) It's a delicate thing to arrange, the killing: he deliberately kills the man, hangs around a bar where he knows the man will be in town. Then he deserts. He does not want to desert (he loves the army) but he is wounded in the fight, he gives the guy a fair shake, by "Fatso's" knife; this makes him afraid to go back for fear of being suspected. (It is important that there be no legal entanglements such as courtrooms and trials, I dont want a detective novel) hence there must be no witnesses, and he would have gone back to the Company had he not been wounded. As it is, he goes to a whore downtown with whom he has "fallen in love" (for sheer hunger of female companionship) and she hides him out in her apt.

. . . .

Prew's whore girl friend, Alma (her house name is Lorene), I have pretty well figured, a couple of their scenes I have written, but this love story is really subordinate to the affair of Warden and Karen, the real love story. The thing with Alma is that she came into the profession cold bloodedly to earn enough money to raise herself and her mother to a higher social caste back home in Oregon. (I am drawing her from a whore I knew.)

. . . .

I'm constantly worried about the plotting taking the life and the truth out of it. I read over things and I think, O Christ, this is shallow as hell. Yet I can't see any other thing to do. I guess I have to do it, and yet I apparently dont know enough to do it, at least not without much, much time. The only thing I go by is that all the plot must come directly from the personalities and from their particular scheme and manner of life. The plotting must be fitted to their living, that their living must never be changed to fit a plot. That way it's very much harder, but I know it's right. I have a tremendous fear of degenerating into commercialism and unreal people, and melodrama. Sometimes I feel maybe I'm too conscientious for my own good.

. . . .

Also, I worry about your having advanced me so much money. I didnt even know then what an unprecedented thing $1000 dollars was for a novel before it was written, especially without having published anything. That certainly bespeaks your faith, but I have trouble remembering it all the time. I worry about the responsibility I have toward you personally. I have divined, or felt I did, that your backing of me was done against considerable opposition—nothing that you said, just what seemed to me to come between the lines.

And it is taking so damned much longer than I thought, and over half of it not even done in first draft yet.

Yet, one thing I do know, whether I ever learn the form of technique: I can write, with true emotion and perception and the right values of the things I've seen. Of course, that doesnt do one a helluva lot of good if you're not published, publishing is the end of writing after all. In fact, I can write so damned well that that is my main trouble. I can write anything, I can write everything; but I havent yet learned how to make it properly selective. Any time a scene hits me emotionally I can sit down and write it, with the true emotion. But too many scenes lead off into tangents and blind alleys from which I cant extricate myself.

. . . .

Ever Sincerely Yours,
James Jones

P/TLS

To Jones's long letter of March 16, 1947, Perkins responded on March 28, 1947, with a letter praising the young author. Perkins admitted that he still could not visualize the whole novel and therefore could not completely understand the parts.

Perkins urged Jones to read and reread Tolstoy's War and Peace *and to neglect works on the art of fiction. He thought well of Henry James's* The Art of the Novel, *E. M. Forster's* Aspects of the Novel, *and several other similar books, but he was firm in his belief that Jones should not be reading them until he finished his novel. He did, however, send him Robert Henri's lectures on art, published as* The Art Spirit, *for it "by inference enormously illuminates the problem."*

Perkins spoke of Hemingway's spending five years on For Whom the Bell Tolls *and reassured Jones, who was worrying about the time he was spending completing his novel: "You are right on time, except for the fact that time is the enemy of us all, and especially of the writer. But don't become obsessed with that feeling, as Tom Wolfe did."*

Perkins was afraid that Jones would become "sort of muscle-bound" if he spent too much time thinking about plot and theory.

Perkins's letter greatly encouraged Jones, and he immediately answered.

TO MAXWELL PERKINS

ROBINSON, ILL.
APRIL 9, 1947

Dear Mr Perkins,

I very much appreciate your fine letter. It did me a world of good, as did the book you sent, which was perhaps the best thing you could have sent me under the circumstances. I suppose I have told you that I am often amazed at your insight into things. And of course you have had much experience with writers' problems, so that you have got to know the signs I guess.

What I needed back was my old egotism, I guess. For a long time I have understood your remark quoted by Malcolm Campbell [Cowley] in the *New Yorker* profiles,[1] that the trouble with literature in our time is that there aren't as many rascals as there used to be. It's funny, but it's also very very deep. Only I would have said son of a bitch instead of rascal, I guess. He has to be one, because he has to want to write bad enough that he will stop at nothing and hurt anybody no matter how much he loves them. There is something to write about there, too; and I dont think anybody ever did it yet. Because—if the man tried to change his character for the better it must, necessarily, be at the expense of his writing. So he has a bad choice. And I think maybe that's what I've been trying to do maybe. Anyway, I have let it go by the board now. In so doing, I have posed myself certain questions I am forced to answer, ones I can no longer put off or tell myself they dont exist. It makes me face a whole new way of life, and I am very glad it happened. I'm getting back my old enthusiasm that life somehow had sneaked away from me without me knowing it. It took your letter and Henri's book to make me face it.

One of the things I've worried about is the sense of reality, of it actually happening in what you write, when I am forced to write of things that did not actually happen to me that I saw and heard and felt. In plotting this book I am writing of things that never happened at all, and I am always a little afraid the feeling, the true feeling, will not be there underneath. In some of these scenes I know it isn't, and I must get it in. But I think also that the way I was feeling before had something to do with it. A writer should not go to his typewriter like a battle-fatigued businessman, I think. However, I think I can do them now.

What you said about a novel never being wholly satisfactory is also good for me. One can be too much of a perfectionist.

[1] *The New Yorker* pieces about Perkins appeared in the April 1 and 8, 1944, issues. Jones misremembered Cowley's name.

And you are right about reading about writing while writing. I have stopped it and intend to stay stopped.

I think too it was right about the muscleboundness. I was, but I am getting over it. I like that one very much.

I am sending back to you today the original of *Laughter.* I dont know what you'll do with it, but it should, I feel, be with you. It is yours, till the time comes to revise it.

You see, one of the things I am faced with as a result of overhauling myself is that I must get out of this town. I know now I can no longer stay here and write as I wish to. Probably it's because it is my hometown and is so small. I have hated the prospect because of several reasons, not the least of which is that I used my thousand bucks to outfit a perfect place for working, with some outside help. A very wonderful place, and I have hated to face the necessity of leaving it. But since it is in this town I know that I must. It is terribly depressing, it makes you lose your faith in yourself, to be viewed as a sort of ne'er-do-well who is living, as one of my acquaintances phrased it recently, "a country gentleman's life of a little reading and a little writing." And here it goes much deeper than that. . . .

This is all probably beside the point, but that's the way it is, and I wanted to tell you. I expect probably to come to New York when (or if) I get the state bonus they are putting out. Since I was overseas almost the whole time I'll get around $660. In the meantime I am continuing working on this book and am working also on a few short stories along hoping to sell some to *Esquire* to fatten the poke.

You are very encouraging about the time element, and I do think I was becoming a little obsessed with it, as I was with the theory of plotting.

I think maybe I'm all right now for a while, I think you can rest on me for six months or so anyway. But I would greatly like to hear from you, sir.

Ever Sincerely
James Jones

P/TLS

Jones responded again to Perkins's letter of March 28, 1947. He mentioned favorably Paul Brunton and Yoga, reflecting Lowney's interests. The "trance state" was used in the stockade section of From Here to Eternity; *the trance state allowed one to endure solitary confinement.*

In his letters to Perkins, Jones was careful not to divulge his relationship with Lowney Handy, nor did he describe the financial help the Handys were extending to him.

TO MAXWELL PERKINS

ROBINSON, ILL.

JUNE 23, 1947

Dear Mr Perkins,

Sorry not to have answered your letter before. It certainly was a fine one. And it means considerable to me. You seem to have a certain intangible intuitive faculty that is of tremendous help, without ever actually being anything you can put your finger on.

Your letter was forwarded to me when I was down in Tallahassee, visiting my brother, getting in some fishing on the Gulf and some sun and tramping the woods. The kingfish run was on then and we had a fine time trolling them, several days.

I am working fine now and feeling high. God, there is no abyss like that of a writer who wants to write but cant and sits around all day wanting to write and not able to and every word he types is horrible. The X factor in all art.

I think the key was in your other letter where you mentioned the <u>intuitive</u> woman writer and in Henri's comments about the Yogis and that the thing was to attain the "trance state" first and that then the art was a natural result. I think I've been, as you said with the man tossing his hat, trying to calculate and figure too much. I've stopped that now and am trying not to worry and just let it come out, because apparently it all is there, in your mind, in the subconscious, and the trick is to throw your conscious mind out of gear and just let it flow thru.

That knowledge has turned me recently to an interest in the Yogis and their various paths of attaining the Overself, as Paul Brunton and Emerson call it, which exists someplace in every man's mind, the God in every man. I've been reading a good bit about them and of them lately. (Is Paul Brunton the man Maugham drew his protagonist for *The Razor's Edge* from? I've a hunch he is, altho Maugham seasoned it up a lot, and apparently didnt know much about Yoga.)

Anyway, the trick is to release the trigger of your conscious mind, it seems to me, and then things write themselves that you have forgotten you even knew. If you could only just reach that state and maintain it, it would be wonderful. Only I cant, and none of the Yoga paths seem to help me any because I'm not interested in spiritual attainment but only writing and in putting down the truth of life.

To do that I have to, as you suggest, put technique, plot and calculation aside and just let it come out willy-nilly. Except that I am learning to say these things indirectly and in action, instead of telling them showing them. It seems to me, altho rather hazily, that if you as the writer retain something that you do not say, no matter what, and then write the rest in action and conversation, there is an element of emotion that you catch that you never get any other time. Now I'm writing scenes and series of scenes that run to 30 and 40 and even 50 pp without a break. But they are all action and talk, as you said once before a long time ago. Maybe 50 pp about what happened between four people in one evening. I greatly fear that in the end, before it is all put together, I will need an editor like yourself as badly as Tom Wolfe did, to help me put it together. With what I've done the last three weeks I've already got enough to make a book, without having touched half of the material I plan to use.

I still plan on coming to New York when my bonus comes through, and I have to report for a pension exam next month. My pension is what I've been living on for the last six months, practically. If I should lose it I dont know what I'd do for living expenses.

But, if I can keep working the way I am at present, I dont intend to come to New York permanently, like I did before. I have a fine place to work, and comforts here that I could never have in New York by myself. And if I can work here, its smarter to stay. So, I sort of plan on making a temporary trip there. When I decided that, I figured I'd like to have something definite for you at least to get your teeth into when I came.

I've been working on some stories the past few months. When I couldnt work on the book, and was stymied, I would work on one of these for a week or two. I have five completed now, all of them good, and one of them which I think is just about the best story I've ever read. I think it beats "The Undefeated," because this story has more of a universal sense of the world's problems, tied in with those of the characters. And I think it beats "The Snows of Kilimanjaro," simply because that story, which is the best I've ever read I think, is a sort of freak story without the universal appeal that makes every reader think: this happened to me. I call it "The Way It Is,"[1] and its a war story. I sent the five of them in to *Esquire* some time ago, hoping to get some money, and got them all back because as the man, Geo. Wiswell, said, and I quote: "But we simply cannot run stories just because they contain good writing." He would have taken that one, which he called a beaut, but it was a war story. The other four had not enough of the action and excitement they were looking for now. I'd like to send them someplace else and sell them, but I was hoping *Esquire* because they pay so well and I dont know anybody else that pays much money except the [*Saturday Evening*] *Post*, and I'm sure the *Post* wont want them, altho I'm going to try them.

Here's how good that one story is: When I get blue and low and cannot write I sit down and read it over again and I am high again because I know I wrote it. It has a sense of action

[1]The story eventually appeared in the June 1949 issue of *Harper's*.

in it, a sense of this happening now instead of being a story about what happened then, that is something I've been trying to achieve for a long time and never did before, and havent very often since.

Anyway, I have these five done, and I have at least three others I'm working on now, along with ideas for a few more, and I was wondering what about a book of short stories, to be done and come out before the *Eternity* novel? I'm working on them some now, in the evenings, after I quit working on the book and I ought to have them done before so very long. I counted the stories in Hemingway's *Winner Take Nothing* and *Men Without Women* and they each had 14 stories. I'll have eight, and possibly a couple more, but they are longer than most of the stories in Hemingway's two books. What do you think of that? But still, I would rather not make any definite commitment as to time, its just an idea. Because I seem to work much better with a freer mind when I do not feel any sense of time pressing. But its an idea and I wanted to let you know about it.

I certainly want to come to New York, at least for a while to see you, I feel there is so much I can learn from you that will help me, but I would rather wait at least until I have enough of these stories to make a book. I feel that I have not earned it yet, sort of.

I'm working on a scene now, or rather a series of them, with Maggio and Prewitt and two queers where Maggio gets sent up because he's drunk and the MPs beat him up. And it's running into well over 30 pp without a break and not half done. But I'm not letting it bother me because I can fit it in later somehow I'm sure. And it is truly very wonderful writing.

sincerely,
Jones

p/TLS

Jones's last letter to Perkins arrived after the editor's death. Perkins had been ill for months and died on June 17, 1947. According to A. Scott Berg's Max Perkins: Editor of Genius, *before Perkins was taken to the hospital, he "carefully instructed his daughter Bertha to take two manuscripts by his bed—one of them* Cry, the Beloved Country, *the other, pages of* From Here to Eternity" *and make certain they were placed in safe hands at Scribner's.*

Burroughs Mitchell wrote Jones about Perkin's death. Jones decided, without having met him, that Mitchell was the editor at Scribner's with whom he should work. Their friendship and their working relationship were to be long ones. As Mitchell wrote in The Education of an Editor, *"We were very different, and yet about certain essential things, we thought alike." Mitchell found Jones gregarious, forthright, humorous, and intense. Mitchell came to know Lowney well, also, and he perceptively noted: "In those young days, Jim was by no means an easy man. For all the gregariousness, he was strung tight; he could become harsh, even savage, lashing out when something outraged or disgusted him. What made all this the more difficult was the peculiar dogmatism with which he had been indoctrinated by his mentor, Lowney Handy." Mitchell, cast in the same mold as Perkins, was not dogmatic and was an effective counterbalance to Lowney.*

TO BURROUGHS MITCHELL

ROBINSON, ILL.

JUNE 30, 1947

Dear Mr. Mitchell,

Your letter came today. There is not much for me to say. Some things you feel you cannot write because the words have been used too many times before and have grown old and you do not like to use those words because they are a sort of indignity to what it is you feel. Anyway I guess I do not need to say it to you.

I did not know about his death before your letter. I do not read the papers any more at all and I do not read the literary mags. Anyway, if it would have been in the Chicago papers I would have heard, and this afternoon I went down to the local library and looked through the literary mags they had but there was nothing there. People here did not even know of him, just as they have not read Tom Wolfe.

I do not have many contacts. I have never been politician enough to ever learn to make them or to use them. I do not have many friends and those I have are mostly very scattered. And even those I have neglected, purposely, partly because I want to be free of them to work, partly because it somehow seems the more I learn the wider the gulf I create because I just cant go on repeating the other things I learned before.

My parents both died when I was overseas, which is probably just as well, and the relatives I do have are estranged from me over the question of whether I should go to work or write. That includes my uncle and my sister and lately my brother, who are the only ones left now. And so I have sort of had for Scribner's and for him and his faith in me the feeling a young man usually has for home. My father told me once when I was a boy in one of his less sober and more maudlin moments that any time I got in trouble if I would get to him and tell him first, before anybody else told him, he would always back me to the limit and that is sort of what I felt for Mr Perkins somehow, and through him for Scribner's. I had read about Tom Wolfe and him and the feeling that was between them and had transposed myself there in Wolfe's place in my mind, although of course I never said it. But I guess in life such a thing only happens once between any two men and there is never a repetition of it.

The thing about him was that above all else he was an individual and as such respected the individual in others. Such a thing is increasingly hard to find any more. There are too many editors of the Bennett Cerf variety, who became editors because they nursed a secret ambition to be writers. That was not true of him I think because that bitterness that always grows out of such a thing was not in him, and they would do better I think to get out and try to write, if that was what they wanted, and leave the editing to men like him.

There is a wind and rain storm here tonight and the after-glow hung on the clouds a long time and I do not think it maudlin of me to say I think its fitting.

It was a very hard letter you had to write me, an awkward situation and probably not easy. I went to Scribner's because of Mr Perkins and what I'd read of him in Wolfe and I think once I even told him that but I find that now I still feel like Scribner's is that home. I would like to know who it is I am to work with from now on, because I would prefer to work with one man, an individual to an individual. Rather than with a group. Of course you did not say exactly and I do not expect you could. But I would rather get it all straight now. From your letter and from the time or two he mentioned you, and since you are the one familiar with my stuff, but mainly for the first two rather than the last, I would like to work with you if it is all okay there.

I have had the feeling for a long time that I should come to New York, that he might die, that I should not selfishly but for writing go where he was because there was so much that I could learn from him. But as I said, life does not ever put two such things together; his time of that was with Tom Wolfe and not with me.

I had planned to come in the fall provided I had enough done to give him a thing to get his teeth into. I will still plan on that now although it may be longer because I want to get as much done as I can. Lately it has been coming much clearer and the writing much easier and better and maybe I can finish it this year. But I will still plan on coming there when I can make it. Maybe you and I with what he gave to you can learn about it all together and then there will be that much learned for some other man someday to use.

The fine thing about him was that he was not only the usual

punching bag for writers but he was like a hillside too, where
you hollered out the words you wanted most to hear and the
hillside sent them back to you just like you wanted to hear
them and then you knew there was somebody there, after all.

This has been the ending of a thing that has been happening
to me that was the perspective he said he thought I needed to
revise "Laughter." And that is that, in the end, it is always
between the man and himself that the fight is made without
bitterness and knowing what it is and that, in the end, each
man must make his own fight himself.

There was a time not so long ago that I would have gone
off on a bat someplace and sweat it out but now I think I will
go back to work tomorrow.

I keep thinking of Tom Wolfe's phrase: "O lost, and by the
wind-grieved ghost, you can go home again."

Ever Sincerely Yours

James Jones

If you could send me something, newspaper clippings or magazine articles if there are any, that tells about it I would be glad.

P/TLS

TO BURROUGHS MITCHELL

ROBINSON, ILL.

JULY 21, 1947

Dear Mr. Mitchell,

I am returning the clippings [about Perkins]. Sorry not to
have sent them sooner. I was working hard when they came
and hung on for several days and did not want to bust it up.
And I wanted to copy a couple of the articles before I sent them
back. I copied the one from the *Herald* June 18th, which I thot
the best, and the one from the *Asheville Times*. I was a little
surprised at how poor they all were, how far they came from
expressing the truth that was the man.

Also, the article in the *Sat. Review* made me mad as hell.[1] I'm going to write them and ask for a copy of that July 12th issue to keep. When you read an article like that from one of the top litterateur organs you know why I don't read them, and why a man like Mr Perkins was so rare. I'm convinced that the main attributes of genius are guilelessness and innocence of spirit, and that in some subtle way these release the latch the conscious mind keeps on the deep subconscious. As Wolfe said once, "I'm convinced that to be a genius a man must be something of an ass." And went on to tell how Tolstoy read nothing for seven years but the novels of Dumas.

With my own experience in New York, and with things like that article I'm going to do a novel someday on the litterateurs that feed off of innocence in artists and would-be artists and try as they do to kill that same spirit. There's a hell of a story in that, all of the Bennett Cerf school of literary schmucks.

I dont know anything about clipping bureaus, how expensive they are, or if they keep files that you can purchase later. Maybe you can tell me. But I kept the Romeike address and intend to write them for a group of clippings on Mr Perkins if I can get them, as soon as I get the money next month. Also, working on the Stockade stuff as I am now, I'll ask for a complete file on the Lichfield Trials, if they have that. I can use a lot of that, I've saved some clippings myself, but not many.

I was up to Danville Friday for that compensation exam. I was pretty worried about it, because I'm living more or less on that pension at present. But I dont think now that anything will happen to it. The doc I saw was a medical M.D., and not a psychiatrist, and was a decent guy. As I told him, I've never seen a psychiatrist who was not a little off himself and a subtle sadist to boot. There's something there to be written someday, too; what with the time I did in the prison ward at Cp Camp-

[1]Harrison Smith's "Midwife to Literature," *Saturday Review of Literature* (July 12, 1947), concentrated on Perkins and his relationship with Thomas Wolfe and took a superior attitude toward Wolfe.

bell I can write it. Freud's chaotic subconscious may exist, I think it does, but still deeper, under that, there is a subconscious whose prime characteristic is order, and as long as psychology ignores it and subsists on the Freudian alone we're going to have the evils of men without faith in anything larger than their egos and this school of complete materialists in psychology.

I'm taking today off to write some long neglected letters, and am sending the five stories *Esquire* turned down in to the *Post*. I dont expect them to take any of them, of course, but I'd like to try them before I start the literary mags because they pay so damned much better, and I can sure use the dough.

Always my best to you,
James Jones

P/TLS

TO BURROUGHS MITCHELL

ROBINSON, ILL.
AUGUST 12, 1947.

Dear Mr Mitchell,

I waited till I heard from Romeike [the clippings service] before writing. No soap there, either on Mr Perkins or Lichfield. But I did send for and get the issue of *Saturday Review* that wrote him up. In regard to that, I guess I told you I wanted sometime to do a novel on the litterateurs, agents, hangers-on, etc.; and that article will certainly come in for a big part in it. I've never seen one done satisfactorily, altho Wolfe wrote them up well. It's the thing I would like to work on after this one on the army and after "Laughter" is revised and done.

But then, I seem to have so many books teeming in my mind, countless books. And while they go on teeming, I am knocking myself out trying to get even one written, writing and tearing up three-fourths of what I write. There's a helluva long breath between the conception and the completion. While it may be good, it is not pleasant to be your own worst critic. No theme, however great, is anything unless the writing matches or surpasses it.

I guess my greatest trouble is in the struggle to achieve form, overall form. I was reading yesterday in Craven's *Men of Art* about Michael Angelo and how he created his own oversize heroic universe, peopled it in proportion and lived in it. And it struck me that Tom Wolfe did somewhat the same thing with his novels. He created form, of his own, and withdrew to live in it. I ache to do something like that; I ache to discover an unsevered thread that will run continuously through everything I write. Am I clear? I, for instance, I seem to find no connective meaning between "Laughter" and this one.

For instance, I have five good stories done, I told you that, and another one almost completed that I've been working on at odd times. And I have three or four more in process, anywhere from just a note to almost done, that I work on now and then. And I know them all to be good, yet there is no place for them at all. I can bring them all out in a book sometime maybe, like I wrote Mr Perkins in that last letter, yet even then they will be separate, no connection between them at all. And apparently the only way to get them out is in a book, because nobody wants to publish them. I've had them turned down consistently since I wrote that letter.

Well, anyway, I got off on a tangent. (I seem to do this when I'm working too, all the time, which bothers hell out of me.) (I never know if I should leave it in or take it out.) What I started to say was that since I can't get anything from Romeike on the Lichfield trials, and have no other connection to go about it, I would certainly appreciate it if you would try and dig up a dossier on it for me. I'm just arriving at the place where Prewitt goes to the Stockade and it would be wonderfully helpful.

There is no news yet on the pension since I went up to Danville for the exam. I really think it will be all right, but if

I'd lose it I'd really be up the creek without a paddle. It destroys my confidence that I cant sell any of these stories, because I'm just incapable of writing hack for anybody; I'm having all I can do to write for myself. And without this pension to live on I'm screwed.

I work very slowly, and painfully. Now and then I'll write like mad for a week or two and knock myself out and then it's a page or two a day until another spasm seizes me. In the over-all, it's very very very slow going. And I cant help worrying because I've never, to date, completed anything. For almost four solid years I've done nothing much but write and havent earned a penny at it, and havenot [sic] published a word, and see no immediate prospect of doing so. Truly, there seems to be no place at all in our society for the artist who is really in earnest. And all the dumbjohns always hollering about what's wrong with art in our time. All of which shows the importance of being earnest, I guess.

More and more I think the system of patronage practiced during the Renaissance was the reason for the Renaissance. The artist then not only had an honored place, but he could earn a living. More and more I seem to be drawn to the Renaissance and reading about it, more and more to the classics like Stendhal and Tolstoy, because every book that comes out any more is touted as the Novel of the 20th Century, and it's a fulltime job to separate the wheat from the chaff. I had to give it up myself because it got me clear down.

You mustnt mind me. I seem to work by fits and starts. And this is one of the fits.

I wanted to tell you I got my bonus, $600 worth. After I paid off my debts, I sent the $500 that was left to my account in Findlay and it's waiting there for my trip to NY. Eventually, I must come there and get you to help me cut and patch and put this book together, once I get enough of it done so that it will be at least coherent. It really has the makings of a great book, honest; if I can but realize it. I've written so much now that I cant find half of it, and still there's half of it to write.

If it's not too much trouble, I'd appreciate your looking up the Lichfield stuff for me.

I think maybe I'm afraid you people there will lose faith in me because it's taking so goddamned long, without even a coherent end in sight yet.

You know, if anybody (excepting scientists) wants to find Order in our world, he just simply has to create it himself; he cant find it anywhere else, because it doesnt exist, unless a man prefers being led through the shoots by the butcher's lamb and feels safer lying to himself.

Ever sincerely yours, and again, dont mind me,
James Jones

P/TLS

Jones went to New York in November 1947 to confer at Scribner's about his novel. For the first time he met Burroughs Mitchell, who had read his works, and they had good talks about From Here to Eternity. *Jones also found John Hall Wheelock, the distinguished poet-editor, to be profound. Jones's letter to Lowney described in detail his reception at Scribner's.*

TO LOWNEY HANDY

NEW YORK
[POSTMARKED NOVEMBER
16, 1947]

Dear Lowney,

So much has happened that I cant even write it all, or attempt to, but I wanted to write to you anyway and remind you I love you. Got your note last nite when I came in. Had meant to write you yesterday but didnt get up early enough and I had to go over to Scribner's.

It was sure good to see your handwriting on the paper, tho.

When I got in Monday I just stopped long enough to clean up before I went over to Scribner's. (Have sitz bath only, no shower.)

Talked a long while with Mitchell, then he took me out to lunch at Cherio's, the place Cowley tells about where Perkins always ate lunch. He didnt say so, but I guess he had planned that all along. The sailfish Perkins caught while visiting Hemingway was on one wall. Perkins went there, I found out, because he liked martinis and they make the best martinis around.

Mitchell is much younger than I thot, only 33. And looks much younger. Looks younger than me. He is very shy with a sort of coverup that comes out in exquisite manners. Wears very conservative clothes with a funny kind of high collar, almost like the 1910s, but not quite that bad. He is the only man at Scribner's who was in this war, was an EM [enlisted man] for a while then became officer, in the navy. Use to be a reader for pulp mags before navy, said he really knocked himself out by having to read so much stuff, most of it crap. Knew Perkins from before because Perkins published some kind of non-fiction book for his father, and badgered him for a job for a long time. It was only after he came back from the navy that Perkins finally accepted him. My guess is they needed a man with war service and that Perkins, with his intuitive shrewdness, could see the boy had grown up. Our idea about him being Perkins's successor is true, I think, but in a different sense, not so obviously, not so patently. He is the youngest man in the office, I think, and is afraid, I think, that I will feel slighted because they [assigned] me to him, also that I might not think him good enough to be my editor. I havent found out yet why he is not writing, but I think its because he is a gentleman, a real gentleman, you know, not a pseudo.

(Yesterday he introduced me to Wheelock, who is really fine, <u>really</u> fine, and Wheelock remarked in the conversation that Samuel Johnson wrote that no man could be both a writer and a gentleman. That was while we were talking about Tom Wolfe, and Wheelock had said that in next month's *Atlantic* a portrait of a Scribner's man is coming out (forget name but will get it), and the portrait is so true that it is cruel, even while recognizing the man was a nice fellow. Will tell more about this conversation later.)

Mitchell is especially strong and adamant about the part on the Stockade and is very interested in my getting it down true. I mean he really wants to see it written. He told me several things he had heard of and seen, such as the brig marines guards running prisoners through the gauntlet with belts, etc. He really wants to see that written, I can see, altho he is reserved sort of and did not come out with a harangue or anything like that. He says my reproduction of the army talk, the idiom, is remarkable, and we talked about the subconscious and memory, conscious and automatic memory.

Yesterday I took in the queer scene and the whorehouse scene and the stories. We had talked a lot about queers and about how they had written about them always with this *Weird Tales* effect, and that nobody had really written them right. He was a little shy (you know what I mean, he tried obviously to show me [he] was not bigoted, but he was still shy about talking, altho he talked all right, you know?) He asked if I'd read Gide and I told him no and he said he'd read two of his books and that they both were concerned with homosexuality, but that he felt that Gide had sentimentalized it, had not written truly. Thats perceptive on his part, and true, he's a good man, and I must make him feel that I want him for [my] editor. You know? Then we talked about Hemingway, and that his style of understatement was really a sort of inverted sentimentality, and that this new school of writers with their weird effect when writing of queers was the same sort of inverted sentimentality, just like Gide except they had gone to the opposite extreme. He likes Maggio tremendously, says it is so true of so many guys he met himself. I asked him to read "The Way It Is" while I was there yesterday, after we talked to Wheelock. He read it while I sat in the library they have on the editorial floor which is of all Scribner's books they have published. I saw the new edition of *Look Homeward, Angel* on one of the shelves. He came in then, tremendously enthused with the story, said I had done something completely new with making it go in and out of the man's mind and at the same time using physical action synchronized with it so that the two tied right together. He showed me a couple of the places, because I didnt even know I'd done it. He was tremendously enthused about it, and about the way I handled abstract thinking in dialogue and action, which is new too. This was after we had talked to Wheelock and I asked him if he would ask W. to read it too, and he said sure. That was a mistake on my part, tho he didnt show it, but he needs to feel I really want him for [my] editor.

The conversation with Wheelock was fine. He is a very searching man, and in the conversation asked me a lot of profound questions about how I work. Whether I work gorgingly in long stretches and then have to lay off a while, how I am physically when I work. I told him I did work that way, but that I was trying to learn to write four or six hours a day only, because you did more in the long run and did not make yourself sick. I told him about how I got indigestion and constipated after working so hard and he nodded and smiled as if he knew and had done it too. He has magnificent eyes, a long square topped head and a long haired moustache that sweeps back to the sides. He said I could recuperate easily now while I was still young, but that when a man got older he could not recuperate so easily. So I told him about how I thought that every real artist's work was really a striving toward discipline, like you and I talked about. I also told him about the Yoga breathing exercises I had fooled with; he asked me if I had trouble sleeping when I was working, and I told him how I put myself to sleep with rhythmic breathing but did not explain the process. Also told him about how I kept a glass of water on the desk, after learning how the Yogis kept a vessel of water by them. He was very interested in this and asked if it increased my energy. I did not go into great detail, but intend the next time I talk to him to explain about Prana. We talked a lot about Tom Wolfe, and he told me how the elevator man used to bring his car up to the fifth floor at night and pretend to be working, just so he could listen to Wolfe and Perkins yelling and swearing (Wolfe swearing) while they worked on the *Angel*. He said Wolfe had too little artistic self-criticism, but on the other hand Hem had almost too much. Said Wolfe was like two people, gentle and amenable at times and wildly raging at others. And I said I thought that an artist's work, like I had said before, was always an attempt to bring these two parts of himself into an integrated whole, and Wheelock smiled that warm smile the way you and I look at each other when we know a thing and said he thot so too, and went on and elaborated it some. I told him how much I liked the panther poem, and he smiled sort of sadly, and shyly, and said that was written a long time ago. Said he wanted to talk to me again.

They really work very hard there, reading all the time, the editors. He, W., had read "Laughter" and the first 200 pp, but not this last, but intends to. Also, Mitchell said he wanted——
——(cant remember name) Hem's editor to read it.

Oh, yes. I asked Mitchell yesterday pointblank what all of them there at Scribner's thought of me, as a writer or potential writer. He said they thought very highly of me, and that was when he took me in to see Wheelock. He had said Monday he wanted me to meet him, and had gone in and asked him a couple times, but apparently he was busy. I guess that was what it was that was bothering me, and I think he knew it. Mitchell brought it up, what I had asked, when we were talking with Wheelock. And Wheelock said they felt I was going to write some [of] the most important books that were going to come out now, in this new time. I was proud but embarrassed, you know, and when I didnt say anything, Wheelock smiled and said something about editors having to read so terribly much and naturally got so bored with having to read so much, that their opinion could be taken highly, both professionally, technically that is, but also because they had to read so much that something had to be very tops to be able to impress them so they would make a statement like that.

We talked a little bit about Jeff, Wheelock didnt know about him, and about how I had knocked myself out when he came down this last time, and how I had written him to stay away. Wheelock said he knew what I meant by pouring myself out on someone, but he said while it cost me I probably would gain by it sometime because I would have learned things to write about about Jeff. We all laughed at that.

Tomorrow I'm to go over to *Time* and see Mitchell's friend.

They said it would be alright for me to bring a portable and copy off the stuff about Lichfield.[1] It sure helps if you've got some connections, you know it?

I have tickets for three plays, only one of them outstanding, and it's one Mitchell told me about. *Medea,* a Greek tragedy by Euripides which has been freely adapted in verse by Robinson Jeffers and is starring Judith Anderson, who is a great tragedienne they say. I never heard of her myself. It's selling out way ahead, and I couldnt get a ticket before Nov 25, next Tues., and only got that because some guy was standing in lobby and had two tickets and wanted to sell one of them.

I think I'll probably not stay near as long as I expected. I'm enjoying it and all, but I cant work in a hotel room from which I know I must move in a cuple days. Besides that, I miss you some. Not frantically, like before, but with a taste of Xmas Eve the way a kid is the night before, and there is a hollowness

[1] Jones wanted background information on the Lichfield trial. Colonel James A. Kilian, who was commander of the 10th Reinforcement Depot in Lichfield, England, for over two years during the war, was charged with condoning brutality in the stockade. The trial went on for many months, and *Time* on September 9, 1946, summarized the testimony of former inmates in the stockade: "Men had been beaten there with fists and rifle butts till they were unconscious, then revived and ordered to clean up their own blood. Prisoners who complained of hunger were gorged with three meals at a time, then dosed with castor oil. Hours of calisthenics, of standing 'nose and toes' to a guardhouse wall were routine punishments. . . . There was even a ghastly, sardonic slogan among Lichfield guards: 'Shoot a prisoner and be made a sergeant.' " The Army tried to justify its "get-tough" policies, but the prosecution was able to show that many of the six thousand who went through that stockade were minor offenders; some had been AWOL for only a few hours.

Colonel Kilian was found not guilty of "knowingly" condoning the heinous acts of the guards and guilty of "permitting" them. He was fined five hundred dollars. Jones used details from the trial in the stockade section of *From Here to Eternity.* The verdict of the court undoubtedly further reinforced Jones's disgust with the caste system in the Army and his identification with the misfits who were subjected to such officially sanctioned brutality.

in me that is always there. It does not upset me, only makes me lonely and sort of sad. I dont think I'll stay much more than a couple of weeks.

Am invited to Mitchell's apartment for dinner Saturday night. Has very sketchy living quarters he says, two and a half rooms. I'll know more tho, from my viewpoint, when I see it. I like Mitchell, a lot.

Monday night went up to 52nd St for Jazz. Heard Bill De Arango's quintet, the guitar player in *Exquire Jazzbook*. He's good, but its gone to his head, his publicity, I think. Sidney Bechet was across the street and I went in twice, but both times he was not there during a break, and I didnt hear him yet. It was getting late, almost 3 AM, and I went home. Last night went to Eddie Condon's, and heard some good stuff too. Condon is really a commercializer, with ratty eyes and tiny ears, and I dont much like him. But the others were fine. Joe Sullivan, the piano player, plays during the intermissions. He's the one in our Sidney Bechet album that has the three piano solos by him, Timothy, and Chimes. Chimes is the best, the one you and I both like. I requested some numbers and got to talking to Sullivan. He was drunk and somehow very pathetic, and he got mad at me over some obscure remark about blues, and asked me what the hell I knew about jazz, and I said only records, and he said you cant know them from records, and was this what he had spent 12 years for? 12 years listening to all the old ones, Hines, and Johnny Dodds and Baby Dodds and Jimmy Noone. I got a big thrill out of hearing him mention those names. I apologized to him and agreed I was just a punk and had never heard them except on records, and told him how it made me feel to hear those names that I had on all my record albums and loved so well and that I didnt blame him for getting pissed off. It ended up I bought him a drink and we shook hands and he started calling me J.J. and I promised him an autographed first edition of *Eternity*, in about two years. He was like a kid, so pleased I was going to send him a book I'd written, and wanted me to come back some more.

It knocks me out now, when I think about it. I guess I'm really a provincial at heart, but I guess everybody is, who is honest. I have been using your technique of the cornfed boy fresh to the city since I got here and can get anything I want from anybody.

I'm going to quit now. Am trying to get a seat at the ballet that is running for a few more days here. They are doing *Swan Lake* and *Romeo and Juliet* one night and something French *Les Patineurs.* I've never seen one, except that movie, and I want to see a good one.

Someday not so far off, you and me will come to town and do all this and then it will be perfect, and there will not be anything I will have missing.

Oh, asked Mitchell about an advance, and he said he thought it could be arranged, but that everything I took came out of my royalties and that I ought not to ask for more than I really need to get by. So I dropped it momentarily, after telling him I was $600 in debt. I'm still going to ask for $1000.

All my best to good ol Doc and to Jimmy if he's there.

Forevermore,
Jim

Bought Parker pencil to match pen. Am going out to see about winter slacks. Wont buy very much more, I guess. Money goes fast here, especially in jazz nightclubs. 50¢ a beer; 85¢ a bottle, but you have to buy something if you want to sit & hear them.

Dan Topping was at Condon's last night with two gorgeously decked out cunts, one dyed redhead, one dyed blonde. He bought a lot & ol Eddie was sure sucking his ass.

s/TLS

Burroughs Mitchell wore Perkins's mantle gracefully, and as Jones worked his way slowly through the tortured composition of From Here to Eternity, *he wrote to Mitchell just as he had to Perkins. He often mentioned his problems with style, and he was concerned about literary influences. He was ambivalent about Hemingway but continued his praise of Wolfe. His letters to Mitchell, though, never strayed far from the central occupation of his life then: the writing of his novel.*

TO BURROUGHS MITCHELL

ROBINSON, ILL.
DECEMBER 7, 1947

Dear Mitch,

. . . .

You people have been wonderful to me. I dont need to tell you that. If there's ever been a writer who's been advance[d] $2000 dollars for a just-begun novel and who has never published anything, I never heard of it. There's something about the office there that makes me know how much it's worth. There is room there for a man to elaborate, to enlarge, without being cramped by petty rules on every hand. I dont know how to say it, but you know what I mean. Nobody will ever know how glad I am I broke off with Aley and then swallowed my pride (I had to do that, you know) to write Perkins another letter and ask him to look at "Laughter" again. But then maybe it's been Kismet, all along the way. Personally, I'm inclined to think it has.

I had a little trouble getting started when I got back, getting into it, but now I'm in and I'm going good. I hope I never get to believing I'm a genius; I also hope I never get so I dont believe it, either.

Wheelock wrote me a wonderful letter. I dont know if you read it, or a copy of it, but in case you didnt I'm quoting a sentence of it to you. It's the first time I've ever seen in words just what I'm really striving to do in writing. He saw it and defined it, when I couldnt even define it myself, a thing I've never been able to word. It's somewhat what I meant when I wrote you that I wanted to combine Tom Wolfe and Hemingway in my writing. Here's what he said: "Without romanticizing anything there are moments when from reality itself, presented with fidelity, an exalted kind of poetry is wrung." That really hits it, if anything ever did.

I'm writing him, thanking him for it. I dont see how a writer with anything on the ball can help from realizing it if he works for you people. You people seem to bring it out of him, almost supernaturally.

. . . .

Yours,
Jim

p/TLS

Soon after returning home from New York, Jones wrote to John Hall Wheelock. Without mentioning Lowney by name, he spoke of two ideas he had gained from her: that he must deny himself a wife and children in order to pursue his art and that he was interested in the occult. Lowney was intrigued by the occult and by Eastern religions, but Jones was never a true believer as she was. He was, as Emerson and Thoreau were in their taking ideas from Oriental religions, an eclectic, picking and choosing what he would believe.

TO JOHN HALL WHEELOCK

ROBINSON, ILL.
DECEMBER 8, 1947.

Dear Mr Wheelock,

I want to thank you for your letter. With me anyway, it's very important to know that you people there are behind me personally, and believe in me personally, as much as you do.

I have, in a way, put all my eggs into the single basket that is writing and if the splits are weak and break I've lost them all, and there is no justification at all for my having even lived. But then I guess you know that. Metaphysically speaking, in denying myself a wife, and children, and a job I can be more or less proud of—while at the same time providing myself with the spiritual and financial freedom to really write—I am in a hazy sort of way forcing Fate to be beneficent to me, in writing; because Emerson's Law of Compensation applies here as everywhere else, and what you dam up and restrain one place must necessarily flow forth someplace else.

In your letter you said a thing that startled me with its insight. It impressed me so much I quoted it to Mitch when I wrote him back, and I underlined it in the letter. It was the first time I'd ever seen set down absolutely clearly what it is I've been working to achieve in writing. I had never been able to even define it myself, having only a vaguely hazy idea of what it was. I wrote Mitch once, and I think maybe I told you both that morning we talked, that I wanted to combine the spiritual insight and poetry of Tom Wolfe with the pellucid clarity and reality of life moving Hemingway has. That was as close as I could come to saying what you defined concretely for me when you said in your letter that "without romanticizing anything there are moments when from reality itself, presented with fidelity, an exalted kind of poetry is wrung."

There will never be a better definition of what I want to achieve in writing.

After I got back here I looked up all of your poetry I could find in the local library. I had never read more than a few scattered poems in different anthologies, and of course my favorite, "The Panther." There wasnt much, only in anthologies, but quite a few I hadnt read. (They're going to order them, however, now; now that I'm a bigshot, they even let me keep books without being confined by the two week limit.) Anyway, I read enough of them to see that you had done considerable reading in Eastern philosophy and its ramifications, like we talked about. There is something there that intrigues me, although I dont know exactly what it is.

Anyway, there was a new book here for me when I got home, and I wanted to mention it to you. It's called *A Strange Language*, and its by a Pundit Acharya. I think you'd like it, and there's wonderfully fine material in it. It's written in a very odd way, a poetry in prose that is really excellent. You said not to send you any books, and this is the only copy I have, but in case your bookstore there doesnt have it, you can get a copy of it for a buck or so at Samuel Weiser's Bookstore at 117 Fourth Ave.

I was there several times when I spent that winter in NY in '45. They have a special section at the back labeled Occult Books, and while they sell other books too, they seem to specialize in occult stuff. I bought a few and found that some of them were very good, but that others were if not insane, completely evil. I dont know why I say that, I'm not one to go around saying this or that is evil, because basically I dont believe it, but that is the only way I can say the way these books made me feel.

Also, when they found I was interested some in occult stuff, they wanted me to meet Manly P Hall and go to hear some of his lectures in Town Hall.[1] Another thing, this guy called Norvel[2] is one of their boys, and this last time, at the Woodstock, right next to Town Hall, I noticed Norvel was lecturing at noon, to women only. Now I've seen some of Hall's books, and somehow they give me the same feeling that the other bad ones did, so I never went to see him, and refused to meet him.

But somewhere there's an angle there that I've not clarified yet to myself. There's some kind of sinister racket in that whole deal, but I cant figure it out. But if one could understand and get inside and see, I think there's something to be written there, something that needs to be written. Maybe its only that I've got a darkly romantic imagination, but I dont think so. Anyway, I hope someday when I'm in NY and dont have so many other things to do to go down there and pretend to be sucked in and find out what I can. It would make fine stuff to go into this literary novel I talked to Mitch about, as a sort of secondary plot. There's something indicative about America and American life lying in it somewhere.

I didnt mean to go into it at such lengths, but I thought you might like to have a look at it yourself, since you are interested some in those sort of things, as I am, and I truly think you'd like that little book.

Mitch told me he was going to let, or have, or ask, I guess, you read those five short stories I left with him. I would like to see what you thought of them, but I dont want to put any more load on than all your other reading.

As I wrote Mitch, my NY trip was a success, because I got two complete short stories out of it to do, once this book is

[1] Hall wrote on Rosicrucian and other mystic subjects.
[2] Probably Anthony Norvelle, who wrote on astrology and metaphysics.

fixed up, and I also got the answer to a third short story I've had hanging fire for months because I didnt know how to finish it; all this in addition to what I got that'll help me on this book.

But of course, I dont mean that that is all I got, either. I enjoyed the lunch with you tremendously, and also the talk we had that other day. I hope when I come back with this manuscript that I can return the favor and take you out to lunch someplace.

I am glad you and Mitch believe in the book the way you do.

Yours,
Jim Jones

p/TLS

Lowney usually spent part of each winter in Florida. Jones was
with her in Venice, Florida, in 1948.

TO BURROUGHS MITCHELL

VENICE, FLORIDA
JAN. 20, 1948

Dear Mitch

Got a wire last night from Weeks, in answer to my letter.

PUBLISHING TEMPER OF STEEL MARCH ATLANTIC PROOFS SENT AIR
MAIL VENICE. KEEN TO SEE YOUR NEW WORK REGARDS
EDWARD WEEKS

He didnt say anything about the other stories, so I guess it's
possible he may keep some or all of them and run them later.
I was surprised he picked "Temper of Steel," because you
remember we talked about it. And he picked it over "The Way
It Is." He may have picked it for the writing of the flashback,
or he may even have picked it for the very fault you and I saw.
But the only way I could figure he'd pick it over the other one
is that he saw and got the point I was driving at. Maybe I'm
idealistic. It may be the seeming dilettantism of Lon was what
sold him. Anyway, I'll be able to work it over, before we ever
get a book of them out.

I never explained to you just what I was trying to get across
in it. Lon, you see, is really a killer, a man who kills with no
compunction whatever, and not the dilettante hanging around
cocktail parties. What you didnt like was the old stuff about
dilettante cocktail parties, but I meant to show Lon as the result
of the tremendous advance in indoctrination since the last war,
a member of Hemingway's generation, you know? Could it be

Weeks got it?[1] Whether he did or not, I'll have to rewrite it, because I want everybody to get it, not just the editors.

I'm not taking any time off for stories now, either. All goes on the book. It's coming along fairly well, some fine writing but much sweating, but I can feel myself getting into harness, like I was when Jeff came that time and spoilt it.

With Best,
Jim

P/TLS

---

[1] In *The Ice-Cream Headache and Other Stories,* Jones referred to "The Temper of Steel" as having a "well concealed" point. At the end of the story he published this gloss: "The point is in the reference to Archie Binns and the quote about chivalry being dead, and in the boy's comparison of his own coldblooded killing of the Japanese to the comparable scene in *All Quiet.* This is what modern warfare has come to be, with all of our blessings, and God help us for it."

Jones built upon his own killing of a Japanese soldier in this story, as he was later to do in *The Thin Red Line.*

Jones, still in Venice, Florida, added this postscript to a letter to Burroughs Mitchell on February 25, 1948.

You know I had a dream shortly before I got your letter. Dreamed Scribner's had called me in (on the carpet, sort of) and were very disillusioned with me, that I had let them down, badly. They picked my book apart, very logically I must say, told me how it was really very bad, in every way, and that their $2000 was being marked off as a loss, part of the game, and they [were] dropping me, like a hot rock. Afterwards, you talked to me, very sadly, saying you didnt exactly agree with them, but you could see what they meant, and wished me luck and said I'd surely sell it to somebody else. But I didnt want to sell it to anybody else, and took it and burned the damn thing up. It was a very bad dream; I suppose it came from not hearing from you for so long, altho consciously I hadnt given it a thought because of what you said about writing letters. Its like with sports, I guess; you build yourself up (at least I do) and give a false impression of your prowess, but all the time underneath you are worried as hell somebody will make you prove it; and I say I dont care if you people dont write, and I dont, of course, but in the subconscious there is always that fear, the one you dont even know is there, until sometime you dream it and it is horribly real and it takes a long time after you wake up to realize it isnt. For a couple days, every now and then, my mind would work as if it had happened really and not just been dreamed. I mean, I'd remember it as a memory. Odd, what?

P/TLS

In his early letters to his editors at Scribner's, Jones did not mention Lowney in any detail, but in a long letter to Mitchell, Jones did describe her teaching methods.

TO BURROUGHS MITCHELL

ROBINSON, ILLINOIS
MAY 6, 1948

Dear Mitch,

. . . .

Lowney has been working with two fellows here, who want to write. . . . Lowney started them out on copying, picking stories by different good writers, or even chapters out of their books. Although first of all she had them copy Hammett's story "A Man Called Slade," in order for them to conquer the circumlocution that most beginners have. . . .

She had them copy "Snows of Kilimanjaro," I think, and then a story from *Between the Dark and the Daylight* by Nancy Hale—"Those Who Lived and Died Believing," and "That Will Be Fine" by Faulkner, and "The Ears of Johnny Bear" by Steinbeck, Tess Slesinger's "Life in the Day of a Writer." She had them copy 20 pp from Tom Wolfe's *Face of a Nation* that Wheelock edited, letting them pick their own sections. . . .

Some Rebecca West from *The Harsh Voice,* some Fitzgerald from *Tender Is the Night.* . . .

I dont know what all else they copied. The principle was to not let them copy too much of any one author at a time, so as to be influenced by his style. Later, I think she had them copy the Vets scene from *To Have and Have Not,* "Francis Macomber," "No One My Grief Can Tell." These were not SOP. The point was for each to copy toward his weaknesses. For instance, if one loved poetry she put him to copying the tersest stuff she could find, like Cain, Raymond Chandler, William

Irish. If he was a Hemingway addict, she put him to Tom Wolfe or Chesterton's "Lepanto," like that. It's really intriguing as hell to watch how it works. I think I mentioned *Challenge of the Unknown* by [Louis K.] Anspacher to you when I was in NY. The theory used is based on his chapter entitled "Psychic Manifestations in Art and Literature." You can see clearly in it how what you put into your subconscious is what must come out, later, all mixed up like jam, apparently unrelated. John Livingston Lowes tried to show the same thing in his massive tome *Road to Xanadu,* but he got muddled all up with so many trees making the forest invisible. Anspacher does it better. Its a clear explanation of how an artist creates, although I've found that with me (and with all of them, I guess) there is still some X factor that is unaccountable. . . .

Yours,
Jim

P/TLS

James Jones and Lowney Handy were together in Illinois or Florida most of the time during the writing of Eternity; *but every now and then one or the other needed to get away, and some of their correspondence during their periods of separation has survived. At times that correspondence is intense and personal, but some of it is banal: reporting comments on their travel, the weather, and activities of friends and relatives. In the winter of 1948–1949 Jones was living in the house in Robinson with Harry, and Lowney was in Tampa, Florida, working on a novel,* But Answer Came There None. *She was in an agitated state and regularly took sedatives. She railed against Harry's mistress and talked of divorcing him and eventually marrying Jones, though she said she would first give her young lover time to be a celebrity.*

Together or apart, Lowney constantly subjected Jones to psychological warfare. "Before I could learn," he wrote his brother, Jeff, "I had to be broken. *And boy, I mean broken. Lowney cut the ground out from under me until I had absolutely no place to stand. I was completely lost. Every way I turned for aid or escape, Lowney was there and cut me off."*

She cut him off in a variety of ways. In late January 1949 she wrote to Jones from Florida suggesting that one of her brothers could find a girl for Jones to satisfy his sexual needs. He replied on January 25 that he would not allow her brother to be a procurer. He was, instead, going to win Lowney back. They were both romantics, he wrote her, but she had turned to the asceticism of Yoga while he continued to yearn for "Love of a woman, a mate, a comrade, an equal, a meeting in body, a meeting in mind, a meeting in spirit."

TO LOWNEY HANDY

[ROBINSON, ILL.]
THURSDAY 27TH [POSTMARKED
JANUARY 27, 1949]

Dear Lowney,

Basically—

I'm making a carbon of this so I can re-read it myself, but I've been thinking hard, trying to make it coldly, and maybe I'm learning something about me. But if I write it to you, then I have to formulate it in sentences intelligibly, whereas I myself I just make notes that I cant even read, later.

Basically, it comes down to ego-stimulation. You remember the saw that "love is closest to hate." Nature put sex in all life to take care of the mechanical reproduction of it. In humans, naturally, with a conscious mind, there must be some corresponding emotion. Two people fall in love (they think), that is nature working on them to keep alive the race. In their minds, however, the first result is ego-stimulation. Women are not supposed to let men fuck them; therefore, the man's ego is tremendously stimulated to think that this woman will give him what she will give no others. There is nothing he can not do for her, he worships her—because she makes him feel he may have Greatness in him. They build great dreams and plans. On her side, the woman is pleased at all the loving attention the man gives her, she likes to be pampered, looked after, and she believes this man has singled her out from all women, to give her his worship—her ego also is tremendously stimulated; she herself feels the touch of Greatness within her. Her children will be great artists, or, according to the type of mind she has, they will all be President or newspaper owners.

This is a valid relationship. It is actually good for both of them. AS A MAN THINKS SO IS HE. They think they are Great, they are Great. Okay.

That is "young love." "Innocent love." "Blind love." Yet,

it has been the instrument that has set many a man off on his trip toward Greatness, merely because the woman in the case thinks he is Great, or will be. That is true of me with you.

However, it is not true of you with me, is it?

Well, back to the hypothetical couple. They have this love, which is valid—for its place and time. Both their egos are stimulated, they are able to wall themselves off from the world that hurts them within each other. Maybe they get married maybe they dont. Maybe they dont even sleep together. Whether or no, they are together, replete in each other.

I know in my own case, it is when my ego-stimulation is at its highest that I do the best work. I remember the day Fay[1] came when I was finishing up "The Way It Is," and she even sat in the room here and jabbered and it did not bother me. I talked to her as I finished rewriting the ending and then went on and copied the whole thing. Part of that was that I was showing off to Fay as a writer, and having my ego stimulated.

I've got this far but I'm not sure I can carry it on. Something happens to our hypothetical couple. I had it in my mind before, earlier, but I worked. I was high over it too, felt I'd discovered something. Helped me to iron out a spot that had been bothering me for days.

Anyway, something happens to them. In some way or other the great high of ego-stimulation between them drops. It may be that the outside world comes into it: the man has to work maybe, at an office job, he is away, the woman suffers because he puts part of his mind on working instead of all on her. That something must happen is inevitable. They couldnt live like that forever. Even if they are millionaires with no work to do, and are not interested in any other sex affairs, they cant keep it because its like you use to say I'm going to have a record made of that: Jim, you're great. Jim, you're a genius. You got tired of saying it; the truth is, after the first flush wore off you

[1]Lowney's sister.

didnt even believe it. But I wanted you to believe it, because it built me up to write.

But with us, the first thing that caused the loss of ego-stimulation was when I made a pass at Doris and you saw I was not the single minded lover you had thought. Your ego dropped. I caused it there, I know it. And I could cut my hand off ever since you told me in the Keys. I had never dreamed it before, silly isnt that? Still, you covered it so well. I asked you if you'd mind if I laid Doris and you smiled and said no go right ahead. Your pride. But I didnt know. Even now, I feel sick over it, physically sick, every time I think of it, even though I know something else would have caused it if that hadnt.

Oh, god, sometimes—

Anyway, something causes our hypothetical couple to begin to diminish in stimulating each other's egos. Domesticity and getting used to taking them for granted can cause it if nothing else.

Then, once they stop stimulating each other's ego (Nature already having done its work), the reaction of each is to work on the other so as to get back the great high sureness of the stimulated ego. (Like in *Rogue's Legacy* the fat whore says of Villon, Praise is meat and drink to him, he will do anything for it, I will give it to him and he will forget Katherine) At the same time each of our couple set about to get ego-stimulation in some other way. When you found Harry was unfaithful at the first, you went into club work, the country club, finally when you had sucked all of these dry of all the stimulation for your ego you could (honestly, to yourself) get from them, you went to school to learn to write. That in itself was ego-stimulation, but also promised the even greater ego-stimulation of writing great writing, of great art, which is just about the final step of ego-stimulation, further than that one cannot go. One can be famous and a great writer.

In my case, I was a punk kid in the army that couldnt do anything and was not looked up to be anybody, least of all a woman in marriage or love. I went into writing then. The U of H gave me a great ego-stimulation. I was the fair haired boy.

After I left there though, back into the army, into combat, my ego suffered worse than it ever has (except possibly the last four years with you), at the thought of <u>me,</u> Jim Jones, being <u>killed,</u> and all for nothing and nobody would ever know I had lived or died.

But with our couple, while turning to something else, they also attempt to reput into the other (both of them) the old ego-stimulation that was once there. They begin to try and make them over. The result of that is a conflict, each trying to make the other over into his own picture of him, and it becomes a battle that is hate and it becomes dominating.

The funny thing is, when I first knew you, Harry had you dominated. He even had you convinced you were just about to go crazy. You remember that? You had forgotten it, hadnt you? My love saved you from that. Now it is you who dominates Harry. But Harry didnt use to be a dominated man, before I came. He was the dominator. Remember the Saturday in the kitchen with Nola? It is only the last year and a half or so that he has completely receded into his sentimentality, his "rose glasses" as you say, that he is helping the world thrugh [sic] us (which he is) ((as long as you keep the finger of me over him)), a sentimentality which enables him to believe himself useful.

I guess for a long time at first from what you both have told me, you dominated him. I suspect it was a battle still, then, with neither one winning, neither becoming completely dominated. But when I came along, you were about beaten. Your writing was only an escape then (as mine was).

It has become the same battle between you and me, you using Yoga, me using sex (there are millions of ways besides sex).

You dominate Harry now, and also Don, and Willy, and even Tinks.[2] You are a teacher, which is almost as infinite a

[2] Don Sackrider, Willard Lindsay, and Tinks Howe were protégés of Lowney's.

way of getting ego-satisfaction as is being an artist. You did that, basically, to escape being dominated by me.

Apparently, there seems to be no happy medium. Sometimes I wonder if Harry could get me out of the picture completely if he wouldnt even perhaps win again in the battle for dominance. He works on me some. Last night, for instance. I'll tell it later.

But our hypothetical couple, who love each other and thus feel bound and dominated because they are weak enough to love, also hate each other for being the cause of each others bonds. Usually they end up like my mother and dad, your mother and dad, Harry's mother and dad, Dr and Mrs Wallace, Mr and Mrs Stewart, one or the other winning, until the loser finally withdraws into an impregnable tomb where he can no longer be reached and hurt by continued loss of ego-stimulation through the other one dominance. As I said in my last letter, there are all kinds of tombs. There is the tomb of Mrs Wallace's literariness, there is the tomb of Mrs Stewart's laxatives, there is the tomb of drink, the tomb of sex affairs, but all of them tombs, not realities which instead they are created to shy away from.

That is a black picture. But I refuse to believe that there is no more than that. I insist that there is a love that can exist between two people that can be equal, and undominating, terribly ego-stimulating (and thus fine art-producing) for both parties. I insist there is a greater fuller love between two people, but like you say you cannot find it by changing and switching like Hemingway. Hemingway has ended to be the absolute dominator, of his wife, his servants, even of all Cuba damn near, and would the whole US if he could. To do that he has had to refuse to see himself truthfully as the dominator, which ethically he hates.

Might not this apply to you a certain amount? You had ended by almost whipping me, using mainly an ethical ground in the sense that you have made me feel guilty for all I did to you (which I certainly did do, no doubt of that) ((but which also, you refused to have an[y] tolerance about)). I escaped in sex dreams. I am not doing that any more. I had ended by dominating you until it looked like you would never write. My old disbelief in your writing even helped. But I dont have that any more, either. Because I saw enough of your stuff before I left that I know you've got it made if you only keep working.

What I am trying to prove, both to you and myself, is that I have nothing to be guilty for, any more than you have. You would have made a Bill Crebs out of me, or been one yourself. But we cant either one quit there, Lowney, or we are both finished.

I will become Hemingway one way—through sex, if I no longer can count on the ego-stimulation of your love.

You will become a Hemingway another way—through domination, of Harry, of Don, of Willy, of Tinks, you say you want to be free of them, but do you? when you are talking of taking them to Mexico with us three? Either that, or else Harry will step in as the heavy husband, as soon as your love for me is acknowledgedly finished, and your writing is done.

(He has been working on me to go out and sleep with something, anything. Last night, for instance. He is being honest, yet at the same time he is not being honest, he has an angle.)

Maybe you think he cant step in, not now. But he still holds the pursestrings. And if you left him and became the mistress of somebody else to get what you wanted, you would have the same thing to contend with. That has always been one of your threats, your escapes to save yourself.

The thing is I dont think you are looking at reality completely yourself. You talk about your pupils too much. You have helped them, surely. I've helped them some too. They are not my pupils, though. And certainly, I know I have never been your pupil.

I'm not tearing you down or nothing. What I'm saying is there is a love that exists, beyond dominating, and that love is only possible for you and me through each other.

I'll be able to write a great love novel someday, dont you think? It will end as a tragedy, of course. But yours and mine must not end that way. It has been too great a thing, for both of us. It has made both of us, though it nearly destroyed us both a thousand times.

As for me, I dont want sex anymore, but I do want it occasionally with you. If I have to go without for months at a time while we are apart working until we can get enough money to set everything up right so we can be close but still free to work, then I'm willing to do that. I'll go without not only because it destroys you for me to do it, but because I dont want it otherwise.

Its never been for you a wildness. But it has been a pleasure for you, the pleasure of tenderness and of love and being needed and needing. The mild pleasure of physical contact of hands and arms, the look of shoulders. I think thats just about all it is to me too.

I had a piece thrown in my lap last night, and turned it down right in front of me—not because I felt guilty about you but because I just didnt want it. It was not your body, your kiss, your anything. Tinks called me up and said he had a piece picked up for me, a girl from Iowa who was broke and on the bum, a pretty girl. He had a date with Dorinda, and wanted me to come over and take her up. I was reading Stendhal and almost didnt go. Harry and I talked about it a long time. I didnt really want to go. Harry thought it might make me feel better, if I had one. I tried to tell him it was not sex I wanted but the contact of love without dominance. Then I wondered if I really did? So I decided to go over and see. We drank a couple of beers over there, Tinks, Dorinda and me doing most of the talking, but the girl putting in a vague stray remark every now and then that showed she was following. She was reasonably pretty and young. Then we came over here with some beer, the four of us, and played some records. Tinks and Dorinda left, to pick up Tinks mother after a couple hours. The girl and I talked quite a while. She had just jumped on a bus and left Iowa on the spur because she couldnt stand it any more, she said. She is looking for romance, and adventure, been married (to a man she didnt love, she said, because the one she did love was killed in service). I could have had her. Tinks had gotten her a room the night before at the Woodworth but she had checked out. I could have had her just for staying all night. And she was affectionate. She didnt take hold of me or anything, but she was kittenish, like you stroke a cat, she had that look, but I didnt have any sexual desire for her at all. We talked, and I finally got the idea of me and Tinks putting up bus fare and sending her over to Mary Ann to get her a job in one of the bars. Mary Ann's worked in all of them. I drove her back to the hotel and paid for her room.

The payoff was driving home. I was mulling over it all, and I could see that I had gotten my ego-stimulation, not from sex, but from talking to all of them, from being the writer to them, (Tinks and Dorinda) and from showing off my room, and also from offering to take care of the girl. Sex was not in it.

Well, I got to quit and mail this. I copied up the first ten pages of Ch 36 today, finished, and its good. I did it all by myself. I wont have to have you read it and brag on it, after [all]. But what I do want, need, is your love, Lowney.

You said you were with me all the way. It isnt all the way yet, not by a long shot. Whenever I'm away from you it will not be all the way. But you also said, "after you've made the fight—I'll be waiting for you."

Between us, we can conquer it, Lowney. We must. We must have love without dominating, with the ego-stimulation love gives you. There is no joy in life without love, everything is drab, meaningless. I'd just as soon not be alive, as not have your love.

Forevermore,
Jim

Your letter of Monday just came. I'm scared. Mail fucks you up so. The poetry was not meant that way.[3] You will know

---

[3]The poem is not attached to the letter.

that by now tho. But it terrifies me, & now I'll have to wait for another letter.

I wrote that because I had let you down so, down there. & because I was so unhappy without you. The mail is so slow, we cross. Now I am frantic. I'm wild. My hands & whole body has the shakes. Dont hurt me, Lowney. Dont hurt me. I'm having so much trouble as it is, being gone from you. I didn't send a message with Mitch's letter because I didnt want to bother you.

Oh, Lowney. I didnt want to hurt your work with my problems. But I've already done it since with two letters. I quit work this morning, at 9:30, to write you this one because I thot I had it & the answer seemed so clear. Now I'm afraid this one will have something unintentional in it that will give you the wrong idea. I dont want any other women, truly. I couldnt sleep with one. I couldnt get a hard on now, any more, but with you, I bet.—But I didnt try. I didnt want to try. Oh, Lowney, Oh God Lowney.

Forever ever ever more,
Jim

Please, Lowney, Please.

I've just re-read your letter. So many subtleties and in-nuendoes. I dont know where I am. Write that you love me. I dont want sex. I want your love. Even without sex entirely, I want your love.[4] Oh, Lowney. I'm all gone inside. Letters are bitches. Harry's gone to Findlay. I'm going to drive the jeep to Vincennes and call you. I'm shot. I wont be able to work if I dont.

s/TLS

---

[4] Jones wrote a love-without-sex scene between Warden and Karen Holmes in Chapter 54 of *Eternity*.

Lowney responded on January 29, 1949, calling him "Darling" and admitting that she had kept him out of her astral world. Back in this world she had been reading an account of an older woman who ruined the career of a man twenty years younger than she. His letter had convinced her that she should not fence him out of her life. Lowney's letters responding to Jones indicate that she was making a conscious effort to smooth over their difficulties.

TO LOWNEY HANDY

[ROBINSON, ILLINOIS]
MONDAY 4:30 PM
[January 31, 1949]

My darling,

This is such a fine word. You called me your darling. I call you my darling. Probably 10 million lovers have used it, for lack [of] anything that will say it, and we still use it and it is never old, never trite.

. . . .

One thing, that has come out of this time: you have swallowed your pride enough to admit to me that you do need me—to need you.

. . . .

Where you say: "You say you've fought it out. Each time is a little more." I am humble before that. I have fought something out, yes; I have fought out that sex is nothing without love, and love nothing without you, without Lowney. (I love your name, it fits you so.) I have fought out, but that does not mean I have earned your trust back, the love you had at first, yet. You give it to me now, yes, but I know in myself that I must keep on earning it. I must never let you down as I have in the past. I will love you every day of my life, love you until you purr like a cat eating cream, love you with sex, love you with understanding, love you with closeness, love you with faith, love you with love—and I will never atone to myself for all the pain I've caused you. I know only that I must make you so happy you will trust me utterly and be frightened to death at the thought of ever leaving me.

Where you say: "I must be appreciated." You are, and will be, appreciated. And you are right, it is more than pride. The greatest gift any human can give another is himself. I dont blame virgins, all women, for putting such a high price on it. When they give it, it should mean something. It should be valued—not virginity, but the giving of oneself to another. You dont know how you will be appreciated.

(So many things to say.)

I remember someplace in them you say: "There are some people you just can't get over." God, you don't know what that means to me to have you say that to me. I want to be needed too, and I've always known I could never get over you. If I came home thinking to sleep with some other woman, it was because I thought maybe that way I could forget you, since you did not want <u>me</u> any more. But I couldnt even do that.

Thats where my faith is founded. I know now for sure you can never get over me, and that I can never get over you. It is as simple as that. Just that we are a man and his woman who love each other, a woman and her man who need each other. We are in love. Dont ask me why, or how. It just is, and must be accepted. We have loved through more than one eternity, to be able to love so much.

. . . .

Words just fail me, Lowney. I cant explain. Its just love, overpowering, all embracing, unbeatable, thats all.

You say, another place, "I need for you to need me." There is no word to say my happiness at reading that. Because I need for you to want me to need you. And where you say, "I think I have a jealousy knowing some of it (the book) will be written without me" and "the book sort of grew with me there all the time." Oh, it did. It is as much your book as it ever was mine. I've tried to tell you that before. You dont know how much a happiness it is to have you say that. It has always been "our" book, without you and the part you have put in it, it wouldnt have been attempted, let alone written. That is another bond between us. They will give me the credit for it, although I'd be as willing to put your name on it with mine, dont let me getting the credit hurt you. I dont want credit, I want your faith in me to do great things, and your love. And you say, "In the near future you'll need me with you to begin something else." How true that is. If you stopped loving me tomorrow, I might be able to go on and finish this book. I could never start another.

I havent done much since I got home. It goes much slower without you there to read it. I did not know how much I depended on your judgment. I would write something, and then show it to you, and forget it. If you said okay, I knew it was all right; if you said rewrite it, even though I bitched and groaned because of sheer laziness and fear, still I knew it needed rewriting. Now, I have to do that too, and it is much slower. Its hard for me to judge it objectively. But I'm doing it, though. Slower, yes, but everything I've got up to now I am absolutely sure of. . . .

To date I've done 19 pages—not counting that four pages I rewrote when I was rereading the first of Book IV. Twelve of it is copied up, and I'm satisfied with it, but the other seven I'm sweating over still. As soon as the chapter is done and copied I'll send it down, and you can fine-tooth comb it. If you say rewrite it, nuff said. If you say okay, then I'll already have it copied up, two copies, and I wont send the original out till you send the carbons back. Even if your help wouldnt help me, I'd send it anyway, because you deserve to be in on the finish, after sweating out the rest of it. I want you to feel its your book, too. At the end, you wont only have your books, but you will know that you also have mine, to your credit. And someday, I mean to see the world knows it too, darling. The time is not yet, but it will come, when we can write our own ticket to all of them. I cant say how truly happy it made me to have you say "I think I have a jealousy knowing that some of it will be written without me." Truly. Because when you say that I know you love me, and I know as long as I write you will always love me.

I ran onto an interesting thing in the Stendhal biografy. Around 1800 Stendhal wrote in his journal that I cant quote but that it should be possible to write down what actually happened and by selecting the details give the full picture of the emotion. Who does that make you think of? pray? Not Hemingway, by chance? Also, Stendhal made a note around 1800 that he wanted someday to write a book about one day in the life of a man and all his thoughts and what happened, just like, the biographer even says, James Joyce did over 100 yrs later! Also, the biographer points out earlier that there was a great revival of Stendhal around 1900 in France. I dont think the biografer saw it, but to me it is obvious that Stein studied Stendhal, and helped both Hemingway and Joyce from him. But Hem had never given the credit to him. You can see he was a liar from the very beginning, which helps to explain how he could fuck up so badly. Thats one thing neither you nor I have ever been.

Stendhal wanted love too, as much as you or I. But he was not willing to adjust or sacrifice to get it—until he was too old and the two women had both died. Then he saw himself as the fool he was, as all men are actually, and that is what he wrote, as honestly as he could, and what made him great. We can learn from him how not to fail ourselves, and in so doing be even greater. I dont hate people any more, I had gotten so I hated all of them, yet now I never really trust any of them—but you. You I trust, fully. I didnt until now. I could see too many fallacies and mistakes in you, when you preached to Willy and them, ones you would not admit. You did hurt me over Willy down there, my pride, yes, but also <u>me</u>, the thing that is <u>me</u>. But then I did not see you were doing it as an escape because of how much I had hurt you, so that really I had only myself to blame, as we all have in the end. Thats whats so great about Dos Passos *USA*. You are right, that it is holding the hurts inside yourself that loses people everything. Its good for us to be apart, and I'll struggle on here as long as I can. When it gets too tough I'll let you know, because I know if I need you you will come. Knowing that, I do not need to be repeatedly proving it to myself by calling you, like I use to.

Also, I think this time alone down there is helping your writing more than any single thing has ever done. I have never helped you as much as I should have, I've been too scared that I would fail myself—as one may easily do on each new book, no matter how many great ones he has written. But also, you would never listen when I criticized. You just told me I didnt believe in you. Yet, you tore my stuff to shreds repeatedly, and though I complained like hell, I ended by taking it. I think now when you do come home, I will be able to go through it with you and help you what little bit I can, because you will be willing to listen. You'll probably bitch almost as much as I do over your criticism, but you'll listen. The only way to get good is to admit how bad you were. Which you made me do. But I could never make you do.

You say, "Most of the trouble originates in me." But thats wrong. No more than half originates in you, and probably not over 35 or 40%. You worry about not doing something worthwhile with your intellect, yet but for you I wouldnt have ever been anything. You dont count that. Okay, then you will write a great book yourself, with your intellect. And I will help you do it. I should have helped you more before now, even though you refused advice; I refused advice, yet you made me take it anyway. And when your book is done and a satisfaction, I wont count it. Then we'll be even.

Of course, you'll have to help with every other book I write, too. I will need you with me to begin something else. It just looks like I'm always going to need you, and theres no way we can get out of it, I guess, is there?

As if we wanted out.

You're right that we need to get a light on sex. I'm beginning to think its only our different definitions of it.

(Harry came home and I quit to eat. I'll try and get back in where I was.)

In the first place you say, "a predominantly sexual love." To my mind, there is no predominantly sexual love. No matter what I've said in the past, or done—both as an escape from the fear of losing our love, and as a bald masculine pride—I say now that love cant be predominantly sexual. That doesnt mean, though, that two people in love cant have sex every night, if they want it every night. You are right that "you have a tendency to extract all of the meat of love—the delight and pleasure in the hours in bed." I did do that, but I did more because I was frantic for fear of losing you—I could <u>see</u> I was losing you—and I was grasping frantically at whatever straws I could seize. It wasnt that way at the very first with us, if you remember. I was ravenous, yet even so, that was a warmth there that heightened everything, like the way we would look at each other glintingly when other people were around (especially Robinsonites), we knowing what we had had shortly before and would have again. You, now, resent it if you feel I take too much from you in sex; I will try to remedy that by adjustment (like you said); yet at the same time you would be terribly hurt if you thought I <u>didnt</u> want to sleep with you, wouldnt you?

Somehow, I feel we wont have much trouble with sex when we get together again. Somehow, now, I feel like it will already have ironed itself out.

You say, also, earlier, "Maybe I have little enough sex—but I place a value on me as an individual." I dont think you have little sex, I've always thought you had a lot. . . . The thing with you is, nobody has ever been able to lull you with love enough to awaken the sex that is in you. I did maybe for a little while, or rather I was just beginning to (remember how I use to say relax your mouth?), but then I had to go and spoil it all with my harebrained kid's ideas I'd picked up out of novels like Hemingway's. There is tremendous sex in you, you neednt worry your head on that, sex as love and sex as nearness and sex as giving pleasure and taking pleasure, it hasnt been awakened yet with trust. I think it will be when we come together again, if only by the fact of my being true to you (not from willpower, but from being incapable of doing anything else but be true to you).

. . . .

You say, "Perhaps out of hurt you wrote me the letter, so casual about your need of sex, so determined that sex and love were one and the same for you and whoever could furnish the sex you could love." You misunderstood my first letter, it wasnt the hunger for sex that made me suffer but the hunger for your love, and the fear that I was losing, had lost, you—even while I was trying to wean myself away from loving you. That was what I meant when I spoke about the suffering. When I mentioned the whorehouse, it was as a second best, a last resort—but even then it wouldnt have worked if I had been able to find it. Nothing, no sex, no woman, no nothing, could fill the empty place in me when I think I could have lost you.

You say, "But if we can gradually wear these down—adjust more—theres nothing that will approach the happiness and love we'll have forever." And when I read that, I sing all over and its all I can do to keep from crying, with my happiness.

And now, you telling me about what Mrs Mahlon's cousin said about your figure! What have I been trying to tell you all along? But you refuse to believe (because you think I'm either prejudiced, or lying) and you believe Mrs Mahlon's cousin! You have the most beautiful [body] I've ever laid my eyes on, and I mean that (IN or OUT of a bathing suit). Oh, if I could only see you now.

But I'll hang on. If it gets too bad to stand (not for want of sex, but for hunger of seeing and being with you, my darling, the sex comes second, or maybe third), if it gets too bad to stand I'll write you. But right now, I am determined to give you the time to work that you want and need, and place my own selfish hunger for you with me in the background. I can prove my love to you again, that way. And I must prove my love, and then go right on proving and proving my love to you.

You closed with "Forevermore: and never doubt that I love you, I cant help myself." There is nothing you could say that could make me prouder, happier, or greater than that. So I repeat it back to you, as hungrily and sincerely as you said it.

Forevermore: and never doubt that I love you, my darling, I cant help myself.

I'll write again tomorrow.

I didnt write Sunday. You'll never know how long that day was. Even after talking to you Saturday night, it was so long from then until today when I could get and read the letters.

I'll write tomorrow. I want to mail this before the evening pickup.

Stay there and work. I am waiting and shall be waiting.

You're right about the money, and the sense of guilt about Harry, and taking his money. We must finish our books and be free to have ourselves to ourselves, for a while.

Why couldnt you and I go to Mexico alone next winter? And then Harry fly down for his vacation? You are right that if we took the boys or one of them, they should be lonely seeing us so happy, and then you would do like in Naples and go out of your way to be nasty to me in front of them to save their feeling[s], and hurt mine. Honestly, I'm not being selfish but it isnt fair. Not when I mean more to you than they do. I think part of our greatest trouble up to now is trying to be unselfish with others and sacrifice our love upon everybody's sensitivity.

Anyway, it will work out.

Write to me. Write and tell me how you love me. How you need for me to need you. Oh, Lowney, Lowney, that was so lovely, to hear you say that.

Forevermore: and never doubt that I love you, my darling, I cant help myself, you just cant get over some people, you meet them and there is a look between you, and you are bound together to the grave, and to beyond the grave.

I love you

Jim

s/TLS

Jones and Lowney weathered the 1949 crisis, but certain funda-
mental problems were still there and were festering. Lowney, it was
clear, was not going to leave Harry. He was superintendent of the
refinery in Robinson, a position of power and prestige; he let her
lead her own life; he supported her and Jones. As Jones matured,
he was less willing to accept domination. He also felt guilty about
cuckolding Harry, a man he admired and respected, and he was
seemingly becoming aware of the psychological implications of his
relationship with the much older Lowney. Years later, in Go to
the Widow-Maker *(1967), Jones fictionalized part of his problem:*
"As Carol Abernathy [Lowney] in one of her better moments once
chuckled and said huskily as they lay in bed, 'Christ! You're the
only man I ever heard of who got to live out his Oedipus complex!'
Grant [Jones] had laughed, at the time."

Jones's letters to Mitchell during the late winter of 1949 gave no
indication of his emotional state. Jones continued to describe the
progress he was making as he neared the end of Eternity.

TO BURROUGHS MITCHELL

ROBINSON, ILLINOIS
FEBRUARY 25, 1949

Dear Mitch,

. . . .

I've done the next entire chapter—right. And am part way
through the next. Both are within the Stockade; and I'm finding that Stockade part is about the roughest writing I've ever
tried to do up to now. It goes very slowly and very agoniz-
ingly. I think it is because I was never actually in a Stockade
per se, but only in a prison ward in the hosp where they
brought the boys after they beat them up. There is a basic
problem there, in the writing of it and getting it right, that it

would take pages to go into so I wont. I dont know if I could ever explain it. Maybe I could give a rough idea of what I'm trying to hit on it, though: All the new books since the war are occupying themselves with the problem of <u>Evil</u> with a capital E—like Buchenwald etc. and all that—and trying to understand it. But they've all failed for my money, for the same reason that they've all failed to write about homosexuals. You remember we talked of that once. The fallacy lies in the concept of Evil with a capital E, and the attempt to understand it as a thing outside of oneself that is observed. Whereas, it is actually a thing inside of oneself, not objective at all but subjective, which they all are either unable or else ashamed-and-afraid to understand. What I mean is, we are horrified at Buchenwald yet every man if put in the position of the guards and overseers would have ended in the same way doing the same thing. Given the same place and position in History, every man would be Hitler—or Shakespeare—or, to stretch it, Christ. We all think we could have been a Christ or a Shakespeare, but we will not all believe we could have been a Hitler. We will not any of us believe that. So that, viewed from that angle, there really isnt any Evil with a capital E. We just think there is and torment ourselves with it.

. . . .

Yours,
Jim

p/TLS

Harry Handy helped Jones buy a jeep and a trailer, and when the wanderlust struck Jones he could travel. Lowney (and sometimes Willard "Willy" Lindsay, who was studying with Lowney) often accompanied Jones on these writing excursions to Memphis, Tennessee; Albuquerque, New Mexico; Tucson, Arizona; and Hollywood, California.

Lowney and Willard Lindsay were with Jones in Memphis in early May 1949.

TO HARRY HANDY

MEMPHIS, TENNESSEE

[MAY 8, 1949]

Dear Doc,

They are getting ready for the Cotton Festival downtown with lights, bunting, etc. Front Street on the river is closed off for about eight blocks for the carnival concessions. Gypsy Rose Lee is the main attraction; she and husband were parked right across street from us for several days here in their trailer, but left to park it on the show grounds. When they left, they had trouble getting hitched up and I went over and helped (at Lowney's knifewielding insistence) and then went back and showed a Scribner's letter and asked if I could find a copy of her book downtown would she autograph it.[1] She said yes, isnt that a coincidence, we are planning on selling them in the show; also, my new book too. Hubby, an Armenian I think, invited me to come around to the back of the tent. I havent yet, but intend to. The Gyp dearly wants to be taken for a writer now, apparently, instead of a stripper. She was very flustered.

. . . .

[1]Probably *The G-String Murders*.

All my best love to you, dear Doc,
And may you have many happy returns
of the new refinery.

. . . .

Kove and Lisses
Mack[2]

s/TLS

[2]Jones often signed letters to Harry with the name "Mack," a reference to "Mack the Knife," the song from *The Threepenny Opera*.

Lowney returned to Robinson, leaving Jones in Memphis. She continued to have problems with her health, often resorting to self-treatments: faddish diets; enemas; megadoses of iron capsules. She wrote Jones that she was thinking of checking into Barnes Hospital in St. Louis for treatment.

TO LOWNEY HANDY

[MEMPHIS, TENNESSEE
MAY 29, 1949]

Dear Lowney,
  . . . .

I'm sorry to hear that about Barnes. I find, looking deeper into myself, there is some obscure fear I have of having you go into a hospital, not because you will die (tho there is that fear too), but mostly because it seems to take you entirely away from me, out of my reach, into a social structure where you are, and perforce must be, Mrs Handy. I've even imagined you falling back in love with Harry—I saw a Joan Crawford movie, psychologically wrong of course when you analyze it, but smoothly done and well acted and it upset me quite a bit. I'm learning more and more to cover up tho, so that no one suspects how upset I may happen to be.

I was hoping you'd get better, just resting, that it was only frustration here and nervous strain that was causing all of it, but I guess its more than that. I guess I have to admit it, for your good (which is my own too). You ought to have a checkup, anyway, at the least.
  . . . .

Forevermore,
Jim

s/TLS

Lowney, who was with Jones on the jeep-trailer trip west while the concluding chapters of Eternity *were being written, received a letter from Burroughs Mitchell praising the novel.*

TO HARRY HANDY

[ALBUQUERQUE, NEW MEXICO
OCTOBER 9, 1949]

Dear Doc,

    . . . .

You will have had Lowney's letter from Mitch by now. They're very impressed at Scribner's, as well as anxious. I've been hoping that the letter will show you, or rather repay you, in some measure for what you've done. This book never could have been written without you in there doing the backing up, just [as] it couldnt have been written without Lowney in there helping me with the writing. Its going to be one of the best books thats ever come out in this country, if not the best, including *USA*. And you're responsible for a large part of it, buddy.

    . . . .

All my best love to you, Doc,
Jamie Mack-Jones

s/TLS

From Albuquerque, New Mexico, Jones sent Harry a comic message on a card with a picture of Ernie Pyle, the war correspondent. Jones was ambivalent about Hemingway, both the man and his work. During World War II Hemingway sometimes called himself "Old Ernie Hemorrhoid, the Poor Man's Pyle."

His Home In Albuquerque That Ernie Pyle Loved So Well

Jones had a small disability pension (less than fifty dollars a month). He had to make periodic trips to a veterans' hospital for examinations in order to continue to receive his monthly check. He normally went to a hospital in Illinois for the examination, but when he was traveling, he made arrangements to be seen at nearby VA hospitals.

TO BURROUGHS MITCHELL

ALBUQUERQUE, N.M.
OCTOBER 30, 1949

Dear Mitch,

Here is the piece de résistance, the tour de force, the final accolade and calumnity, the climax, peak, and focus.

Here, in a word, is Pearl Harbor.

From here on it is all down hill.

I had a rough time with part of it, but I think it is right now.

We stayed over two days extra, so I could finish it; partly because it would be so hard to work back into it after the move; but mostly because I would have been a son of a bitch on wheels to live with moving, if I had to give up on it, and both Lowney and Willie[1] knew it and wisely chose to suffer cold and close quarters rather than me. Not, of course, because they are as anxious and enthusiastic as I am to get it finished.

Friday, I got up at 2 AM and worked four hours before I went out to the Vets Hosp for my pension exam, at Lowney's suggestion, because we all knew a day off would throw me and particularly one as trying as an exam day. It always upsets me like hell.

How the exam will turn out I dont know; they never tell you any more than they can help, which is usually nothing. But I'm keeping my fingers crossed, knocking on wood, not walking

[1]Willard Lindsay was with Jones and Lowney on this trip.

under ladders and all that. God knows what I would have done without it all these many years; there is a limit to even Harry's and Lowney's ability to dispense generosity, if not to their desire. It was about like up at Danville, the last time, and they didnt take it away from me then.

I was a wrung dishrag when I got home.

Well, anyway, here is Pearl. And I, personally, believe it will stack up with Stendhal's Waterloo or Tolstoy's Austerlitz. That was what I was aiming at, and wanted it to do, and I think it does it. If you dont think it does, send it back and I'll re-rewrite it. Good isnt enough, not for me, anyway; good is only middling fair. We must remember people will be reading this book a couple hundred years after I'm dead, and that the Scribner's first edition will be worth its weight in gold by then. We musnt ever forget that.

If this note sounds overly enthusiastic, you must remember that I have just finished a chapter.

> My best to Helen, Wheelock, and Bruce,[2]
> And to yourself,
> Yours,
> *Jim*

P/TLS

---

[2]Helen was Mitchell's wife, and Bruce his son.

In addition to his small government pension, Jones received financial help from Harry Handy. Harry, though, was not wealthy, as Jones explained to his sister, Mary Ann, when she requested money. She was in Miami, in difficulty with the law, and needed to get away. Jones responded in an undated letter: "When your wire came, Harry was out of town. Lowney couldn't have raised five if her life depended on it. Today when your letter came, Harry had been gone two hours on his way to Chicago on a business trip. Even if he was here, he couldn't help with dough. You got to realize that Harry lives from month to month on his salary. He really lives on credit which is possible for him in his position when you and I couldn't do it."

TO HARRY HANDY

[TUCSON, ARIZONA
NOVEMBER 18, 1949]

Dear Doc,

. . . .

We got the money of course, and it was very welcome. I think we had about seven cents, all told. That noon, before it came, we . . . needed a quart of milk and a loaf of bread so we compromised and bought the bread and used canned milk in the gravy.

This chapter I'm working on now is the one where I kill Prewitt off. I kind of hate to do it in a way, I've got so used to the son of a bitch being around. But my first loyalty goes to the book I guess. Then there will be about three more chapters, after that. (Or four.)

This is an awful shitty letter, but I'm awful tired. Not physically tired so much, but empty. The morning always takes everything out of me.

I'll try and do better next time, though.

XXX

xxx

ooo

///

mack

s/TLS

Jones completed Eternity *in California on February 27, 1950. Lowney was also in Hollywood but not living in the trailer with him.*

TO BURROUGHS MITCHELL

NORTH HOLLYWOOD, CALIF.

FEBRUARY 27, 1950

Dear Mitch,

I am on my third martini (your recipe) and this will just be a short note. I'll write you a more comprehensive letter in a couple of days. I've been working all day to get it all finished up, and I'm too pooped for much of a letter. I havent written you sooner because I've been expecting and hoping to have it finished up to send.

I know you have been worried about the ending between Karen and Warden. After you read it, I dont think you will; I think you'll be able to see what I had in my mind and could not articulate. I think you'll agree with me it couldnt have been any other way.

I really feel very peculiar. Not elated. Not depressed. But peculiar. Maybe humble. So little of what I think this novel is and may be is so little due to me. I want to tack on a kind of series of acknowledgments, at the end, later. I'll write it up in a few days and send it on.

. . . .

I've got a lot of short stories to work on, and this novel on Russell.[1] And I plan to help Lowney with her book.

Lowney is a very peculiar person. She has a psychological necessity to put forward the worst side of everything. Consequently, I feel there is a lot of material and purpose to her book that you have not been acquainted with. It is anything but a

---

[1] The Russell novel, greatly changed, became *Some Came Running.*

suspense story, really. The murder part of it is incidental to the rest, for me at least. It had a lot of fine possibilities.

The sad thing, the funny thing, the really ironical thing, is that she has put so much time on me, and on Willy, and Don, and several others who have not panned out as well as either of these, that she has neglected herself. I intend to see that she does not go on doing it. The truth is, I'm excited about the damn thing. Her book.

. . . .

Yours,

Jim

p/TLS

Jones sent the following telegram to Harry Handy when Eternity was completed.

HOLLYWOOD CALIF

FEB 27 1950

HARRY EDWIN HANDY & FAMILY

OHIO OIL CO ROBINSON ILL

FINIS. CONGRATULATIONS TO YOU BOTH AND HEALTH AND
EVERY HAPPINESS TO THE NEW ARRIVAL. YOUR LOVING SON.

MACK

s/

TO BURROUGHS MITCHELL

NO. HOLLYWOOD, CALIF

MARCH 18, 1950.

Dear Mitch

First, I'd like to ask a favor of you. Lowney has gone home
now, due to lack of funds, and I would like for you to send her
a copy of Perkins' *Letters* there to the Robinson address.[1] She
saw it here—she was in Frisco visiting her brother the Navy
flyer and his wife, when it came, and I met her at the plane with
it in my hand—needless to say, she was as thrilled over it as
I was. And I would like for her to have a copy. If you could
have Mr Wheelock fix it up, just like he did the one to me, with
the card and the publication date written on, and then address
it to her at the Robinson address, and send it soon, before it hits
the stands, I know she would be very happy to have it. And
I would appreciate it greatly.

I would enclose the money for it now, but I'm caught very

---

[1]*Editor to Author: The Letters of Maxwell E. Perkins,* edited by John Hall
Wheelock, contained the texts of three letters Perkins wrote Jones.

short at the moment, but I would send the money to you first of the month as soon as my check comes in. Will you do this for me?

As to the book itself, there isnt much I can say. I think it is a magnificent memorial to Perkins. Apart from the invaluable help it ought to be to anyone who seriously wants to write. I'm writing Willy and Don and the rest to get a copy soon as its on the stands. They can learn much from it. I have already. Of course, for me, there was the additional thrill of seeing my name in a book for the first time. It is not the same as seeing it in a magazine, which is mentally and intellectual a passing thing and physically is flimsy and destructible. There is such a sense of permanence about an actual book. If at any time, for any reason, I get the least bit low, all I have to do is open it to page 297 and read footnote 2 and then I believe it again. He was a great man, a real genius to my mind, and I say that unembarrassedly, and this is a fine way to preserve him—at least, as much as is possible to preserve what he was and did. I keep thinking of all the priceless conversations that are lost for good, and I wish a wire recorder could have been turning somewhere near. Such things are impossible of course. It is only the romantic in me that wishes they were not. The rest of me is glad they aren't, because—well, its like when I broke that Randall-made knife I wrote you of once; it was perfectly balanced and made for throwing and so I practiced throwing it and eventually I broke it, as I knew I would, and it hurt terribly but still I could not have refrained from throwing it, just to save it. Since then I've gotten another one, but no knife I ever own will measure up to that one. This is an extreme analogy, as he said in one of those letters to me, perhaps even an indelicate one. What I'm trying to say is that you cannot always be counting the cost, because counting the cost is a profession in its own right and belongs in the realm of the CPA. When you count the cost of anything, it becomes a life work in itself. But you know what I'm driving at.

I was very glad to see that young picture of him. I've studied it a lot. It is fine. There is a lot in it. Whoever picked it did a perfect job.

I am not doing much of anything. Reading a little, loafing a lot, and writing letters sporadically; I've a lot of them to catch up on. Its always different when a thing happens to you, it never is what you expect. All the imagination in the world will not make up for having an experience happen to you; there are always myriads of little things that are so incongruous that you could never imagine them up. I find that I am relieved of a great tension; if I am driving the jeep down the freeway and begin to think about a tire blowing, in the back of my mind is this thought of how I wouldnt really mind dying so much now. There is enough of it there now that they could print it; maybe it wouldnt be quite as good as it will be, but it would be printed.

But the loss of this tension has another effect, too. I am like a rubber band that has been stretched over two nails for a long time and left there; you take it down from the nails and it hangs together all right. But if you try to stretch it again, even the least tiniest bit, it will crumble. Not snap, or break, or burst, or pop. Crumble.

Thats one of the reasons its taking me so long to work through this stack of letters I have to answer. I get completely pooped out over nothing.

Outside of that, I'm doing nothing. Just waiting, for you to get the things to be done ready. To be frank, I feel a little like the fighter who has climbed in the ring and is shuffling his feet in the resin, and hears the stir that means his opponent is coming down the opposite aisle, but does not turn around and just goes on scuffing his feet in the resin in the great deep silence.

One of the things I would like you to remember is that the things we change in this book for propriety's sake will, in five years, or ten years, come in someone else's book anyway, that may not be as good as this one, and then we will kick ourselves for not having done it, and we will not have been first with this,

as Perkins and Hemingway were with the other, and we will
wonder why we thought we couldnt do it. Writing has to keep
evolving into deeper honesty, like everything else, and you
cannot stand on past precedent or theory, and still evolve. You
remember that.

You know there is nothing salacious in this book as well as
I do. Therefore, whatever changes you want made along that
line will be made for propriety, and propriety is a very incon-
stant thing.

   . . . .

Yours,
Jim

P/TLS

Burroughs Mitchell and Horace Manges, the attorney for Scribner's, found many words and passages in Eternity *which they felt should be omitted. Jones was ambivalent about the censorship of his novel.*

TO BURROUGHS MITCHELL

NORTH HOLLYWOOD, CALIF.
MARCH 29, 1950.

Dear Mitch,

The manuscript came this morning. I had already studied your letter quite a bit. I ran through the manuscript hurried[ly] today, looking only for your markings to see what you would want out. Your letter had made me more than unusually amenable to the cuts. After seeing them, I guess I am not quite so amenable, though still, I think, fair. There are some of them that I agree with entirely; others I agree with partly; some I do not agree with at all.

The last paragraph of page 1, Chapter 6, and first paragraph of page 2 can be cut entirely. And I think will help it. If I would have wanted to save any of that, it would have been the imagery of the gassy bubbles etc., but even that is a mixed metaphor, or simile, or whatever.[1] I had read it over before the manuscript came, in the carbon.

The part about Ike I disagree with. It may be close to burlesque, but so was Ike. You'll never know how much. Maybe I prefer it almost burlesque, now that its mentioned, tho I hadn't thought of that before.

Now as to the sex cuts. I agree with you in principle. Both the part of the selling, and also the part of accustoming the reader gradually. Still, I feel you have perhaps leaned over

---

[1] The "gassy bubbles" section, a naturalistic aside, was excluded from Chapter 6.

backwards in your accustoming. I dont think as many need be cut as you have marked. For instance, the one place where it is used in the first chapter ought to be left in, I think. It is the only use of "The Word" in that chapter, and it is not used at all in the second.[2] I actually think the leaving of that one in, there, and then going on for quite a little space before using it again will have a tendency to help prepare the reader, of itself.

There is another place I want to mention particularly. That is page 21, Chapter 9. The scene between Warden and the clerk. You cut most of that about the painters, I noticed. I dont know if you felt it superfluous, or if you cut it back a ways, just to avoid the one word there, "cunt."[3] That whole thing about the painters I want in because it shows a particular depth of character in Warden that I want. Neither am I romanticizing him. The guy was like that. I used to be the "intellectual Type" like Mazzioli; and I would come up with things I thought would catch Warden, and then he would come back with something amazingly out of character for the role he liked to play. I mean, he <u>had</u> read a lot; he <u>did</u> know a lot about art; about damn near every intellectual subject.

As to the word itself, I have seen it published—in America. The word is used once in Faulkner's *Wild Palms,* in one of those italicized stream-of-consciousness parts. I read it in the little 25¢ pocketbook edition. If it can be published there, and that book circulates over most of the country, surely it can be printed in *Eternity.* The thing is, to have used any other word there, such as "snatch" or "pussy," or some other slang word for it would be to take away all the psychological shock that I want to show in the clerk Mazzioli. The paragraph after

[2] I have examined Jones's carbon copy of the manuscript, and Mitchell did excise "The Word" (the same word Mailer had to misspell in *The Naked and the Dead*) many times.

[3] Mitchell did not restore the comments about Titian's "Venus of Urbine," perhaps because the word *cunt* was used. Most of the section on art was removed.

Warden says it, that starts: "Mazzioli was deeply shocked." I have put a comma after "Deeply" and added the word "profoundly."

I want that word to be left in there, Mitch. I am willing to sacrifice the use of it in Chapter ɪɪ (though I definitely dont want to, unless I must), but in Chapter 9 it is necessary to the effect of the scene and the depicting of both their characters.

About the scene in Chapter ɪɪ itself, I do not like the way you have cut it. I will grant that it can be cut some. Still, you in your cutting have excised all mention of his masturbating. The positive mention of that, someplace there, is necessary. You see, Prew is a proud man. He would not do it unless forced so completely to the point that there was absolutely no escape. I dont know if I am making myself clear. But that is necessary, not on account of the loneliness and frustration and that alone, but on account of the pure subject of the fact that guys are <u>forced</u> to masturbate in the Army. Have you done any reading in Kinsey's book? That is the point of the scene; not simple frustration and loneliness and that.

I dont know if I can make you understand. You think I put those things in arbitrarily, just for simple shock value. But it isnt that. You see, you were an officer. Officers are inclined to be a little more polite about such things. For instance, the word "cunt-pictures" in Chapter ɪɪ. That word is as much a common term in the Army as "latrine" or "chow down" instead of "eat." (I said I was willing to sacrifice that one, and I am, because it can be given up.) But the thing is, it is to be crude "cunt" that us American men of the lower classes, especially in the Army, are interested in. It isnt love; the love only comes later, if at all. In fact, in a great many cases it comes only grudgingly and with great reluctance on the part of the male. I dont know if you follow me. But that term, and not the term "pinups," was the term used in the Army. The use of it implies a whole host of things that are absent when it is left out, and that would take pages of "delicate" exposition to portray, and then you would never show it.

Then also, in Chapter 11, you cut out the little thing about Red having the wet dream. I want that to stay in. I saw that, with my own eyes, and—with very little variation—I saw it a great many times. If it is illegal as written, then maybe I can cut it inside, a word or two here and there, to make it a little more palatable, but I want it in. Christ, Mitch, the people of this country dont know what the hell goes on in it. Maybe thats why they're such sanctimonious bastards. But if Joyce can have Molly Bloom remember how she tossed him off into a handkerchief, then I can have that about Red's wet dream.[4]

There are lots of other places. For instance, you have cut absolutely every place where the phrase "piece of ass" is used. Yet I have read plenty of times the phrase "piece of tail" in other writers.

Well, anyway the purpose of this letter, now, is to find out what you want me to do if I dont feel like cutting a lot of this. I am willing to cut considerable of it; but I feel you have gone too far the other way. We ought to be able to compromise on some of it.

You see, if you take it all out like that, the whole thing is going to sound like a historical novel of the *Amber* ilk which cunningly hints at everything but never has the guts to say anything. You understand me.

As for Hemingway worrying about being considered a "dirty" writer, I think thats almost what I would call fatuous. I've heard of it before, the same remark. Fatuous on Hemingway's part, I mean. Well, anyway, that is one worry I do not have. I dont care if anybody thinks I'm a dirty writer. Maybe I am. After all, I've only my American background and training to pattern after.

But the argument here is the legal angle, not my spiritual development. I think some of this can surely be left in. Not as

---

[4]Jones was not successful in saving this wet dream episode or many of the other explicit sexual scenes mentioned in this letter.

much as at first, perhaps, and I grant that. But surely a little more than it is now the way you've cut it.

. . . .

Yours always,
Jim

P/TLS

The Colony Years,

1950-1956

*A*t first Jones agreed to most of the cuts suggested by Mitchell. *He did not want his book "to be a Henry Miller 'limited edition,' " he wrote Mitchell on April 3, 1950. He described how he had revised a masturbation scene in Chapter 11, changes that would make the scene less objectionable. He asked his editor to make asterisks by passages that Scribner's believed absolutely should be changed because of the obscenity laws. Jones insisted he had no knowledge of those laws.*

By the end of the month Jones was expressing reservations about several of the changes Scribner's wanted and asserting that certain passages should be published as he wrote them.

Jones returned to Illinois and turned his attention to the building of the Colony for writers, long a dream of Lowney's. The Colony was in Marshall, a small town north of Robinson. At this time Jones, who was without funds, could contribute only physical labor to this project, but the prospects were good for large sales of his novel and future financial support. In the years to come Jones was to be the major donor to the Colony, but in the summer of 1950 Harry was providing the funds to get the cow pasture turned into a campus for writers.

TO BURROUGHS MITCHELL

MARSHALL, ILLINOIS
JUNE 28, 1950

Dear Mitch,

. . . .

The "Marshall Plan" is coming along pretty well. We've about reached the place of having enough necessities done now that we can relax somewhat and stop working on it mornings, just afternoons now, because what remains to be done will be a long time in the doing anyway. Water and sewer lines are in now, and the electricity, and we've got enough old brick laid into patios for the two trailers that its comfortable (you see, we've had a long bad spell of phenomenal rain this year—its almost ruined the corn crop all over—and for a while the water was an inch deep in the grass around the trailers; we needed the brick walks and patios to take care of that). Also we've had a hell of a time with the road in, that we had to build. The drainage still isnt right on it, but thats the next big job.

You see—well, here. Maybe I can give you a picture. You see, Highway 40 runs east and west through Marshall, and out on the west side of town, just at the city limits sign, is this big old white house with half a dozen big oaks in the yard, Harry's homeplace, and his mother has lived there for years. Behind the house is a deep, pretty steep natural draw heavily grown with brush and willows which is the natural drainage for that side of the town. The city street drains empty into it. Then up on the other side of the draw, still part of the Handy homeplace is this high ground that was a cow pasture. Thats what Lowney tells everybody it is and always calls it: "converted cow pasture." Well, to get water and lights over to it we had to dig a 2½ ft ditch from an outside faucet over at the house clear down one hill across the half-swamp in the bottom and up the other hill. I did that part, me and Bob Smith, a boy who quit school at the U. of New Mexico to come up here, after meeting us out there last fall. The wiring, which required the setting of poles and other professional stuff—such as having to run our line <u>under</u> the power line which runs down through the bottom, and then <u>over</u> a phone line which goes across the hill on this side, both specified requirements of the electrical code—the wiring was done by some of Harry's boys from the plant.

Well, anyway, we're over here, and now occupied afternoons with finishing off around the camp. The cabin itself, which is being refinished entirely in plywood inside, wont be done for quite a while yet. The cabin is Lowney's, hence she is still down at Robinson and drives up three or four times a week to see how things are going. Willy also, now that his family has finally accepted him as a genius and therefore step[s] lightly mornings while he works, is down there, and working hard.

Our road does not come in off the highway, but from a side street two blocks north. Up here there are two trailers, and one tent (brick floored, and with a tarp-canopy porch also brick floored). Bob is in the tent (Willy's old one, of Albuquerque days), and I'm in my trailer, and the other trailer belongs to Alma Isley Akers and twin daughters June and Jane (aged 12), who are from Oklahoma City, and whom we all met in Colo Sprgs last year. It was Mrs Akers whom I wrote Jack Wheelock about several months ago, that I had sent her a copy of [Wheelock's] "Golgotha," when she was going through a bad time. Well, the typewriters are really going mornings, as you can imagine. We've even got the twins working, copying fairy tales. Alma is copying Hemingway, and Bob a mixture of Hindu Yoga and Hammett and Raymond Chandler. You would be amazed what this copying system, which I wrote you about a long time ago, does for them. Take Willy: he is, after about two years, at the place of technical (and mental—spiritual, if you will) proficiency that I was at about two or three years ago, after working at it for at least five years! And the twins—god, man! if I had only had somebody to get on my tail and put me to work when I was twelve! It makes me sick to think about it, what I've missed. And they are quite serious about becoming writers, too. The copying, of course, is interspersed with periods of working on their own stuff—except the twins. The whole thing is Lowney's invention, and it is to her whom the entire credit belongs.

God knows what it will be like by the end of the summer. Don Sackrider is expecting to get out of the Army any time now, and come up. And a boy named Dan Towns from Ft Worth (whom you may have read about in the newspapers; he is the instigator of the "Towns Tri-Continent Expedition," that was to take a party of jeeps from the tip of Chile to Alaska via the Pan-Am Highway, but which fell through because he could not get the Willys people sufficiently interested to donate the jeeps, even though he had the endorsement of the Governor of Texas, Frank Buck, a couple Senators, the US Chamber of Commerce, and I dont know who all else. You probably have read some about it.)—well, he is expecting to quit his job and cut out for here in the next month or so. And then there is Warren Pearsley of Rapid City, S.D., one of the most erudite individuals with whom I have ever corresponded; he is expecting to pull in some time this summer for a month or two.

Its really an amazing thing. And of course, behind it all, is the guiding-light, whip-cracker, and guardian-angel which is Lowney. Keen Rafferty, head of the Journalism School at the U. of New Mexico, who has been in town for a short stay and has been up a few times, and who will probably be here himself for a while next summer, and is almost wildly enthusiastic about the whole thing (Bob Smith was more or less one of his proteges), said last night that he thought Lowney has the most intelligent, and demanding, and yet most feeling eyes he has ever seen in a human being. I guess that would describe them. Anyway, I know I never would have written neither what nor as much as I have, had she not stood over me with the club, like the mother standing over the future concert-master as he sits at the piano with one eye on the clock.

Both trailers have bathrooms, but the one in the cabin isnt finished yet because of the rain, and Bob is using mine now, but a separate bathhouse with a side for boys and one for girls, complete with a utility room for washing clothes, is under construction at the moment, and we expect to have up about three more surplus tents before the summer's over. After we sell *Eternity* to MGM we'll convert those into permanent cabins; but Lowney says we ought to keep the tents anyway because most of our clients have had it too easy all their lives anyway and its good for them. I know living in a tent's sure helped Bob, who use to be a campus esthete and intellecshull.

There are flood lights mounted on each of the four light poles, and in the evening we sit out on the brick between the trailers around the rough hewn rustic picnic table and the breeze that comes across the hilltop under the big maples makes it almost chilly enough for a wrap and the fireflies of which there seem to be millions stand out starkly against the deep black of draw that hides the Handy house across the way but you can hear the big trucks grinding by all night on the Highway, and a quarter mile north through the trees and brush faintly the big floods and the speaker-system of the softball park.

I'll get this second batch of galleys out to [you] as soon as I can.

   . . . .

I dont know what the customary procedure is with the original manuscripts, or whether they are considered to belong to the writer or the publisher, or any of that. But after we're all through with it and its no longer needed, I would like to have the original manuscript of *Eternity* back, so I can present it to Lowney as a surprise. God knows if anyone deserves to have it, she does. And I think she would like it.[1]

Say hello to Jack Wheelock for me, and tell him I'll write him sometime soon. He might be interested in seeing this about the "Marshall Plan," as Harry's named it.

My best to Helen and young Bruce,
and to yourself,
Jim

p/TLS

---

[1] The manuscript was given to Lowney, with the understanding, Jones insisted, that it was to be returned to him after her death. All his efforts to reclaim the manuscript were unsuccessful.

TO JEFF JONES

MARSHALL

OCTOBER 3, 1950

Dear Jeff,

I've been meaning to write you for quite a while, but since I got back from NY I've been working on two stories, rewriting and cutting one ("Greater Love," that you read), and starting from scratch with the other, "The King," the one on Bunk Johnson.[1]

While I was in NY, Mitch and Wallace Meyer, one of the old guard there who has been Hemingway's editor since Perkins died, took me out for cocktails with Marian Ives, a quite good agent they have both worked with a long time and whom they wanted me to meet, and the two new stories, plus the ones I got back from Moorepark, are to go to her to see what she can do with them. They are trying to find me a good agent, to take that part of it off my hands. Moorepark turned out to be pretty third-rate; I looked him up, and gathered that most of his letters to me were just talk; about all he handles are second-rate English books trying to get Amer. rights on them. Anyway, Miss Ives had never seen any of my stuff, and that afternoon Wallace Meyer was quite eulogius in his praise of it, saying he would get a set of the galleys for her to read when he got back from Cal. on vacation. One thing he said was that he still had a copy of the original galleys of *The Sun Also Rises*, that he meant to keep forever, and that he had got a set of *Eternity* to keep with them. Of course, it was quite good for my ego (or bad). They gave me to believe that Miss Ives was the type who if she really likes a writer's work will go to almost unbelievable lengths to sell him, hence their desire to show her my stuff.[2] Anyway, she should by now have the stories, and

---

[1] "Greater Love" appeared in *Collier's* in 1951, and "The King" in *Playboy* in 1955.

[2] Marian Ives did not become his agent.

I should hear something soon. I'm hoping greatly that "The King" might be sold to *Esquire*, which would mean considerable more money than *Atlantic* or *Harper's*.

They really treated me royally, while I was there. I met everyone in the editorial staff, all of whom are fine people, and old Mr Scribner, the one they call CS. "Young Charlie," his son, has been called back into the Navy. Several times Mr Scribner stopped me to ask if I had enough money, that they wanted me to enjoy myself while I was there, as well as work. And if I didn't I was to ask for more. I was bucking for this $2000.00 advance, which I've later got, so I did not ask for too much.

Mitch and I had three sessions with the lawyer, Manges, who is a sharp boy, and went over the 50-odd galleys he had pulled from the whole that he felt would cause trouble. I think in Owosso you read the love scene between Prew and Lorene, well a large part of that had to be cut. All the part on the Unguentine imagery—the "Unguentine Galley" Manges called it.[3] And there were five or six other places, most of them ones you have not read I think, so it would be useless to explain them. One thing we had to cut was all mention of "one-way, two-way, and three-way girls." The scene with the queer Hal, the part of his pornographic picture sitting on the desk had to be cut out completely—just the picture, not the scene. All in all I think we patched it up pretty good; some places I was even able to twist the cutting to my advantage and give a whole new twist to particular scenes that had not had it before. I think they were all quite pleased with my reaction; I think they were scared I would blow up and go temperamental, but I didn't.

As far as the words go, Manges had a "score sheet" he had kept while reading, and there were 259 fucks, 92 shits, and 5 pricks. He did not count the pisses for some reason. Well, Mitch and I went through later, working in the Scribner of-

[3] The "Unguentine" section on the relief provided by sex was not published.

fice, and cut the fucks 146, the shits to 45. This was all subject to Manges' approval, and after I left he agreed to everything but words, and Mitch and he cut the fucks down again to around 106 and some shits, Mitch says he don't know how many he is tired of counting small words. I can sympathize. Manges wanted, Mitch wrote me, to cut the fucks to 25 or 6, but Mitch balked there because they had promised me to print the fucks in unprecedented scale. As it stands now, Manges thinks he can successfully defend it in New York, but he's not so sure about Mass. Mitch said in his letter, Well, to hell with Mass.

I was disappointed of course, but then this is a practical problem, not an artistic one which, if it were, I should balk on; but it isn't. And if you are going to print a book and sell it you have to get it under the wire as legal. Otherwise, you might as well write it and then file the mss away. And I want to be printed.

Manges was a very nice fellow, otherwise, though very adamant. The upshot was that I rewrote several scenes in his office library (44th floor of Lincoln Bldg, right across 42nd from Grand Central) with he and Mitch sitting there. I ended up by horsetrading him: "if I take this out, can we keep this." Mitch said later I had saved several places he had been very doubtful of keeping. It got so it was a joke between the three of us. One time, after a bad spot, I leaned back and said to Mitch, "Would you do me a favor, a personal favor?" "If I can," Mitch said cautiously. "Well, when they do the cover design—(which isn't done yet)—will you have them put a little black star in the upper righthand corner of the design?"

You see, Manges had been telling us about working for a pulp mag chain that had lost their mailing privileges, and he read their mags for three months straight every week. To get the mailing privileges back in states that had banned them, they put out a "Star Edition" they called it—to keep from saying "Expurgated" I guess—which had been censored by Manges.

Mitch was delighted and said he would, so the black star will be on the cover of *Eternity*. It had just struck me, you know? and I hadn't thot of anything else, but now I suppose it will become a part of the Legend, someday. I didn't do it for that, tho.[4]

   . . . .

Yours,

y/tl/c

---

[4]The star did not appear on the dust jacket but is on the spine of the first edition.

From Here to Eternity was scheduled for publication on February 26, 1951, and Scribner's began a large-scale publicity campaign for the the novel late in 1950. Jones and Lowney went to Florida, where Jones worked on a novel, eventually to be published as Some Came Running.

TO BURROUGHS MITCHELL

FORT MYERS BEACH, FLA.
NOVEMBER 8, 1950

Dear Mitch,

. . . .

We've had rather a hectic time, getting ready to move, moving, and getting over moving. Things are beginning to come into focus again now. I've been making some notes, and trying to get the stuff sorted out. Out of a series of unrelated accidents, which commenced with Harry's wanting me to get in a scene that happened to him over Russ Meskimen, I've concocted a minor character that has me excited as hell. Harry was at the Shackamak cabin (scene of "None Sing So Wildly,")[1] when the one-armed ex-Marine husband of Katy, Russ's girl ("pig" is the vernacular) whom Katy had married from a standing start in a pique at Russ, and then had regretted same and run off and come back—when this husband came down from northern Indiana to claim his legal property, i.e., Katy. There was nobody there but Harry, and the ex-Marine and a chum charged around and tore up the cabin and raised indignant hell accusing Harry of conspiracy, looking for Katy. If you can imagine Harry, who is the perfect Midwest aristocrat type, inbred somewhat and an absolute gentleman, coping with the outraged morality of the ex-Marine and chum, then you have the meat of the scene.

[1] Collected in *The Ice-Cream Headache and Other Stories.*

Well, the problem was to fit in a character who could be of the same type somewhat and could be in the same position so as to have the same scene. To do this, I hit on the idea of giving the Teacher[2] (who will play the White to Katy's Black) a father. Naturally he must be cultured; he could on the other hand not be rich. Upshot: a professor at the small (created) college where Teacher works, who has a small income is about to retire as book opens and does retire during course of it, drawn outwardly from a high school English prof at Robinson named Atwood English. Then, because Teacher must have some good contact by which she might assure Russ a good chance at publication, I decided to make Prof a distinctive minor major poet, somewhat in the manner of John Crowe Ransom, who is related to the Revels of Flat Rock (12 miles from Robinson, in our county). With this background, I can also use him in this book as I used Jack Malloy in *Eternity,* to get over the ideas I want to get said. A sort of fuddy-duddy, yet astute, and acute, white-haired Father, who is against Russ at first but, because of a natural hero-worship for the romance of Rebels, Gamblers, and general Physical Prowess, eventually turns to the side of Russ and pleads with daughter to marry same. Which she cannot bring herself to do, because of this sexual aberration.[3]

I'm excited as hell over him and the prospects which he opens up.

   . . . .

Yours,
Jim

P/TLS

---

[2]Gwen French, the teacher in the novel, is largely based on Lowney Handy.
[3]In the final version of the novel the sexual problem of the teacher is finally revealed: She is a virgin.

It was obvious to the editorial staff at Scribner's and to Jones himself that a movie would likely be made from his novel. Eventually Columbia Pictures purchased the film rights for eighty-two thousand dollars.

TO BURROUGHS MITCHELL

FT. MYERS BEACH, FLA.
DECEMBER 2, 1950

Dear Mitch,

As far as movie rights are concerned, I have only two desires. The first, and main one, is that I get as much money out of the sale as I can, and to hell with how they butcher it up. I'll never try to buy it back after I see what they do to it, as Hemingway is supposed to have done with *Farewell to Arms.* I dont give a damn what they do to the movie; the book will stand by itself after the movie is forgotten.

The second concern is that I would like, if at all possible, to get a couple months work or so out there on the script. I would like to have this written in the contract if it can be done. I want this because someday, along with all the other goddam novels I want to write, I want to write a goddam novel on Hollywood. A really good one has never been done, with the possible exception of *Last Tycoon* which was not finished. And, if I make a little money in wages while doing this, I will not complain of that either.

Your most enthusiastic constituent,
J Weatherby Jones
(Call me Mack)

P/TLS

The editorial board members of the Book-of-the-Month Club found From Here to Eternity *"one of the most impressive novels they had read in many years." The board put out a special statement in the club's booklet: "In spite of its unusual quality, we decided to present it to our members as an alternate, instead as a regular selection, for reasons which will be clear to all who read the book. It is not the kind of novel to be put in any reader's hands without warning. Its barrack-room language is unvarnished, and some of the episodes will come as a shock to readers who have led sheltered lives." The statement went on to defend the work and concluded, "It marks the advent in American letters of a young writer who, thoughtfully and with a born talent, is following in the great tradition of the novel." J. P. Marquand published a laudatory review of the work in the booklet, and Jones wrote him a letter of appreciation.*

TO JOHN P. MARQUAND

FT. MYERS BEACH, FLA.
FEBRUARY 4, 1951

Dear Mr. Marquand,

. . . .

When Scribner's flattering ad came out in the *Publisher's Weekly,* I remember that I wrote Burroughs then that I suddenly felt as if I had lost my book, that I felt as if I were the author of two books, one the one I had worried with and sweated over and that had been alive to me, the other the one that had been printed and bound and advertised and would be laid out in rows for the public's eyes. And that the people who read the one would do so without ever even knowing or suspecting the existence of the other, because I had lived with the people and they werent book characters to me and I still remembered the living prototypes from whom the fictional characters were made up. I said that I felt in a way that I had myself destroyed my book, in making it.

Well, I still feel that; but not as much as I felt it before; because I can feel along with it that you for one read the first book that is buried underneath the second, and knew it was there, and recognized it, as perhaps, after all, only another writer can.

   . . . .

Sincerely,
James Jones

H/TLS

Jones was in Hollywood during the spring of 1951 to write a treatment of Eternity *for Columbia Pictures. He was on good terms with Harry Cohn, head of the studio. In a letter to Mitchell, Jones characterized Cohn:*

> *He cusses a lot, very obscenely, and this horrifies most of the people who work for him, but Cohn does it deliberately to bait them; he also insults hell out of people—if they take it, he does it more, and worse, if they dont, he likes them. If they tell him to go fuck himself. Which I more or less did, once I had figured him out, and we got along very friendly. I like him. He's an uneducated self-made tycoon with a private barber, and he loves every second [of] it.*
>
> *Anyway, when I got home, I sent him a Presentation Copy completely unasked for, and inscribed it: "From one old fuck-up to another, no strings attached." And down at the bottom of the page put: "Now for Christ's sake, <u>read</u> it!" (He never reads a book, only synopses.)*

Jones did not complete a satisfactory film treatment of his novel and did not stay long in Hollywood. He returned to Marshall to work on his new novel and to help with the Colony. He did more work on the treatment, but it was not used.

TO BURROUGHS MITCHELL

MARSHALL, ILL.
MAY 31, 1951

Dear Mitch,

. . . .

Right now, I am trying to get through with this damned treatment and get back to Dave Hirsh, who excites me more the more I think about him—and mainly his explosive effect upon the town of Parkman Illinois; thats what really intrigues me. His advent will change damn near everybody's life in the town, one way or another; and we'll get a damn good ironic picture of social structure in action.

Things are moving rapidly at the MARSHALL PLAN. We now have five tents set up. The new cabin, which you will occupy, is being rushed ahead for interior finishing and getting the plumbing in. Lowney has been carefully culling her mail, and now has three new people who are coming in before long.

. . .

I'm going to have to have some more money. We dont have room now for all the ones we've got, and are building a "barracks" of five cells with room for a bed and a desk. Thats going to run around $3500, and will be done in two weeks. Also the much-needed cookhouse, onto which we're going to tie a ramada, screened in with a fireplace and tables to eat, like a mess hall. Dont know how much that'll cost. In addition, I'm finally buying this stretch of land next to us, which I told you about last fall; another guy has been angling for it, and Ralph Montgomery is planning to sell and move by the 4th of July. I can finance the deal, but will have to put about three thousand down on it, and this must be done soon.

Because of all this stuff coming up, I'm wondering if it wouldnt be the best thing to just take a large payment of $10,000 or $15,000 from you folks which will run me till December, rather than causing you bookkeeping work by taking little dribbles along from time to time. I know its causing you all a lot of trouble, its coming along like this, but these things just cant be helped.

. . . .

Yours,
Jim

T/TL/C

By the first of August a $10,000 payment from Scribner's was almost gone. The building of the Colony at Marshall had been expensive, and Jones had bought a Chrysler ($4791.28), a new trailer, camera equipment, guns, and clothes. He had only $400 left in his checking account and needed Scribner's to transfer more money to him.

From Here to Eternity was a commercial and artistic success. Early in 1952 Jones went to New York to accept the National Book Award, and it was during this trip that he met Norman Mailer, William Styron, and other writers. He saw a great deal of Mailer and Styron during that New York stay. One night when they were in Greenwich Village, Styron put his arms around the shoulders of the other two and said, "Here we are, the three best writers of our generation. . . . !"

TO LOWNEY HANDY

HOTEL NEW WESTON
NEW YORK, N Y
[FEBRUARY 8, 1952]

Darling—

Here's a hundred that should keep you going till I see you.

Am meeting editor of *Holiday* this afternoon.

Also, meeting Mailer, Bourjaily, young Marquand, Styron, Willingham with Mitch & with Harvey Breit tomorrow nite.[1] Do some drinking (light) and talking.

Will tell you all about it when I see you. Should be a good time.

[1] The exact date of this meeting is not clear. The letter is not dated but was postmarked February 8, 1952.

Your watch band should be ready by Monday, when I leave, so I can bring it with me.

Love
Jim

s/ALS

When Jones went to New York, Lowney was deeply afraid that he was going to escape from her. She suspected that he was sleeping with secretaries at Scribner's, that women were throwing themselves at her now-famous protégé. She even suspected, or pretended to suspect, that Jones might be infatuated with other men. In her fight to keep him, she was willing to attempt to make him doubt his own manliness. Lowney began to make calls to find out what Jones was doing.

TO LOWNEY HANDY

HOTEL NEW WESTON
NEW YORK, N Y
[FEBRUARY 13, 1952]

Dear Lowney,

When Mitch told me yesterday you'd called, I tried all day to call you. Stayed all night with Mitch & tried up till eleven, when I knew if you were there you'd be in. Tried once more this morning after we got back to town, in a vain hope. Your letter was waiting for me, too. So I assume you've gone on your binge in Miami.

I write with that knowledge in my mind.

I told you before I left that trust and love are what make people big. You agreed. I hold tight onto my mind that if you did go to Miami for a binge you still wouldnt be able to do it. But if you <u>did</u> do it, I still wouldnt care because I love you, and God knows I've done enough to you in my time.

But I want you to know: This time I havent.

The particular night you called that I know of (when you later called Mitch), I had a late dinner with Bill Styron and went to an Italian movie, and we sat in a bar and talked until after 3 way down town, then we walked, and talked. I got back here around 4:30. There were no women involved, and no queerdom—if you suspect that, too.

Monday afternoon I was packed and checked out of the hotel, when I went over to Scribner's & found Mr. Scribner had just died of a heart attack. I volunteered to stay for the funeral. They didnt ask me to, and said there was no need, really, unless I wanted to. I said I did. They were all pleased.

I stayed over first because I wanted to meet Mailer, who is a hell of a fine guy. I am leaving Thursday night.

You are wrong to think I'm caught by New York. But I have met a lot of serious writers whom I've liked, and I'm glad I've met them.

The other times you've called I dont know when they were, but several nights I've been invited out to dinner and spend the nite because they all live in the suburbs & its a three or two hour train ride back into town. Harry Brague's,[1] Cal Whipple's, Meredith Wood (B.O.M.C. Pres.), others. Oscar DiLiso, one of Mitch's writers, and good. I've taken it all in & soaked it all up, not worrying because I knew (or thot I knew) you trusted me.

There are lots of things I suppose I could do now—get drunk, pick up a woman, etc. etc. But I'm not going to do any of them. . . .

Your watch band (bought Harry a sterling Dunhill liter), which I was having sent because it wasnt done yet, I can now bring with me. But instead I'll have it sent on, so you'll have it in case you do decide to leave. But I hope you wont. I hope you'll trust me.

If you do, leave my stuff there. I'll drive down and get it. I'm still going ahead with getting the trailer, unless you write different to Robinson.

It would be a shame, if now you've got the kind of love you want, after paying such a high price for it, that you yourself would destroy it. I hope you wont. I believe you wont.

You should know me better than to think I would bring anyone in the Colony without your o.k., & if they didnt do the work first.

[1] An editor at Scribner's.

And you should know me better than to think I'd puff up under flattery. Men are made big by belief. So are women. And I believe in you.

All my love forevermore,

Jim

I wired Harry.

s/ALS

*Jones usually left Illinois during the coldest part of the winter.
In 1952 he and Lowney were in Tucson.*

TO BURROUGHS MITCHELL

DEC. 17, 1952
TUCSON

Dear Mitch,

. . . .

I was thinking just the other day that since the publication
of *Eternity* our letters, yours and mine, seem to have mostly
degenerated into business letters. No more the old fears and
lamentations and "deep" discussions, the self-exposures and
the need for succor. It shouldnt be that way between us. I'm
sure that as an editor, the most affective part of that profession,
the most interesting and most emotionally stimulating, is that
"soul" side of it. I know it would be so to me, were I the editor;
and I know that for me the writer it was always the pleasantest
part. It was upon that always that the deepness of our friendship was based, for me.

I seem to have acquired a great fear of sentimentality, any
more. Only rarely do the emotions I feel really break through
the increasingly more rigid wall I've been building. I think it
shows in my work, too. Maybe critics have something to do
with it. No matter how much we always scoff at them, we still
hang eagerly on their word when it comes, and are hurt if they
deride, flattered if they praise.

I've been having a hard time lately. Both here and the last
work done in Marshall before I left. I'm always scared to death.
I think I have self-critical judgment like Jack Wheelock once
said I had, but I'm never sure. I dont know that I have.
Something indefinable tells me when what I've done is good—
or at least passable—almost never good. But its nothing I can
put in words, even to myself. And maybe it isnt right.

I dont know if I can say it. But there seems to me to be more and more an increasing tendency toward the juxtaposition of paradox in what I do. Not only in chapters and scenes, but even in paragraphs, even in sentences. Is that right? Is it fair? Is it fair to do, I mean? That can become a stylization too, a slick way of doing it. Many many times I find myself turning from the first instinctive way I tend to do a scene, turning to the harder more difficult way to do it. I mean, I will have a powerful emotional picture in my mind of a scene, of a chapter ending, say, which can always be done affectively to have a powerful emotion to end up on; but instead of doing it that way I will purposely avoid it, and do it some other way, which takes longer and is much more unpleasant—and, I always wonder, is it worth it? Is it that much better? Maybe I'm turning away from the very thing I need most? Its certainly the thing that made *Eternity* so universally effective. But when seeing it in that first instinctive way, instead of just writing it as I once did, without thinking, I find myself mentally understanding what I am doing and thus destroying the emotion in myself, and hence in the writing, beforehand before I even start to do it. Do you know what I mean? And if I still were to go on and do it that way, I would be prostituting it; lying.

But more than that even, what worries me is time. TIME. Some days, particularly the last two, three months, I work all damn morning on a single four or five line paragraph—and then sometimes dont get it. Rarely do I turn out more than one page, almost never two. Dostoievski, Tolstoy, Conrad (who was slow!) wrote their books in a year or so at the most.

Another thing that bothers me is that I'm now almost 200 pages in, and have hardly got to the story part yet, gotten into the story of it. At this point Dave has not even met a "pussy interest" yet—(I hate to say "love interest"). Yet there are supposed to be, not one, but two, for him—the two main forces working on him throughout the book. Will the whole damn thing have to be re-written? After taking so damned long to get down on paper?!! Then the time and effort isnt worth the waste. All that time, and that sweated blood—and God knows I do sweat it!—will just be thrown away, completely. Never of any use at all. And I aint getting any younger.

Should I try to restrain that strong emotionalism? Or warp it into constantly portrayed paradox?

God knows I live in fear, active, livid fear, undulating around me like a living constrictor. . . .

Yours,
Jim

p/TLS

While Jones and Lowney were in Arizona for the winter, Harry Handy was in Illinois making plans for the bachelor house Jones was having built near the Colony in Marshall. The eighty-five-thousand-dollar house tied up a great deal of his money, and Jones was later to believe that Lowney had encouraged him to build it to keep him in Marshall and under her domination.

TO HARRY HANDY

TUCSON, ARIZONA
JANUARY 25, 1953

Dear Harry,
  . . . .

Should you select the interior trim for the living room?—What do you mean by trim? The molding, etc? if so, yes. But if you mean the entire finish, no. I dont think we ought to decide definitely on that yet. I liked the picture we sent to [you], but it was only tentative, and I'm not sure that thats what I'll want. It was just to give you ideas. I want to be in on the final selection, before we make it definite.

  . . . .

Yours,
Jim

s/TLS

Because of expenses at the Colony, for the building of the new house, and taxes, Jones needed to borrow money, even though he had a sizable income from sales of Eternity *and funds from the movie rights of that novel. He wrote Harry about his plight.*

TO HARRY HANDY

TUCSON, ARIZONA
FEBRUARY 17, 1953

To Harry,

Lowney showed me your letter yesterday, having to do with the financing of the house. After I write you, I'm writing to Woody Burnett[1] about borrowing some money right away that can be drawn from.

The position Im in is this: in order to reduce taxes, Horace [Manges] had fixed it by official letter request from me to Scribner's for them not to pay me any more than $20,000 a year. I will have that forthcoming in the June royalty payment; and carried on the books almost as much again to be paid next year. But I simply cannot draw any more than that or the agreement for tax purposes becomes void. . . .

Urine,
Jim

s/TLS

---

[1]An official of the Dulaney National Bank, Marshall, Illinois.

TO BURROUGHS MITCHELL

MARSHALL, ILLINOIS
JULY 31, 1953

Dear Mitch,

. . . .

I was surprised that you liked Burt [Lancaster] the best. Both Fred Zinnemann and I, and also Dan Taradash, felt that Monty [Clift] actually took the picture right away from everyone.[1] I'm anxious to see what Lowney will think. In spite of that gentleness you mentioned, which I think was there, he was the only one who really seemed to come alive to me. The rest, except Frank [Sinatra], who was fine, seemed to fade when they got on the screen with him and I suddenly realized they were actors.

By the way, are Scribner's making any provision for a boost in sales when the movie gets going?

Your paragraph—which, of course, was the one that interested me most—about the problems of a writer, thats something that has been bothering me quite a while. Of course, I happen to be depressed this week, so I shouldnt even be discussing it. But then next week I would be euphoric, and that would be just as bad. I really dont know. I think one of my own general problems—one thats always with me—is this tendency I have to try and tell or show <u>every</u>thing, to get down exactly every nuance and subtlety of a scene so that it is easily understood. But you cant ever do that, and if you keep on you

---

[1]Fred Zinnemann directed the movie version of *Eternity*. Daniel Taradash wrote the screenplay. Long before the casting and filming began, Jones thought of John Ford or John Huston as ideal directors, with Zachary Scott as Prew, Stephen McNally as Warden, Joanne Dru as Alma, and someone similar to Carole Lombard as Karen. He later met Montgomery Clift and urged that he be given the part of Prew. In addition to Clift and Sinatra, the cast of the film version included Burt Lancaster as Warden, Donna Reed as Lorene, and Deborah Kerr as Karen.

involute yourself right down to nothing, and you wind up with a lot of unnecessary stuff that is mostly only boring. Not only that, you lose the emotion. I always have that to contend with. That is the main thing wrong with *Running* right now, I think. I should be leaving more unsaid, to be handled by the imagination. That way, it has that drawing-on quality, that crisp feeling of moving along to an end. Really, in the end, theres not much of anybody—or any thing—to help you; and you never know if you are right.

I think one of the main problems with a book, with me anyway, is that I have really believed these people are capable of integrity. Of Sacrifice, of Love, of Hate. I think I really dont believe they are. Like Prewitt and Warden—if I had written them as they really were in real life (which is what I'd really <u>like</u> to do) I wouldnt have had any story. Because they were really only half-acting their parts. When Prew went to the Stockade, he just came out and went right back to the life he'd been living—in real life. Somehow in his mind, he excused himself out of something, so that his integrity was never really put to the supreme test, as it was in the book. And I think this is what I really believe about most people; and yet I dont want to believe that—and I also know in certain cases, rarely I guess, but sometimes, people really can be admirable. But it is really only <u>my</u> vision, <u>my</u> picture of them that makes them so. I was intrigued by these two guys—Russ and Arky—in Robinson.[2] But actually they were just a couple of bums, who posed as being—well, whatever it was: with integrity. I obviously romanticized them. But now I, the author of *Eternity,* and some years older in experience, am no longer satisfied with my former romanticism of them. So I have to find myself a new one. Because to write them as they really are would be so depressing, not only to me, but to readers, that I wouldnt have any book—or any plot either. I

[2]Russ and Arky appeared in the story "None Sing So Wildly." At the early stages of *Some Came Running,* Jones was calling it his Russell novel.

dont know if this makes sense to you. I've been re-reading through *Tender Is the Night,* and I am appalled at how sophomoric it is, and how Fitz, romanticized Monroe Stahr (into a wishful-portrait of himself, of course). But we all do that, and God only knows what makes one bad and one good— writing-wise.

I really dont understand it at all, and I'm scared as hell. Most of my working time is spent that way. It was that way with *Eternity* until I was more than half-way through. Then it began to open up and be fun—even though I did continue to worry.

I worry about all kinds of things. I fear I've lost my drive to write because of being successful. I fear I've lost my ability to really like people. Oh, shit I could go on by the hour. And then, on the other hand, I'm afraid that in my desire to be able to like people, I'm inclined not only to wind up making everything untrue to people, but also sentimental.

Dont worry about me. Right now, this house-building is taking a lot out of me, a lot of my time. I have to be over there about every five minutes to decide something. Also, I'm so anxious and interested that my absorption with the book suffers. What I dream about is getting the house done and just moving in there for twenty years and locking the door and just writing books. I think this last trip to Hollywood has just about filled me up to the neck with the haute monde—with just living in general—with associating with people—until I'm ready to give up living entirely.

Well, when the house is done . . .³

I'm working along, though. I think all I've written—except Chaps III and IV—is going to have to be drastically revised, cut, and rearranged for getting things moving faster.

What I hate, you see—really hate—is these people who are always preaching that Man is basically good. I agree with them, inside. But I hate the way they say it; and anyway, who knows

³Ellipses in original.

if they're right? But how to show this difference in one's writing[?]

Oh, well, fuck it.

. . . .

In this same connection, Ned Brown[4] just sent me copies of [Louella] Parsons' and the trade papers' reviews of *Eternity*. Without exception, they all think the movie better than the book—both because the book rambles, and because it's in bad taste. Whatta ya gonna do?

Best to Helen and Brucie. Have a good vacation.

Yours,
Jim

p/TLS

---

[4]Brown was Jones's Hollywood agent who sold the film rights for *Eternity*.

Robert E. Cantwell, books editor for Newsweek, *visited Jones in Marshall "to find out what success had done" to the author whose* Eternity *had sold almost half a million copies in hardbound and 1.7 million in the New American Library's paper edition. Cantwell described Jones's new house with its secret passageway to a secret chamber and with "a bathroom that makes you think of something evacuated from Pompeii." Cantwell also provided background information on Robinson and Marshall, Illinois, and Jones's early life. Cantwell's "James Jones: Another 'Eternity'?" appeared in the November 23, 1953, issue of* Newsweek.

TO ROBERT CANTWELL

MARSHALL, ILLINOIS
NOVEMBER 23, 1953

Dear Bob

I've mislaid your letter, due to the flurries of trying to get moved in, so am sending this to *Newsweek.* I've been meaning to write you ever since your letter came, but havent done so because of the damned house taking so much time. Besides, I've had to move all my files out of the trailer due to the arrival of young Zweig and cant find anything. Christ, I'll never build another house! Not even if I do get this one paid for.

I think the article was very fine. Especially your flattering descriptions of the secret door and the bathroom. I would like to think of them both that way, but know they are not that good. All in all, you did mighty well by us, I'd say. And there was several damn fine images in there, old boy.

If I were to be upset by anything, it would be that I felt you perhaps saw a certain lack of sensitivity in me that was incompatible with the kind of work I want to do. But if you felt that, you're certainly entitled to say it, and more power to you. So I couldnt very well kick on that.

I think, as a matter of fact, I know the reason. We have

tended here toward an attitude (and viewpoint) of—how shall I say?—materialistic? insensitiveness? deliberately. It is a direct reaction against the hyper-sensitive, esthete attitude of the Bowles-McCullers, Vidal, etc. axis which, at least I feel, is destroying itself and its ability to communicate by—as Crane's poem says: "feeding on its heart, because it is good, and because it is its heart." I dont think I ever realized, until just now, how that might look to an outsider who came in and viewed it without knowing the history. Also, the same applies to the kicking about affirmativeness. Its not affirmativeness itself I bitch about, so much as the mouthing of it by the critics—to the point of, as Shelby Foote told me, making a man like Faulkner feel guilty because he wasnt writing "affirmative." Well, enough of lame, hind-sight explanations. The whole thing really sums itself up into the title anyway, doesnt it: "JAMES JONES: ANOTHER 'ETERNITY'?" All we can do is wait and see. Me along with everybody else.

We certainly enjoyed having you here with your family. You have a standing invitation, all of you. And when I get back to the City I'll most certainly look you up.

You might be amused to know that the article created quite a little furor of hurt feelings in that noble metropolis of Robinson, especially in the *Daily News* office. I understand that the publisher Kent Lewis is writing you a letter correcting several of your factual mistakes; or so Harry said over the phone yesterday. I dont think they're too happy about it down there, and I'm just malicious enuf to be enjoying it thoroughly.[1] In case you condescend to answer Kent, I thought I'd give you a barb: Harry said Kent was writing you that grandfather's house was not built with oil money but with the proceeds of his law practice in Robinson. If he <u>does</u> write you that, you might answer by telling him that grandfather didnt build it at all, it was built—I believe—by a man named King, after whom King Street in Robinson was named. And tell him that the

[1]Lewis's letter appeared in *Newsweek* (December 14, 1953).

exigencies of space did not permit you to give every detail of history that you would have liked to have given.

I'm sure you and your wife will get as big a laugh out of this as we have. Especially since everything you said was right.[2]

Let me hear from you when you have time.

Yours,
Jim

o/TLS

TO BURROUGHS MITCHELL

MARSHALL, ILLINOIS
FEB 3, 1954

Dear Mitch,

Well, heres the first four chapters. Let me know what you think. I think theyre damn good. But, with that strange and by now familiar trepidation writers seem to have, I still want to know what you think. I know theyre good. But I also hope theyre good.

Wont be much letter. Im going right on. Been hot lately. Will read old chapters 3 and 4, to see if they need any stylistic changes. Which you will probably notice some of. (I dont mean new chap 4.) Will probably have to recopy them if only

[2]Cantwell wrote: "The literary world of New York is filled with stories about Jones's pursuit, by high-powered car and whirlwind midnight visits, of various pleasantly alarmed beauties. His local well-wishers express concern about less glamorous affairs with nearby girls, met apparently by chance."

Jones's romantic flings with other women obviously concerned Lowney, but she had little to fear. Cantwell noted Lowney's economic hold over Jones: He had spent from sixty to a hundred thousand dollars on the Colony after the success of *Eternity*, "and Mrs. Handy now says that paying for the new house, the land around it, and keeping up the colony is going to keep Jones busy for the next five years." Her prediction came true.

on account of commas. Will send them on in a few days. Then into the bulk of the other stuff which is very bad.

Ive got an idea that I cant quite explain of trying to lose bulkiness. In punctuation. One of my biggest problems with this fuckin book is to try and say everything and yet lose the bulkiness, in punctuation and grammar. (Not in pages!)[1]

Maybe Ill lose that too someday. Did you ever hear the story of the wise men who condensed the history of all mankind into three sentences for the king who didnt have time to read? Surely you have.

I feel very strange sometimes. Maybe Im going crazy, you reckon? Well, anyway, you will see when you read this. I know I havent got syphilis. Just had a blood test lately!

You know, I really think its something awful good. Also lately Ive ironed out a lot of plot problems, the kind you have to work out so as to keep at least one ball in the air all the time. Youll see that too, when I get this next batch done. Instead of having Dave turn down Frank's offer about the taxi service, as originally planned, and just being a drunk and gambling— which can get dull after a while, even with a good love story— Im going to have him first refuse the offer for his money, but then after he meets Gwen French at this dinner and tries to make her and cant, he changes his mind and takes up Frank's offer, puts all his money in taxi service, and goes to work as dispatcher for it----all in order to stay around long enough to make Gwen French. Who by the way will turn out to be a virgin who talks about her several affairs because she is ashamed of being a virgin. Nice wrinkle, hunh?

[1]Critics attacked *Some Came Running* for its experimental punctuation (especially the lack of apostrophes) and for its narrative method. George Garrett in *James Jones* has made the best defense of Jones's method: "Jones, as he wrote *Running*, was involved in an experiment with language. . . . He calls it working with 'colloquial forms,' by which he means not merely the free and easy use of the living, *spoken* American idiom in dialogue or in first-person narration, but the attempt to carry it into the narrative itself, into third-person narrative."

Also, Im trying to figure out some way of having Dave get hit by a truck on his way out of town with his busted typewriter, so I can have him die in the end. Of course, it would have to be something with meaning and not just a coincidence. What do you think? Should he die or not? Of course, eventually that will write itself. Im not worried. Just thinking.

Well, please write and let me know an hour after you get this. You ought to be able to read it in an hour.

Love to Helen and everybody there.

Yours,

Jim

Have you still got that dedication I wrote when Mary Ann died?[2] Ive lost the carbon. Have Barbara send me a copy, please?

P/TLS

---

[2]After a failed marriage, many dead-end jobs, and bumming around the country, Mary Ann Jones came to Marshall and joined the Colony. She was working on a novel when she died, of a brain tumor, on June 5, 1952. The dedication of *Running* is "To the Memory of My sister Mary Ann Jones who did not live to finish her own in the hope that time will not obliterate from human thought the name used to designate this particular human personality which, had it lived, would surely have made itself remembered." In the family record prepared at the time of Mary Ann's funeral, Harry and Lowney Handy are listed as her foster father and foster mother.

Jones was in New York during the spring of 1954 and spent an evening with John Hall Wheelock, whom he admired as poet and editor.

TO JOHN HALL WHEELOCK

MARSHALL, ILLINOIS
MAY 11, 1954

Dear Jack

. . . .

Im feeling much better since getting home. Not drinking as much, nor staying up nearly so late, and getting some exercise. And working much better. I really got very frightened there in NY. I always do if I go for very long without working. Then I really start drinking. I think I could really kill myself in about six months, with the peculiar kind of rabid wildness I have. I never know when to stop a thing. Any thing. So I have to run away. I have not even been off the place since getting home, and do not intend to be until Ive gotten a great deal of work done.

I wonder if Ill ever be able to pull the two halves of my nature together, the constructive and destructive, and make a unified whole out of them? I always feel like a tightrope walker with a long pole that has two excentrically revolving lead balls fastened to the ends of it. Not only must I balance myself on the wire, but them too. And no net.

. . . .

Always my very best,
Jim

P/TLS

Ben Griffith, a faculty member at Tift College in Forsyth, Georgia, was working on a theory that Prewitt was a folk hero. Griffith's essay was published in the Spring 1956 issue of the Georgia Review.

TO BEN W. GRIFFITH, JR.

MARSHALL, ILLINOIS
JUNE 13, 1954

Dear Mr Griffith

In this rather belated reply to your letter, I can only say that it [is] rather hard for me to theorize about Prewitt, either as a folk hero or as a folk bum. I think both theories are equally tenable. It all depends upon the individual and his vantage point of view.

You have a rather ingenious theory, but I myself cannot subscribe to it, and it was not my intention to create such a folk hero. I only wanted to write an accurately realistic novel about life in the Army and about some Army types I knew. And of course at the same time express something out of some need in myself.

The way in which I write (and deliberately calculate to make myself write, ahead of time) is to start out with certain people, types, with their particular conflicts and then to bring them in contact and after that to deliberately stay out as much as possible and let them and the book write itself. Because of this, I do not ever try to plot tightly. I do not plot a book at all, in the conventional sense.

The main theme I basically wanted to show in *Eternity*— one which I saw often and which never ceased to amaze me— was that the Army had an infallible way of destroying its own best advocates and adherents. The type of which Prewitt was one are almost always the best examples of real combat soldiers. I have seen such men do absolutely unbelievable things in combat. And yet—what amazed me—was that these very characteristics and ideas which made them the best possible soldiers in combat are the very same things which always threw them into conflict with authority out of combat, or even in combat sometimes, for that matter. There seemed to me to be here a very ironic paradox which the smugness of the Army (i.e., society) does not allow itself to see. I wanted to present it so that it had to be seen. I think that had Prewitt lived, and continued to live, he would have eventually become a Warden. That would mean compromising on his part, and the only other alternative was death.

Now I can look back and see that the Army did not really kill Prewitt. Prewitt killed Prewitt. Else why did not the Army also kill Warden? Warden knew the Army would kill Prewitt, if he could not in some way teach him something—something perhaps distasteful to learn—that he himself had had to learn in order to stay alive and retain a modicum of self respect, and personal integrity. I suppose that subconsciously this came over me as the book progressed and caused it to take the course it did. But the tragic essence of Prewitt was from the beginning the sense of foredoomed knowledge that he must die. That inevitability of avoidable disaster is the essence of all tragedy, from the Greeks on down.

Another thing that had an aid in causing the book was the feeling that I have, rightly or wrongly, that it is becoming increasingly harder and more difficult for a man to continue to live today and still keep self-respect and integrity. Live, anyway, in the comfortable way in which we have all come to believe we have a right to be accustomed. Just how much of self respect and integrity is vanity, and just how much of vanity is all (both worthwhile and unworthwhile) accomplishment, are things I am interested in exploring now—and am trying to explore in this new book. But then if you refine a thing down to the point where it accounts for both everything good and everything evil, what do you have? a handful of sand that trickles away between your fingers.

I guess you could say that philosophically—though not politically—I am an anarchist. I am not fanatical enough to believe that such a way of life could be practicable. But I hate to see everywhere today the encroachments of control over the individual. But it does much good, I know too. It does tremendous good for the many and hamstrings the superior few.

. . . .

Sincerely,

T/TL/C

Jones was preoccupied with Some Came Running *and generally distanced himself from the writers at the Colony. With Tom
Chamales, however, Jones developed a friendship.*

TO BURROUGHS MITCHELL

MARSHALL, ILLINOIS
JULY 13, 1954

Dear Mitch

. . . .

We have a new guy here, incidentally, who is writing like
a house afire. (Weve had several new ones—but not like this.)
His name is Tom Chamales and [he] has led a really fabulous
life: Was with Wyngate in Burma,[1] knew Joe Stilwell,[2] at
nineteen commanded the largest guerilla force in the Far East,
Burma, later was in the gambling rackets on the West Coast
and made a lot of money and got in trouble over it, but evi-
dently all this time had always wanted to write. Hes been here
less than a month and has already done over three hundred
pages on a novel of the Far East almost all of which is excellent
writing, and which only a very small portion of will need any
structural changes.

. . . .

Yours,
Jim

P/TLS

[1]Orde Charles Wingate, the British general, led Wingate's Raiders into
Burma in 1943.
[2]Joseph "Vinegar Joe" Stilwell, the American general who served in Burma
during World War II.

R. P. Adams, a member of the English Department at Tulane, sent Jones a draft of his essay on Eternity, *later published as "A Second Look at* From Here to Eternity" *in* College English *in January 1956. Adams also sent Jones "Tragedy, and Also Romance," which appeared in the* CEA Critic *(April 1954). That letter to the editor defined terms such as "Romantic."*

TO R. P. ADAMS

MARSHALL, ILLINOIS
JULY 16, 1954

Dear Mr Adams

I have not answered you sooner because Ive been working very hard but now Ive finally had to take a few days off to catch up on correspondence in order to get all the papers off the floor where they accumulate. (I have to do this every six weeks or so, or am unable to get into my work room because of mail.)

Luckily, or else by some instinct for organization, I read your *CEA* letter first, and so was able to understand your terms—principally "Romantic"—in the article on *Eternity*. Up to now—by my own private definition—Romantic has meant largely childish Byronism. I have used it mainly, also, in connection with the "Romantic Love" theories so overwhelmingly present in American thought and popular music today. I have also used it to mean Sentimentality. —As you can see, it has chiefly been a derogatory term with me.

Before I go any further, let me say that I am not acquainted with modern critical thought at all, at least not of the caliber and dimension in which you are apparently engaged. I do not know who is Professor [Irving] Babbitt, nor [Alfred North] Whitehead to whom you refer I think twice (In *CEA* letter). Most of my experience with critics has been with the newspaper book section variety, or men like Malcolm Cowley and [John] Aldridge who do not I feel go deeply into things.

Therefore, in this letter, Im on pretty precarious ground. It has always seemed to me that critics take one of two erroneous positions: either they are like Aldridge, who professes only the extremely gloomy and "lost generation" view which comes from great personal neurosis; or else they are of the ilk of Fanny Butcher or someone like that, who is always shouting at the top of her voice for "Affirmation"—whatever the hell that is.[1] If that means that humanity will continue to exist on the earth, I suppose I must grudgingly acquiesce (tho Im not at all sure!), but I fail to see why we must all be so damned smug about it.

Well, so much for my experience with critics. Almost everything Ive learned and know and formulated ideas about (Im referring to life here) has been done pretty much on my own, without recourse to current critical thought. Yet I find that I subscribe to practically everything that you say about the modern Romantics. Some minor disagreements perhaps, but in the main I subscribe. Tell me, is this all a theory of your own—about modern Romanticism? Or are you merely extending work started by other men?

Anyway, I cant tell you how excited I was when I read that *CEA* letter. It expresses things which Ive been thinking out for myself for some time, and have had my own terms for. I had never heard the term "Organic Metaphor" before and was excited by your explanation of it; I am assuming that you did not create this term yourself, from the context of the letter.

Of course you see, being basically (and solely) a novelist, as opposed to critical thinker—which is what I want to be, solely—I am by my own choice placed in the position of having to communicate on a very low level, to people who are rarely thinkers at all, if ever. This is different in kind to the type of writing you do in your critical work, where your audience is of a type who have followed such developments probably for some while. Thus, I can account to you for my oft-misquoted statement which you may or may not have heard: "People need

[1]Ms. Butcher reviewed books for the *Chicago Tribune*.

tragedy." Of course I did not mean tragedy in the abstruse humanist sense but in the more personal, life sense, and I said it because I have found so many affirmation-shouters floating around who seem to think that all they have to do is yell loud enough and everything will be the Hollywood ending they all seem to think they have a right to expect. I was saddened to find Faulkner going into that kind of crap in his Nobel prize speech, which everyone else thought so wonderful and tear-starting, but which I was disgusted by and which convinced me that Faulkner has shot his wad, a thing Ive suspected since *Intruder*. Damn it, Im beginning to ramble. Thats one of the reasons I so very seldom write letters like this. For the amount of time and energy consumed in ratio to the amount of communication gained, its much easier to work on a book. Affirmation, though. Affirmation is a false camp for a novelist, I think, because humanity already has enough puffed up vanity about itself as it is. The Boy Scout who does his good deed every day.

Anyway. I was very excited by both the *CEA* letter and the paper on *Eternity*. I think you have come closer to hitting at what I wanted to say in that book than anyone has, and—at least as far as your "humanist-Romantic" terms go, even clarified it somewhat for me. Rather, I mean, clarified what my position is and where I stand. I started the paper on Crane but did not finish it; but have read enough to be able to see what you intend doing with him, and I subscribe again. He was not a "naturalist" but a "romantic"—by your definition. But I wonder would you call the 'Twenties generation of writers (Hem., Faulk., Dos Passos, in particular) romantics—by your definition. Thinking about it, I would think not. It would seem to me that they would be more nearly your true "naturalist," although they were romantic in personal character (using <u>my</u> old definition). I use naturalistic here as those who spiritually subscribe to the idea of the mechanistic universe, a thing which Crane obviously did not. Id like to know what you think of this?

In your *CEA* letter you mention the early success of the

romantic movement which did not last long, and that the refinement of scientific materialism by electromagnetic theories caused the romantics in their turn to go on the defensive. Well of course, the refinement of scientific materialism did have its effect[s]—and is still having them today by even further refinements. (Such as that new theory which refines [Sir James Hopwood] Jeans' theory of the death of the expanding universe, by suggesting that when the expansive force ebbs to the point of being less than the attraction of gravity then there will be involution back in, and thus repeat the process infinitely.)—(More of this, later.) But isnt it possible that the childish bravado of the early romantics like Byron was only an adolescent revolt, in other words the teen-age of romanticism, which was in turn revolted against by the "Lost Generation"? We think of them as romantics now, but mightnt this have been largely personal romance (my former definition)? And isnt it possible that in their development in their writings they became our only real naturalists? Thus rather than being an extension of Romanticism to our own day, they were really an offshoot, a limb of the tree that for a while looked like the trunk and then died? Faulkner's Snopes? Hemingway's Jake, and the Tenente and the death of Catherine, and Robert Jordan? Dos Passos' preoccupation with the proletariat? Of course I am not versed in all these things, your critical ideas, but your theory has excited me a great deal. Isnt it possible they were real materialists? and that more scientific refinements—until we have refined materialism right back into mystery again—have since passed them by again?

Well, anyway. -----But we have called them our romantic expatriates so long. And yet they are not, I think, romantics by your definition. While the earlier Crane, who professed not to be, was.

Well, anyway. The article on *Eternity* is in my opinion the best piece by far that has ever been done on explaining it, and not because it is very flattering to me personally. I have just taken a break and gone through it again hurriedly, also. I had never thought of myself as a romantic—I knew I <u>was</u> romantic at times—but did not think of myself as being in that literary category. But by your explanation of the extension of romanticism, and by your definition, I most certainly and wholeheartedly am one. But who arrived at the connection of the organic metaphor (evolution) and romantics? and how?

I think you are right in almost everything you say about the book—and I think you are pretty nearly always right in your criticisms. If I took exception or disagreed with any it would be that about Hawthorne and Emerson being lugged in against their will, and Kipling—I assume you mean the quote about the Sphinx which has always been one of my favorites, and the Stone Face reference just popped into my head stream of consciousness-wise, when I was writing that scene. Generally, tho, I think Id agree that I do have an insufficient familiarity with them, and with the tradition in which Im working. But then, Ive not known I was working in any tradition, but have always just been figuring these things out for myself. —And, I might add, intend to continue to do, for two reasons: one, so that my processes may remain largely subconscious and therefore closer to their roots, and two, so that I may not be <u>bound</u> by any tradition, or school.

The rest of your criticisms are absolutely right on the head. (Shakespeare of course Ive read and reread, a great deal; more so lately than ever before.) Youre right about my handling of language in that book, I think; this is already correcting itself, without my conscious aid. Also, I guess you were right about the "artless simplicity" thing. Actually, I was only trying to point the difference between the uneducated singers and the snotty clerks. Which you took hold of in your next paragraph.

Perhaps the only thing I positively <u>did</u> not like was your passing reference to Karen "making up to a young Lt Col" on the boat. Perhaps you did not mean it like it sounded, and I am overly sensitive on this point. Ive had Karen called nymphomaniacal by so many goddamned people—usually men!— that I see red where she is concerned. You are a sensitive enough person to know, Im sure, that Karen was anything except nymphomaniacal. She was desperately lonely and unhappy living in a man's world, created for and maintained by—philosophically speaking—men, and she didnt give a damn if she broke some of their rules. Anyway, she was not making up to the Lt Col; he was making up to her. And she withheld judgment and decision about sleeping with him until she could be more sure if he was worth giving all that love that she needed to give, to. That was why I had her pointedly bring her son into the conversation and point him out to the Lt Col. Its very strange, but I find that most men cannot stand the thought of a woman stepping out on her husband because of fear, I guess, and they are always calling her (derogatorily) a nympho. Yet they step out whenever they can get by with it. But then its possible you are not writing down to Karen. I admit Im overly sore on the point.

Another thing I wanted to comment on was your comment about romantics hating machines. I think that was true of me at the time, but I dont think it is any more, and I think this fear and hatred of machines is a sure sign of immaturity in a romantic. There is no reason, in the end, why machines cannot be bent to man's will without dominating him, and have you ever noticed how beautiful machine tools are?

Have you read *The Naked and the Dead* and *Barbary Shore*, especially the latter?

Im getting awfully tired, but theres one more thing I must go into, and that is Malloy. Malloy and the organic metaphor. I dont know where this phrase originated from, but its basic idea has been a basic tenet with me for some time. It goes into a great many other things, chief of which has been a frequent, if rather desultory, study of Oriental mysticism and philosophy. I do not practice standing on my head or other fakirisms (which seems to be the chief view Americans have of Yoga), but it was a conviction in the doctrine of the reincarnation of souls that first started me on the road to the "organic metaphor." I did not see that it was reasonable to assume an evolution of species and of physical life forms, without at the same time assuming an equal evolution of individuals and of spiritual life forms. That all souls were created and put here to serve out three score years and then were judged on the conduct of these for all eternity not only seemed to me ridiculous and unjust— but also prodigal, to say the least. Especially when the law of the conservation of matter is so apparent everywhere else. And it was the intellectual acceptance of reincarnation that started me on the way to finding a personal religion, strange and outlandish as that may sound to you. If that is so, then each new life a soul leads is only another lesson to be learned. The principle explains at once all injustices of birth, both physical financial and mental. Indian philosophies have taught for centuries that God is Instability, though they didnt use that word, and that the universe both evolves and involves. Ive never had any occult experiences, or anything like that, mind you, my experience and acceptance has all been purely intellectual. And Ive developed my own lexicon and my own religion out of it, and it coincides very closely with your "organic metaphor."

I guess that winds it up except for one more thing. I had no knowledge of Faulkner's Nobel Prize speech, and when I read it I was heartily disgusted with him. Disgusted because it is too easy to just say man will survive. That is what all the affirmation-shouters say. And man has so far not even shown enough purely <u>raw</u> intelligence to even convince any thoughtful person that he might even have a chance to survive. If Faulkner had <u>really</u> believed what he said, as opposed to just <u>convincing</u> himself he believed it—out of fear of death, or whatever—this belief would have been in his words themselves; he would have found an original way, and paradoxically integrated way, of saying it, instead of that simple thing he wrote which some found so moving, but which I felt was truly childish. Thats the perennial problem of a writer: of distinguishing between true affirmation, which is not sentimental, and the false affirmation parroted by all the affirmation-shouters, which is so sentimental it makes you sick to hear it. There is no reason that I can see at present why we should smugly believe that we will endure—and prevail—just because we are men.

I would like to know if *Harper's* took the piece.² And I would also like to know what you think of my ideas, and of this letter.

Sincerely,
James Jones

PS—I would like to ask that you not use any of this letter in anything you might publish, or refer to it. I have an unfortunate habit of always getting myself misunderstood in print. Okay?

T/TLS/C

---

²*Harper's* did not accept Adams's essay, and it was later published in *College English*.

Norman Mailer in a remarkable statement presented on the documentary James Jones: Reveille to Taps *and published in* The Paris Review, *no. 103, said of Jones and* Eternity:

> *It knocked me down and half knocked me out. I thought it was an extraordinary book. All the while I was reading it I had a sinking feeling, "Well, you're no longer the most talented writer to come out of World War II. You've been replaced." Extraordinary sensation. I've always felt I understood kings losing their crowns ever since. . . . I once wrote a one-act play about Eisenhower and Khrushchev called "Buddies." They were the only equals in all the world so they had to become friends. In a way Jones and I were the same. We had the same kind of experience, both young, both had written war novels, both had enormous receptions for their books. So in a certain sense we felt like the touchdown twins.*

Mailer and Jones were friends, and they were competitors, as this and other letters to Mailer will show.

TO NORMAN MAILER

MARSHALL, ILLINOIS
MAY 3, 1955

Dear Norm,

Be prepared for what I feel may turn out to be a nice long letter. But then again it maynt.

Your note was very good to get. Im the world's worst letter writer. I want to write them, and sometimes even like to write them, but by the time I get through work in the morning I just havent got it. So I just keep stacking everything up until I cant get to the desk and then have to take a couple days off from writing and answer everything.

Anyway. First, what about the new book?[1] When is it com-

---

[1] *The Deer Park.*

ing out? And is there a signed first copy for me? Second, I want you to sign my copy of *Barbary* for me sometime. Third, are you going to be going through this way this summer to Mexico and if so did you know you were invited to stop off here? Fourth, you can sign the copy of *Barbary* then.

However, this invitation does not include a host of friends and playing companions. Only yourself and wife (and family? if any). Only the other day I had a call from Jack Cassidy[2] from Indianapolis, and told the boys to say I was out of town. I hated to do it, I like Jack, (Did you ever meet him? I dont remember) but I just did not want to get back into that miserable routine of friendship (for Friendship, read: your-Ego-vs-my-Ego) and cunt chasing (for cunt chasing read: Your-Ego-vs-my Ego) and drinking (for Drinking, read: bottle's-Ego-vs-my-Ego) that I went through last year in NY (for NY, read: Every-body's-Ego-vs-everybody's Ego) and got so sick on. I wound up like a man who has taken a purge (unwittingly) and ex-hausted him shitting and vomiting both. I think maybe it taught me a valuable lesson. Anyway I hope so. I honestly dont think Ill ever need to do that again.

Mickey Knox[3] is mad at me right now because I wont answer his letters. I suppose if Cassidy finds out I put him off he will be too. Hes also sick of the slime and crud of Holly-wood, he says. But he wont leave it. Hell never leave it. And its not my job to try and help him out. I told him what he ought to do, but he made vast—and reasonable—excuses. The only logical answer is that like everybody, Mick wants to talk about his distress with everything and have someone to listen and agree and say gee its tough but youre a nice guy—if you only had a break youd be all right. Well, I think thats another illusion Ive worn out. The only real friendship is frustrated

[2]Probably the actor, later married to Shirley Jones, who was active on Broadway and in Hollywood.
[3]An actor friend of Mailer's who was, at one time, married to Adele Mailer's sister.

friendship, unfulfilled friendship; like Millay's poem: Let me lie down lean with my thirst and my hunger. Real friendship is that sudden, short, sharp, poignant-to-the-point-of-pain feeling that you suddenly and momentarily get when you are doing something else, and for a moment think of someone youd like to see but havent seen for a long time, and go on with what youre doing. Thats the only real friendship; but let it try to be satisfied, let it try to be explained, let those two people get together and stay together for three weeks each trying so hard to prove his friendship—and wheres your friendship gone?

And anyway, it all hurts your work. And for people who cant understand that your work is more important than their friendship and get their feelings hurt, what can you say? You certainly cant explain it to them.

Christ, what a diatribe.

Anyway, dont bring nobody but your wife with you when you come. And dont tell anybody else you been invited—anybody I know. Or Ill have a raft of letters from a bunch of people wanting to come too. And nobody else is invited except maybe Billy Styron. Whose address I dont even have. And then the two of you should not come at once—or wed wind up on a big fucking goddam drinking party which would do none of us any good except maybe our egos, which would do us harm.

Anyway, if you get the chance to stop by for a day or two, avail yourself of it.

I have done practically nothing and seen practically no one; not even here in Marshall, since I got home last spring. I spent almost all my time by myself, except for Lowney who cooks sometimes and reads my stuff all the time. I write mornings and work afternoons. Last winter I began an as yet unfinished project of building (starting from scratch, because I knew no carpentry) myself a series of workbenches and a workshop in my garage. Eventually, when I get some money again, I plan to have a bench for handloading and one for working on motors and one for carpentry and one for making ceramics complete with a ceramics kiln. Also power tools for making furniture. Its a hell of a lot of fun and a power saw has no ego and doesnt get its feelings hurt so that it keeps you from thinking about your characters. Right now, this is in abeyance waiting until I get all my yard work done. Ive been trimming and spraying appletrees, weeding hedges, seeding lawn, and various other sundry items. Someday well have a beautiful place here. In fact, we have already—except its not as beautiful as it will be. You ought to see my place, Norm. May and the first part of June are the prettiest time too. —And the main thing is, you can think about what youre going to write tomorrow all the time your hands are doing this job or that.

You know, old buddy, I feel as if I were just beginning to come into the richest and most productive and most mature period of my life. I want to take full advantage of it. I plan to stay right here for the next ten to fifteen years and get a bulk of good work done that will assure me a real place. Ive got eleven long novels already planned, and three short ones—just to prove I can write one, and I dont know how many stories. But the stories'll have to wait a while.

Its funny, but I could have done this all along and had two—or three—novels done by now instead of one. Only one thing kept me from it: me; me and my desires. Desire for love, desire for admiration, desire to be liked, desire to be a big shot, in short. I wanted—I was driven, by my own insecureness inside—to go out and seek every soul in the world and induce them to like me. Heh heh. And all the time they couldnt even see me because they were all trying so hard to make me and everybody else like them.

I know whats wrong with you, Norm. Youre just like I am. And so is Billy Styron. But if a guy can kill out—no, <u>wear</u> out—all desires in him for love—any kind of love—he can find, maybe, within himself that thing hes seeking.

Youre a mystic, thats the funny thing. Nowhere in time or the world could a mystic be caught by the illusion of social welfare except in America today. We, you and I, inherited it from the Depression and the young bums of the 'Thirties, Steinbeck and Dos Passos, etc. But you got a worse dose than I did, I guess. Probably city living at the time caused that. But despite that, youre at heart a mystic, like I am. And that means your problem is really with yourself and not the world without. Just like mine. Thats every writer's problem, no matter what he calls it, the hunger to reassociate with God, and with himself. And for God dont read fucking religion, either. The same holds true for Billy, I think too. Ive worked mine out a little bit in the last year—I think—because Ive learned the only answer for me lies in myself, rather than the exterior world.

You know out of all the people Ive met, Ive only met two real writers besides myself, and thats you and Billy. All of us have our flaws and shortcomings and our blind alleys which we cause ourselves; but the others, like Vance or Aldridge, or Buechner, dont even have that. They are literary men. Will Motley is a literary man in reverse, in revolt, which is chart class first grade stuff. And thats why I take you two so personally, I guess. If either of you fails, its like part of me fails too; and Im sure that both of you feel that of me.

And the whole answer to all of us lies really in the self, in the full—I should say fuller; well never reach the full—understanding of the self, clear eyed and without guilt or reservations. (You know what I think happens to great—really great—writers when they die? I think they all become apprentice yogis high up in the Himalaya mountains.) Because in the end I think its only through understanding of the self that empathy can be reached; and also, a minor point, that the knowledge that Love—as we call it in the popular songs, with a cap L—is an illusion is [if?] reached; is really only a covering mirage for the hidden inner-desire to be loved—I mean, Loved.

(If Adele [Mailer's wife] reads this and gets mad and thinks Im trying subtly to get you to leave her, tell her this is all only theoretical and has absolutely nothing to do with whether you and she stayed married or not. In fact, for that matter, when you come out if you do, it might be a good idea to leave Adele at home—except that if you did she would be positive Im trying to make you.—But then, if you bring her youll be positive Im trying to make her.—So there you are. You see why I dont like to be around people?)

Incidentally, I think I may have met a possible third one to add to the list of you and Billy. Theres a guy working with Lowney name of Tom Chamales on the writing of his first novel who has a chance to someday reach that status of a real writer. Its too soon to tell yet, but hes as yet the only one of any who have been in the Colony here who—unless, of course, some others grow a lot—has a chance of making it. Youll be reading about his first novel some day next year or so.[4]

Well, I guess Ive shot my wad for several months now and can get back to work.—No, what I said about love above was this: if you—if one—looks deep inside oneself, really deep, underneath affections and everything else, I think one will always see that beneath the desire, the love, there is always that frantic hungry ulterior motive of wanting to be loved first. That the giving, the tenderness, etc., everything, comes from the deep-hidden feeling that if you give enough, are lovable enough, then you will be loved—and thus your vanity will bloom like a flower to be shown at the Garden show.

Dont you bother to answer this either. But I would like a little note to know if you and Adele can plan to come out this summer for a day or two, so I can make plans.

I love you too,

Best,

PS—Lowney says that you promised her a signed first copy in your letter, and although she did not mention it in her letter to you she wants it badly, and I am to make plain to you that

---

[4]Tom Chamales did have great promise as a writer. He published two novels—*Never So Few* and *Go Naked in the World.*

the signed copy Im asking for is to be a different one from the one you promised her, so I guess youll have to send two.
T/TL/C

TO R. P. ADAMS

MARSHALL, ILLINOIS
AUGUST 30, 1955

Dear Dick,

. . . .

You are right of course that all art, all fiction, is lying. It must be because it is the result of an individual viewpoint and interpretation. And in that sense everything is. And by that definition I of course go along with you all the way in that the choice is not between truth and falsehood, objective reality and subjective fantasy, but as you say between better or worse, what works the best. But what I feel is, when youve said that you havent really said anything because this is a foregone conclusion, a basic necessity like having an atmosphere to breathe in order to remain alive; and to carry the analogy further this atmosphere while a necessity is still invisible and untasteable, nonexistent to the senses—unless there is a high wind which occasionally happens to frighten us and make us realize how basically insecure is our existence, our rather frenzied clasp of just being. Still, we are not usually aware or conscious of the fact that we exist in air any more than a fish is conscious he exists in water, which perhaps to us seems ridiculous.

Consequently in our work we can discount that, except as a basic tenet, and what I feel is that beneath that—or perhaps I should say above, but beneath is what I really feel—exists a level which we really can know and explore. And I think it all sums itself up into the really basic simplicity of whether or not is one honest. Given that initial tenet of not being able to know if there even _is_ truth, which practically is really unimportant, are we and can we be honest in what we do accept as existing? I think put like that it is possible to say whether we are honest or not. And the whole point of all this is that almost no human I have ever met is honest about himself to himself. And this quality extends I believe to all phases of our "civilization." But what you say about a "whirring in the head about our civilization," that is not what I have. What I have is a very cold-blooded merciless dissecting and <u>positive</u> knowledge about it. I cant begin to tell you how coldblooded and dissecting it is. And also, I know from studying myself that there is a considerable amount of pure malicious pleasure in me at being able to feel that way. I <u>know</u> what it is, and am pleased to be the idolbreaker. —Yet, along with that which is a purely intellectual quality I may say, there is another quality of simple warmth in me: I like people; even though I want to puncture them.

Also, intellectually I believe that until we <u>can</u> become really honest about ourselves, we can never even begin to decide whether our fantasies are objective or subjective. Im not saying very well what Im trying to say. Anyway, the whole cause of all our dishonesty is really founded on a fear-guilt system. Which is why I have such a hatred for morality—in any form whatsoever, backward or advanced. That was what I tried to express in Malloy's philosophy. Moral implies Evil. A contradistinction between Good and Bad. And in order to avoid that—did you ever notice in a Thesaurus how the words all seem to get paired into opposites?—one must throw out everything. I mean everything. Even the soul. One must get below the soul. So when I say civilization and just about all human relations are founded on mutually accepted lies, I do <u>not</u> mean I am confused or have a "headwhirring." I say it totally without emotion or personal feeling of any kind—except of course that rather malicious pleasure of the iconoclast, and if I denied that I felt that and was doing it "for the good of humanity" or some such junk, I myself would be lying—and as moralistic as everything I detest. I dont mean that there is simply a lot [of] systematic lying. I think the foundations themselves are lying, and lies, begun and perpetrated for our mental comfort.

By the way, have you ever read *Worlds in Collision* by [Immanuel] Velikovsky? I wont go into his new theory which deals mainly with making a cut at current astronomy and Darwin's evolution theory; but the implications philosophically in it, for me, are tremendous.

Which brings me to your theory about *Moby Dick,* in which I heartily concur and have for some time. But there again, I take exception to your statement about the symbolism of the whale: "What it really means, as Ishmael comes to realize, is life, which is both good and evil." Do you see how one always falls into this pitfall of opposing opposites? If you had made it read: "is life, which is neither good nor evil," I might have gone along although even that does not express it, you see— because once again comes this semantical and linguistic pairing of opposites: What it really is is neither "both good and evil" nor "neither good nor evil," but somewhere on in between so much as totally outside both statements.

After all, just what is Evil? We call evil that which hurts us, dont we? That which is unpleasant, that which we dont like, that which we are afraid of. But, if one really truly believes in your "organic metaphor," how can we call hurt evil since it is through pain and only through pain that we grow[?] Therefore, one might say actually that "good" is evil and "Evil" is good, because Evil makes us grow, whereas "Good" makes us stagnate, or at least not grow. This of course is what really made Ahab "Evil"—the fact that being hurt he refused to grow and instead and of necessity consequently became destructive. And yet that very "Evil" cannot be called evil because were it not for Ahab, Ishmael would not have grown. In the same sense, religion should not be called comfort, but discomfort. But how often is the phrase "Religious comfort" employed?

Anyway, Im certainly glad you dont think of Moby Dick as a symbol of "Evil," as Ive read so often and every time I do that makes me fighting mad.

Your statement that writers' criticism is highly personal is a very perceptive one, and true. I know this is true of me. Yet at the same time I think that in the end the only really valid basis for criticism is the personal. Youll note that in my letters whenever I criticize a writer it is always based on the personal, on the personality. The reason is that I know these men almost as well as if they were portions of myself. Take Hemingway or Faulkner. I know their work so well that I know their souls and personalities. For instance, I know that *Farewell to Arms* is a direct outgrowth of one of Hem's stories titled "A Very Short Story." Do you know it? Its in *In Our Time.* And its the <u>true</u> story of the love tale in *Farewell.* I had identical, I mean absolutely identical, experiences while in the Army. About three of them I had. And he wrote it absolutely truly. But he did not understand it. And he did not, later, understand it. Did not understand the meaning behind the fact that after his "tragic" losing of the nurse, he went right on and married some other woman (Hadley Richardson) and was in love with her just as much as he had been with the nurse. And not understanding, when he wrote *Farewell* he took this old affair and sentimentalized it all out of reality by wishful and romantic thinking about what it <u>could</u> or <u>should</u> or might have been. Well, now that kind of writing immediately emasculates itself. Its cheating, except that you cant say a man cheats when he himself doesnt know it. I know why he did it, and why the rejection of the nurse hurt him so, and why later he masturbated on the typewriter with it. I know and understand the whole process because Ive had the same <u>identical</u> thing happen to me. But the real truth is that both he and the nurse followed the line of least resistance: i.e., each chose immediate ego-stimulation with some other lover rather than long range waiting. As I think all humans do. And each resented the other doing it. I had a gal who, after Id left Hawaii for Guadalcanal, went ahead in a year or so and married some guy in one of her psych classes, but kept on writing me all the time naturally, while going out with him—as I kept writing her while laying every New Zealand girl I could get hold of—but the point is that this gal was actually hurt and angry with me even though married to the guy, when I finally through boredom broke off the correspondence and no longer loved her (of course, superficially, the correspondence had taken on the label of "Friendship" after she got married).

Well, do you see [what] all this implies? And do you see why I say that criticism must necessarily be personal? The gimmick of course is that the criticizer has to be objective about both the criticized and himself to do it well. But the criticism must be personal because it is from out [of] the writer's personality.

Incidentally, probably one of the main reasons I intend never to marry is because it is more painful for me not to. I think most people marry for the same reason but call it love. But Im afraid of the cessation of pain that would come from having a marriage. (Even though it might cause other, minor pain in other ways.) You would be surprised to see what a real cow this more or less sensitive girl turned into after marrying and socially-righteously having a baby or two—of which I think I may say she is most unjustifiably proud.

By the same token I know what has ruined Faulkner, who at his best was the most devastatingly penetrating writer weve had. F.'s sudden need in later years to become an "affirmative" writer is all due to this daughter of his, and his "fatherly" worry about her "soul"; for soul read open-mindedness. All this is tied in with sex too, and F. has become the prototype of the fathers he used to ridicule and inveigh against. And in turn, he had of necessity become pompous. Again, as with that generation's earlier mistakes, all this is sexual and tied in with sexuality. Phrased in simple terms Faulkner is afraid his daughter might lose her virginity before she marries. Have you ever read Billy Styron's *Darkness?* This book is as far as I can gather from Bill almost wholly a work of the imagination (I always suspect this statement), drawn from a girl he went to school with as a kid and had a crush on. But it is amazing to me, anyway, how almost identically true this story must be to the basic relationship between Faulkner, his wife (whom I once met, and is an absolute vain nothing), and his daughter.

Along with this, your statement about Lucretius saying that what holds the world together is love amazes me. For a man as deep as you are you make some amazingly sophomoric and juvenile statements. It is this kind of myth and "civilization-lie" that I am trying to dig down under, that Lucretius statement. Have you ever read Stendhal's much more penetrating statement that: "As long as one has one illusion left, one can love."? I suggest you get hold of Stendhal's *On Love* and study it, and then afterwards study his *Diaries.* I just jotted down a note the other day, an aphorism to be used in this book on a conversation on Love: The man (spiritual descendant of Malloy) says: "Evil? The search for love is the only evil for humanity." Superficial, half-love between persons may be all right; but [did] you ever see real love between a man and a woman that did not end up as anger and resentment and fury that the other party could make one need him or her so much?

As for other kinds of love, did you ever love a sunset or a tree or a book when half of you did not say to yourself: ["]Gee, what a fine person and how sensitive I must be, to love this object so"—?

. . . .

Yours

T/TL/C

TO ROBERT CANTWELL

MARSHALL, ILLINOIS
SEPTEMBER 3, 1955

Dear Bob

It will please you to know, in connection with my ever giving up the project—this book—, that I dont think I could. Im too insecure and too scared, I think, to even be able to do it if I knew it was going to be bad and that it would be the best thing. If doggedness is a virtue, so must be the fear that causes it then, I guess. However, I dont think its going to be bad. I think its going to be good. Damned good. If I can do what I want with it, I know it will. Because it will be a barbed spear up the ass of the world. For years to come, I think. All I can tell you about it now is that its principally about Sex—what book isnt? Except Kinsey's, of course. But Ill see that you get a copy of the galleys when. If you want one.

Speaking of Sex, I received from Dutton a bound galleys copy of Norman's new book,[1] as he writes me himself, also about Sex. I think its a good book, and I think its true of Hollywood which is its subject. Also, I think as Norman has told me, it opens up new sexual ground. Somewhat. It lacks something, I think, something I cant define, but which comes basically out of Norm, but its still a good book and one he can be proud of. I keep feeling that Norm has never really hit his stride yet, and that everything hes written up to now has only been preparatory, really. Someday hes going to explode on the world like a nova, with a classic. Hes going to have to give up his ideals first though—or rather, face the realization that his ideals like everybody else's are really personal desires, caused by personal hungers, not abstract idealism or philosophy. Ive about reached the place where I dont think there is any such a thing as abstract philosophy, except in mathematics.

All this about Norm is of course not quotable, Bob, even in conversation. You know? Just between us mongeese.

I want to go into some of the things in your letter, connected with that last paragraph of the *Newsweek* article.[2] If I can. I find

[1] Rinehart accepted *The Deer Park* but then decided not to publish it. The novel was then turned down by several publishers before Putnam's acquired it. Jones must have read the Putnam's galleys.

[2] Cantwell ended his "James Jones: Another 'Eternity'?" in the November 23, 1953, issue of *Newsweek:*

Jones is not driven to write by a message to impart, or by the striving for an integration of life that inspired the great tragic novelists—Dostoevski these things hard to write about because of the constant danger—danger? impossibility—of avoiding dichotomies. Have you ever noticed in a Thesaurus how words are always paired in opposites? In the last two years I have found myself becoming increasingly unable to use a Thesaurus for this reason. In like vein, whenever I make a statement such as I will in this letter, I find—even to myself, but especially to others—it is unintentionally implying a moral judgment against its opposite. That is why its hard for me to write of what my basic philosophy is—or rather, is becoming; because Im only just clarifying it myself <u>to</u> myself. And it is that that makes writing letters like this one good for me: I <u>have</u> to express. Thats why I feel that *Eternity* is basically an adolescent book, a good adolescent book, but still an adolescent one: because in it I accepted pretty much of a standardized philosophy: i.e., the underdog, etc. But even so I managed to save it from sentimentality. The Warden (and Jack Malloy somewhat) is the key to that. Had the book not had Warden, and instead contained only Prewitt, it would have been ghastly. And it is through the partially closed door of Warden, sort of, that Im now squeezing into a big room. Its like going through a tiny hole in the ground into an enormous cave with only a flashlight, and you know how big it is and are scared, but the being scared is half the fun and the real creator of your excitement.

Now dont worry: I am aware of the very real danger you

---

and Tolstoy—who figure in his literary conversation. He believes that life is tragic, and that those who call for a serious American literature which will also be affirmative are asking the impossible. But his own approach to his tragic work is vigorous and even cheerful. The philosophical basis of his fiction does not now concern him. For a long time to come he can work from the casually acquired common-sense view of life prevailing in his time and place—a plain man's view of life, sifted, however, by his marvelously intuitive creative gift, and appraised by a quick intelligence that is unburdened with literary and academic matters. . . .
Someday the limitations of his local philosophy may be brought home to him in terms of his fiction. . . .

mentioned in your letter. Of too much questioning about one's philosophy to the detriment of one's real work—which your example of the German philosophers on history illustrates aptly. And I am convinced that today this—what else shall I call it?—"abstractionism" is probably the great thing wrong with our literature, both writer and critic. I agree with you completely on that. That very thing is the thing which today is still wrong with Norm. Billy Styron, who is the only other really good one we have, does not have it nearly so badly.

But then again you are wrong when you think that I am working basically instinctively. Im not. Im working totally consciously and----

(but I gave you a very bad—not bad perhaps but wrong—impression when you were here; partly this was due to the fact that the mere talking of philosophy rather than talking <u>around</u> it has a tendency to externalize and oversimplify it, and mainly not leave room for including its own opposite and thus it becomes a dichotomy unavoidably; so when you were here, instead of trying to talk of my own, I mainly hooted in general at others'; I ran down sentimentalism and resulted in seeming mechanical—no thats not what I want to say;—Let me put it this way: I showed cheerfulness at tragedy, because other people weep at it (crocodile tears); I ran down the literati, but did not state my own literature; the result was that I seemed simple—and knew I was, I guess—when actually I wasnt simple at all but infinitely more complex than if I <u>had</u> talked of my own. Are you digging me?)

----but as I began above, Im working totally consciously and I know it. But Ive taught myself a trick which is to do all my <u>thinking</u> when I am not <u>working</u>. Thus, in effect, I really employ two levels of creativity: the thinking level, and the working level. And I close the door on the one when I open the door on the other, and vice versa. I think up what I want to say when Im <u>not</u> working, and deliberately forget it when I <u>am</u> working. Thus I think up meaning, and organization and direction and often even individual episodes (which are the only things I make notes on), but when I sit down to work I close this part off and write only to make it real, and often in so doing find Ive changed course completely—while still hanging to the original skeleton. But it is a mistake to think I do not work <u>consciously</u>. I do. But when actually writing, I let intuition and instinct say for me what Ive already decided I want to say, but have deliberately and with malice aforethought made myself forget. The result is, I do not employ any conscious symbols or symbolisms in the work itself. In fact, a great deal of my hardest times come when for one reason or another I discover Ive forgotten to lock the door on the thinking, and find it slipping in as symbol.

I dont know if Ive made my method clear to you. The real point Im trying to make is twofold: 1) that the instinctive writer you thought you saw here is only an act, a very deep act, one Ive deliberately made deep, you see? so deep in fact that more often than not I find myself actually living on that level, which is good—because it is this that contributes the quality of reality to the work; and 2) that the acuteness of criticism which you mention as demanding philosophical grasp on the part of the writer is the very thing that, if one is to do the really good work, one must avoid. Now Hemingway sort of pretends this; but in reality he does not do it because he just is not a thinker. As Gertrude Stein said: Hemingway, youre ninety percent Rotarian. It couldnt be said better; it should be his epitaph. And when I derided Dostoievski to you, that was why I did it: the man, if looked at whole, was just exactly what he should not have been: he did as the critics demand and pointedly portrayed conscious philosophical grasp. The result: he could not help but appear—and <u>be</u>—a moralist and a sentimentalist. *The Idiot* is a prime example: no man such as Mishkin has ever lived, and for that very reason Dostoievski destroys before he begins what he would create. The really good things in him, of course, are the incidental things, when he allowed—or rather was unable to stop—his instinct from taking over for him within the framework of scenes. But the scenes themselves will just not hold up. Now: Am I wrong? Take any scene in *The Idiot* and prove me wrong in a letter (I know it better than the others—*Karamazov* I cant even finish).

Now the only difference between us, you and me here, is that you did not realize—which was deliberately my fault really—that I am working on the conscious level.

Now as for criticism, Im not just sure whom you mean as the younger critics you mentioned. Aldridge immediately jumped to mind. Who else is there that you meant? Im not sure. But [if] you were thinking partly of Aldridge, you are wrong. Because he is not so much a has been as a never was. And you were <u>totally</u> right when you implied a dislike of this too-acuteness: that you "reluctantly admired" it. But you were equally wrong when you used "admired"; you shouldnt admire it. Its the wrong approach, and cancels itself before it begins. The critic should do much the same as the writer, and only use his conscious apparatus when he is <u>not</u> working. The reason you admire it is that you believe it is the basis of the philosophical. But your very example of the Germans proves you wrong. And how antiquated are they today, when even the existence of matter itself [has] been analyzed away into no more than an infinite number of tiny solar systems that are atoms, and were we small enough to do it could probably be shown to be composed of even smaller atoms themselves; when today Jeans' depressive theory of the expanding universe has been elaborated and extended to a theory of an alternate expansion and contradiction? They took their science of their day and tried to build philosophies on it, when it itself was unstable and still growing. As it still is. Probably always will be. Well, this same thing would apply to your critics; and the intelligent writer must always keep in mind what is moral (or philosophical) today will not be so tomorrow. He must allow for that. And the only way to do that is to <u>not</u> set up any hard and fast system of philosophy, or "philosophical grasp."

In line with talking about critics, I dont know whom you

mean nor how much youve read along critical lines. (Probably more than me.) So anyway Im enclosing an article on *Eternity* by a fellow named Dick Adams (who has, incidentally, been unable to sell it to any critical—so called—magazine). I dont know how much you know of the current conflict between the Humanists and Romantics, as personified by the present day generation. But Dick Adams' theory of romanticism and the "organic metaphor" (which idea originally came from Alfred Whitehead) is something new, and to me, exciting in itself. His piece on *Eternity* as an example of his theories of romanticism interested me a lot. I dont know what Dick will think of this new book because I doubt if it will coincide with his idea of the organic metaphor; and will be interested to see if he can find a handle on it. Of course, it does follow the organic metaphor, this new book; in its largest essence; but it presupposes that there is no such simplicity that makes the organic metaphor graspable in any one lifetime or social framework. And that is where Im interested in what Dick will say.

. . . .

Best to you,
Jim

o/TLS

Jones tried to distance himself from the life of the Colony, with its many temperamental writers, but that was difficult to do. Dissatisfied Colonists or former Colonists went public with their complaints and their gossip. Lowney's method of teaching, which had first been presented favorably to the public, was later treated with derision. Stories about Jones and Lowney circulated, much to Jones's discomfort.

Jones became aware that the Colonist Jerry Tschappat, who published the novel Never the Same Again *(1956) using the pseudonym Gerald Tesch, was feeding stories about the Colony, Jones, and Lowney to Norman Mailer.*

TO NORMAN MAILER

MARSHALL, ILLINOIS
MARCH 5, 1956

Dear Norm,

First, let me make it plain that I havent any intention of engaging in a feud with you. Literary or personal. And never had had. My opinion of you has undergone some changes, but it isnt unprintable (in the sense you use the word). Someday, if youd like, maybe we'll be able to sit down and discuss the whole thing, though it would probably be a waste of time. Ive not said anything about you to anyone that I wouldnt say to your face; but I dont want to go into it in a letter. Anyway, Im sure my opinion of you is of no more interest to you than what you think of me would be to me. We both have our work to do, our paths to follow, and they appear to be increasingly divergent. But that doesnt mean anything and I agree with you that it would be ridiculous for us to become enemies. And I never intended that we should. So set your mind at rest on that point.

The only other thing I have to say to you is that you had—someday—better learn to distinguish between truthful "sources" and untruthful ones. Both you and also Lowney (I noted) rather delicately refrained from mentioning by name this information "source," but I see no reason why I shouldnt call Jerry Tschappat by his name to you. After all, he may be—and I expect will be—a pretty big writer some day. However, this does not necessarily mean that I will admire him. I have gradually and for the record painlessly gotten over the belief I used to hold (and you personally have had nothing to do with this) that to be a big writer is to be a big person. But just for the record I want to point out some things to you.

After writing you whatever it was he wrote you (and I have seen some of the letters, the originals, that Jerry has exchanged around about his opinions of Lowney & me;[1] so I expect it was

[1]Several of the stories about Lowney and the Colony presented her as domineering. Once the Colonists arrived in Marshall, she controlled their diets (she favored boiled potatoes, cottage cheese, and warm Jell-O); set them to copying passages from her list of approved writers; regimented their time devoted to copying, writing, and exercise; and passed out money for them to make excursions to the red-light district in nearby Terre Haute, Indiana.

David Ray in the *Nation* (February 8, 1958), wrote of his life at the Handy Colony: no breakfast "because you think better that way"; no talking until noon because Lowney believed in the "Eastern conception of the creative value of silence." Each day those who had finished their apprenticeship (copying the masters) turned in their own prose, and Lowney went over it with them, "reinterpreting scenes or suggesting slants consistent with her views on psychology."

Norman Mailer, interviewed for the documentary *James Jones: Reveille to Taps,*" and published in *The Paris Review,* no. 103, was more judicious than Ray. Mailer visited the Colony, and it was his belief that he might use copying if he were teaching writing: "There are worse ways to demonstrate that writing consists of an awful lot of dreary dull work and paying attention to small details." Mailer found Lowney opinionated and uneasy about literary matters. He believed that there were serious writers at the Colony as well as those "who were running a scam, who liked the idea of having free meals, a bed and some good athletics."

Jones himself turned against the basic philosophy of the Colony. In an interview published in *The Paris Review,* no. 20 (1959) Jones said he had once believed that if the worry of economics were removed, then those who

pretty lurid—how we kicked him out, destroyed his soul, kept him from getting his book published, etc.—also what a drunk I am, and what a tyrant Lowney is)—after writing you anyway, Jerry came back here and spent something like six weeks (from shortly before Christmas right up to the day he left to go to New York and meet Putnam's) working on a second novel which up to then had been only a title and nothing else. In that time, with Lowney's close day-by-day, line-by-line help he did around 400 pages first draft. He has since requested this be sent to him, and it has been.

Now, from what I gather, he told both yourself and Putnam's that he was through with the Colony and with Lowney and with me. He was at that time calling her from New York every day . . . , and he kept on doing so until I got mad and told Lowney to make him quit. . . .

Right now, we are in receipt of a letter from him saying that he intends to come back here in May, and that he intends putting an Acknowledgment in the back end of his book like I did in *Eternity* saying that Lowney helped him and that he wrote the book on Jim Jones's money. I immediately wrote him back telling him that I would under no circumstances allow him to use either my name or that of my book in such a way. He did not write it on <u>my</u> money, he wrote it on the Handy Colony's money. Two entirely different things, since I am not the only donor to the Handy Colony. So far Ive had no answer. If I dont get one, Im sending a carbon to my attorney and have him inform Putnam's of this. I have no

---

wanted to write would indeed write, but he had been proved wrong. With sorrow he admitted: "I guess you just can't pick up any Joe off the street and turn him into a writer by setting him down to copying the great books."

In *Go to the Widow-Maker* Jones dealt with the Colony, Lowney, and himself in a slightly fictionalized form. In the novel, the mistress [Lowney] had induced the suddenly wealthy playwright [Jones] to invest $75,000 to build a little theater colony. The mistress was tying up his new money to keep him tied to her. "He allowed her to go on saying in public," Jones wrote, "that he owed it to her, for helping him."

intention of letting him use my name and that of *Eternity* to help his publicity, or show that he is the friend of the "famous"—especially when he is above using the name of the Colony, which wont help either publicity or fame. Now I have a natural instinct against that way of working, and Jerry has a natural instinct for it.

In his calls from New York here, he told us a number of things. . . . For one, he said that Theodore Purdy hates Lowney's guts, and insisted that he would not accept Jerry's book even tentatively unless he promised that Lowney Handy would have nothing to do with any reworking of it. He said Purdy's wife had met Lowney at a party . . . and did not like her and was insulted by her in some way or other. He said Purdy hates Burroughs Mitchell, and that you and Purdy hoped to be able to get me away from Scribner's and with Putnam. He said he got no advance before leaving. . . . He said that you now hated my guts. He said that you, particularly, and some others (he gave no names, but I assumed perhaps it was Vance [Bourjaily] or somebody) were planning yourselves a secret little conspiracy to get Jones away and out from under the domination of that fearful woman Lowney Handy. Both Lowney and I laughed at this at the time, and I told Jerry he was full of shit over the phone, but he insisted then and later that it was so. He said you also had asked him to do a guest column in your column in the [*Village*] *Voice*, and also that later you wanted him to take a job with it permanently. (Still later, he said you couldnt find him a place.) He also said that Purdy was incensed at what you were doing on the *Voice*, and thought you were through as a writer, and that Purdy warned him not to get engaged in any such shenanigans. . . .

Now, I dont know what to believe, or where to stand. As far as that goes, I dont give a damn where I stand. To you I will say only one thing. If you will look, you will find on that little yellow sheet which Lowney sent you that said "Sucker!," that I also added my little bit, below, printed in ink, which said "You sure are!" I note however that you did not write and ask me for an apology. Do you want one? If so, Im afraid youre as out of luck with me as you were with Lowney.

Now, as I said, I dont intend to start any feuds, literary or otherwise. But you know me well enough to know Im not going to sit around and let somebody like Jerry shit on me forever. Or anybody else. As far as Im concerned, youve made some serious mistakes in judgment lately. Ill even go so far as to say that Im a little disappointed in you, for several reasons. But that is neither here nor there. You would probably disagree with me. But as for feuding, thats out. As for being cool, it makes me no difference coolness or not. Ill still be ready and willing to go out with you and get drunk and pick up some broads like we have done in the past, if and when. If not, thats okay too. But as for talking writing, and abstract moral concepts with you, thats as far out as the feuding. You and I dont see eye to eye on what is integrity apparently. Which is as it should be.

Now. I guess Ive covered everything. No, one more thing. As for having rough, mean enemies in the literary world, I couldnt give less of a fuck. And I think you make a serious mistake in judgment when you attempt fighting such people. The only way to treat fools is to shun and ignore them. But thats your business. It appears to me, just as a personal opinion, that the so-called literary world of which you love being so much a part is a pigsty—except that all the nails are manicured, and all the armpits and crotches more or less washed.

Thats why I live in Marshall, Illinois, which is a pigsty in its own little way—but its way contains a lot less of the enjoyable selfdestructive temptations for me than the big literary one does. And if you, or you and Vance, or you and this Purdy, or you and anybody else, are getting ready to try and free me from the domination of Lowney Handy, let me remind you that while all you boys may have great will power and strength of character, I do not, and I need somebody to look after me and keep me from killing myself drinking and fucking, somebody who has some common sense, like Lowney, and also I need somebody to read over my stuff and tell me if it is good or not. Because I never know, like you and Vance and Purdy do.

Now. If you want to answer, do. If you dont, dont. And if I ever see you, we'll have a drink.

Yours,

PS—A letter is the property of the writer, remember? None of this is for publication in the *Voice* or anywhere else. Since we have such different ideas of integrity, I thought I should explain this to you. —And quit worrying about feuds. Write.

T/TL/C

Norman Mailer did send Jerry Tschappat a letter, dated March 24, 1956, saying he didn't want to hear stories about Jones and Lowney. Mailer sent a copy of that letter to Jones.

TO NORMAN MAILER

MARSHALL, ILLINOIS

MARCH 31, 1956

Dear Norman,

Very fine letter. Enjoyed it. Also, even more, I enjoyed—no, thats not the word; I didnt enjoy it—appreciated is better, appreciated the carbon of the letter you sent to Jerry. I am not returning it since you did not mark it so, but if you want it back just let me know and I will return it.

However, there are a few discrepancies in your letter that I want to set you straight on, in an entirely friendly way, pal. Ill get to them further down. This will probably turn out to be another longwinded letter, I guess.

But first of all I am glad to hear that there is no deep dark plot afoot to relieve me from Lowney's domination.

You are wrong, Norm, in assuming that I would ever come anywhere near flying into a rage because and here I quote you: "Because I happened to be right, whether you like it or not, about Putnam's possibly taking the book [Jerry's book] where Scribner's didnt." I think you make a rather smug judgment and a hasty one when you say that. Particularly since there are a lot of circumstances of which you know nothing, in this whole situation with Jerry.

Now as for my (which should read our, both Lowney's and mine) liking Jerry enough to keep him around a few years, youre of course quite right; but I dont see why you make a point of reminding me of this? Did you think I had forgotten it? or was angry at him? I didnt mean to give you that impression if I did. The point is, Jerry has been here four different years now, and five if you count the six weeks last winter. Now each year he has been here, he has invariably wound up by getting himself run off—all except the last time, which was before he went in to NY. One of those times Lowney went to work on him with her fists and knocked him around a bit, and the last time she ran him off told him he had graduated; he could never come back. (As for the fists, which may horrify your bourgeois belief in the sanctity of the individual, I would point out that she did this only after he had caused a great deal of trouble and gotten so cocky nobody could talk to him, and also after he had been tempting me deliberately and in so many words to knock the shit out of him, something which I am glad to say I refrained from, because that was what he wanted, and would have enjoyed it too much, gotten too good an orgasm out of it, and I told him so.) Well. —But all this is not the point. The point is—and I dont know how Im going to get it through that thick humanity-loving, proletarian-loving, rights of man-loving skull of yours—the point is, all of these things, the fists, the running of him off year after year (to the point, actually, where it no longer disturbed him because he always knew he could come back, which was why Lowney told him he couldnt—and convinced him) all of these things have been done, old boy, with_out the least bit of anger (though Jerry didnt know it), and with a careful calculation and thought-out consideration of how all of them would affect Jerry, his person-ality, and his work. You yourself havent the slightest idea of the energy and thought and time and effort that have been expended here on Jerry. And such a pre-calculated, Jesuitical way of working is totally foreign to your mind, Im sure. But thats the way we work here, and thats the way we have to work. Not understanding this, and probably even believing it isnt morally ethical with that adolescent childish idea of integ-rity that you have, you have probably done more damage to Jerry and his career than you will ever even guess at.

The way Jerry stands now, and unless some as now unan-ticipated force impinges upon him and changes the direction in which his free-rolling ball (which is without choice, you know) into rolling off at another angle, what he will probably turn out to be will be another sort-of-latter-day Hemingway. If he escapes being a Maxwell Bodenheim.[1] A perpetually adolescent immature man who can write wonderfully well, but because of his character limitations keeps forever degenerating away from his first good book, or perhaps two.

If you have ever made a really close study of Hemingway through his work as I have, you will know what I mean by immature. The consensus of his philosophical outlook might be worded thusly: Say and do everything you can that will make Hemingway look good, even if it does make a lot of other people look bad. Im sure he believes, as Jerry does, everything he writes. But where does that leave him? Look up his comments on Sherwood Anderson—a snide parody of whom the whole book of *Torrents of Spring* aims at. Also his various comments on Mencken, and on Scott Fitzgerald, and on Tom Wolfe. Most usually they begin: "Poor Tom Wolfe etc, etc" or "Poor Scott Fitzgerald etc etc"—"if he had only known thus and so" (implying he, Hemingway, does know this or that) "perhaps it would have helped his work thus and so."

Well, thats about the size of what youve helped to perpetrate upon the world in helping Jerry get this book published. I hope you feel very pleased, and smug, as your letter sometimes sounds, about it. He is, in fact, so totally immature that he will probably turn out to even be much worse than Hemingway.

Now as for me being angry about you being right about Putnam taking the book when Scribner's turned it down. First, I didnt send it to Scribner's. Lowney did. She worked with Burroughs Mitchell on her own book without any go-betweening on my part. On the other hand, I am remembering some very petty remarks on your part concerning Scribner's, when they turned your book down. These were in a letter you wrote Jerry. He quoted them to Lowney, who with me be-

[1]The bohemian poet and novelist who was murdered in 1954.

lieved Jerry was lying. But you yourself wrote and told her that you had in fact written them. And you went on to put upon Scribner's your own supposition that that house was now not as courageous and forward as it once was when it published *Eternity*. Also, you went on to say—either then or later, in another letter—that since you expected it would be two more years (a petty remark in itself) before my book was done, I neednt worry because Scribner's would probably have changed back by then. Now just where you got that "two years" deal I dont know. Probably from Jerry. I know Jerry has a great fetish for going around telling everybody how I have the second-book-blues (which of course he does not, he implies) and that I might not even be able to finish this book and have to abandon it. The fact is that I am right now at the winding up stage of this book. I hope to have it done by June of this year, and expect to.

Now, all this is rather ridiculous on your part. Whether you were angry at Scribner's or not, you should have learned enough by now, as I have, that whenever you are angry is the best time—and also the hardest—to keep your mouth shut. All this is what I meant when I said that I thought you had made several serious mistakes in judgment lately. I am quite sure in my own mind that when you wrote Jerry all that crap about how pantywaist Scribner's had become you were indulging your own vanity to a potential satellite. Dont be angry now; I find myself doing this all the time myself, and have to lean over backward to avoid it. But you ought to know better than to write such crap to a green kid. I myself am quite sure that your book was <u>not</u> turned down at Scribner's because of any near-salacious material in it. And I can prove that by what is in this book Im working on myself. I think your book was turned down because it was a pretty bad book, and though Ive read both the galleys and the finished version, I dont see how you helped it very much.

Now, its very possible Im wrong about *Deer Park,* and Im willing to admit I may be. But as far as Im concerned, its not a good book, and in fact isnt as good by far as *Barbary*, which I liked very much—when read as an allegory, and not as a novel which of course it is not.

Im punching all this out straight from the shoulder, buddy. Probably Im hurting you. But this is honestly what I feel. And BY GOD! I have <u>not</u> said it to another soul.—No, I take that back; I did say it to Jerry. And of course Ive said it to Lowney. But certainly to no one else. I still believe there are great books in you. <u>Great</u> books. If you can ever get them out. But I certainly doubt very much if youll ever do it while writing a fucking column for the *Village Voice*. Thats another serious mistake in judgment youve made I feel. Certainly, I know that my own ego-vanity could never survive such an operation, and in spite of what you say Im positive yours is at present ballooning—both from the admiration you get and from the dislike you get, just as my ego would also.

But all this is really beside my point, Norm. The real point of what Im writing is this: Jerry had a potential <u>great</u> book there in *Again*. I mean a really <u>great</u> book. I dont know if you have read it. I havent. But, in some moments of her [Lowney's] upset when working with Jerry (my! wouldnt this statement please him: somebody upset over him!) she talked to me about it. The whole plot of the thing centers around this homo affair between Roy and this kid Johnny. The grown-up adult Roy, who should know better, seduces poor little adolescent Johnny who is a victim. What Lowney tried and tried to get him to do, for two years, was to pull a switch. She wanted him to make Johnny, who was of course himself somewhat the seducer, and Roy the seduced. And of course, Jerry could not quite expose himself quite that much. He was willing to expose superficially but not quite that deeply. But Lowney would have handled him, and worked him around to facing it someday, and would have got him to do it right.

If it had not been for one Norman Mailer, my old buddy, who hates to see good art thrown away because it has salacious matter in it. Who hates to see an individual's privacy of soul and integrity impinged upon. The rights of man, buddy, the rights of man.

And—if she had finally got him to do the book <u>honestly</u> and he knew that that was honest—hes not that bad, she would also have got him finally and at long last to face the one thing in the world he hasnt yet faced, and thats himself. And he might then have become a really great writer. And of course its still possible that he might yet. But I rather doubt it. I expect he'll be another Hemingway, only more so. And Im convinced myself that Hemingway is just as bad a pathological liar as Jerry. I used to be—still am, a lot of the time. But Im growing out of it a little, very painfully, I might add.

And so there you have what Im trying to say. Thanks to you, and your political pull with this Purdy who was impressed by you as a great writer, you got Jerry in with Putnam's, and now the book will be published wrongly, and God knows what will happen to poor Jerry. All because, Im quite sure, you were piqued at Scribner's because they wouldnt take *Deer Park* and saw—subconsciously—or perhaps consciously—a good chance to take a dig at them.

Me be angry because "you were right, about Putnam taking the book where Scribner's didnt"? Christ, man! Grow up a little.

Now. Only one more thing. I dont think you have any conception of how completely Lowney works with these writers here. She works with them so totally that when the product is finished, its almost impossible to tell what ideas were hers, what actual lines were hers, what actual paragraphs she suggested putting in. And she does all this without ever once impinging on what the writer himself wants to say. This was true of Jerry. When she couldnt reason with him to change the basic roles in his book, she didnt try to force him to, or try to work him into it behind his back subtly. She let it go, because she believes that what a writer wants to say he should say, even if she doesnt agree with it. But all the time she was trying to get Jerry to grow up a little, outside of working with him on the writing part. I know of only one editor who was able to do that kind of thing with writers, and thats Max Perkins. But even Max didnt go as far as Lowney does, and actually suggest the right paragraphs and put in the right sentences—and not only does she put them in, but she puts them in in the <u>style</u> of the individual.

Up to now she has with only one exception—me—been paid back by these people in exactly the way Jerry paid her back. I could go on and name you a dozen of them. Two of whom, besides Jerry, should have books out within the year. Now, I dont deserve any credit for sticking by Lowney, because Im more sort of a son to her and Harry, actually their son. And in that capacity Ive been trying for years to get her to quit trying to work with these people and do the writing on her own—which with a little hard work she could do. Of course, the tragedy is that she has spent about fifteen years on this work by now, and she is trained in it. She isnt mentally trained as a writer per se. But she could be. And from what I gather from her concerning her experiences in the past year or two, she is just about ready to admit that shes going to have to wind up doing it.

Now, I guess thats all Ive got to say. Off my chest. Except that Ill be willing to bet you—I havent talked with Jerry about it, or read what writing he is doing—but Ill be willing to bet you that when the novel *Again* is finally published, its going to wind up with poor old seduced Roy being the villain—whether a Budd S[c]hulberg type of villain or not.

And I think I can truthfully say we all—Jerry, Lowney, Putnam's, me—owe it to you, old pal. And Jerry has perhaps finally and forever escaped the one thing hes been running from since about five minutes after he was born: Jerry. If so, of course, hes through. (You should have seen the amount of detail suggestion and work Lowney put in on that new work on his new book that he did here just before going to NY.) The whole trouble is, Jerry cannot admit to anyone just how much Lowney has helped him. But until he is able to, hes dead.

Well, now Ive said my little piece, buddy. And Im near the end of this page. I would of course appreciate a rebuttal. Always remember, if you cant find a psychiatrist for the *Voice*, you always have me. Except I wont let my vanity spread so much as to print our arguments in the *Voice*. I want to be a novelist, not a political and moral essayist. Sorry. A dig. But you got it coming.

Anyway, I still love you. And in spite of all, I still think youve got great books in you. I just hope you dont ruin the whole next generation of American writers getting them out of you.

(Goddam it, now I didn't make the finish on that last page.)

Well, Ill close anyway. I wish you would come out for a few days, so we could really hash all this over. But then I dont know what would happen to your column. Anyway, you have the invitation.

And if you think Im a fucking schmuck, old friend, you are undoubtedly right. But you should have seen the little note I <u>wanted</u> to send you, but which Lowney stopped me from sending. If you do come out, Ill show it to you. I still have it filed away, along with all my other stuff on Jerry. He'll really make me a fine character someday.

Well, I got to quit, old brother. In fact, I cant even think of anything else to say. Oh, I suppose I <u>could,</u> if I really put my head to it. But—

Well, write me, anyway. And come if you think you can stand it.

Yours,

T/TL/C

As Jones neared the end of the writing of Some Came Running, *he became concerned that Scribner's might request major revisions.*

TO BURROUGHS MITCHELL

MARSHALL, ILLINOIS
SEPTEMBER 12, 1956

Dear Mitch
  . . . .

I figure, probably, as soon as I have Book IV done completely, to send it in to you there. Since its over three hundred. And then to wait till the end for the sending [of] the rest. If that is suitable with you. It is a natural breaking point, and should not bother me too much by a letdown. Ive held off sending anything up to now because Im quite sure that we're going to have a number of big arguments about the scene of Frank's going down on Edith, though there is no actual physical description of the act. But it is plain enough (or at least I hope so). But I state here categorically that in the last analysis I am prepared to go to the mat for it—with you, or Horace, or anybody else; because it has been built to all through the book and is a very important part of the realization of Edith's character. Another reason I have hesitated to send anything on now is what Helen said when you all were out here. Ive brooded over this a lot—but have managed to keep it down— also, this coupled to the remark that I seem to get from Harry Brague[1] everytime we talk about the book: that, of course, it will need a lot of revision. Id stake everything I know or have ever learned about writing that such is not the case. If there was anything at all wrong with the first part, I have myself taken care of that I think by the Prologue which I wrote shortly before you came. I dont think it needs any changes. A few

---

[1] An editor at Scribner's.

minor cuts here and there perhaps, like *Eternity*. And you remember you yourself told me in so many words that it needed no revision, major or minor. But I also remember that you told Helen: "You talk too much." As I say, Ive brooded about it a lot. Im running on a pretty thin ragged edge to get done, but that is no excuse for your lying to me. And if I ever find out that you did in fact lie to me about what you thought about revision, even in order to help me along as you thought at the time, Ill be through [with] the book as far as you and I are concerned. Anyway, with all of this in mind, Ive decided to go on and send this end of Book IV on in for your opinion of it, etc., once I have it done. As I said, minor cuts to tone up the scenes I dont mind about at all. That was all that was really done to *Eternity*. And I have a pretty good organizational sense, I think. I know its long, but every damned chapter of it belongs in there. I know I offended Helen, I guess, by tacitly in my drunken way—all unintentionally—"putting you in your place" as an editor. I didnt mean it like that at all, in the way she took it. But after all, that is what you are: an editor: an honorable profession, too: but in the end it is really the writer who writes his books, and not the editor. Perkins would have been the first to say so. As would Lowney, and Im sure yourself. Im sorry you havent had a flock of other best sellers like myself, as Helen said; but after all, that is not what I started out to be: a best seller; and was not even my expectation or my basic intention.

. . . .

Yours,
Jim

p/TLS.

Jones wrote Mitchell on December 16, 1956, that he was going to go on a fast for a week or ten days and then spend two weeks completing the manuscript of Running.

TO BURROUGHS MITCHELL

MARSHALL, ILLINOIS
DECEMBER 16, 1956

Dear Mitch

. . . .

Anyway, here is what I propose to do: As soon as our work—yours and mine—is done on the manuscript itself, I want to find out from you just when—and whether—I should come to New York. I shall have to come anyway, I know, when Horace is through working on the book, probably, and horsetrade and battle with him on it. So I would like, if there is anything else, such as the libel possibilities (which Im coming increasingly to doubt: that there are any), to be done: then Id like to get it all done with only one New York trip. And this, of course, will depend upon whether you there decide to wait for Horace to read it until it is in galleys. If you do decide to do this—rather than have him read the stencil copy from Ned [Brown]—that will mean there will be a time gap of how long? two months? before the book is set up in galleys. (I have no idea of the time it will take to do that.) So—anyway, if you decide to wait and have Horace read the galleys then instead of coming to NY now, soon, I think Ill make that Trinidad skindiving trip <u>first</u>, before coming to NY. Then, after that— which might be a month or six weeks, I guess—I intend to get back home here and go right to work on "Laughter."[1]

Yours,

P/TL

---

[1]Jones's intention at that time was to revise *They Shall Inherit the Laughter.* Instead, he wrote *The Pistol.*

New York and Paris Years,

1957-1974

$\mathcal{J}$ones had been under terrific pressure as he finished Some Came Running *late in 1956, and he was ready to be away from the problems brought on by Lowney's increasingly erratic behavior and the strain of writing. He left Marshall for New York, where he hoped to relax. On his first day in New York he met Budd Schulberg, who was a well-established writer, and Jones stayed with him in his apartment. In an interview published in the Summer 1987 issue of* The Paris Review, *Schulberg commented that Jones "seemed at loose ends—somewhere between breaking away from his life in Illinois and not knowing exactly where he could break to." Jones told Schulberg that he needed a woman, and he described what he was looking for: "I'd like someone who looks something like Marilyn Monroe for openers, but who is intelligent, knows writers, who's interested in writing, with a great sense of humor." Schulberg knew just the person for him, a friend of his, Gloria Mosolino, a beautiful blonde who had been a stand-in for Marilyn Monroe, had written an unpublished novel, and knew many writers. When he called Gloria to arrange a blind date, he told her she would like Jones; in fact, he predicted, "I think you're going to marry him."*

Their first date began inauspiciously. Jones arrived two hours late and had already had a great deal to drink. They survived the awkwardness of their first date, began a whirlwind courtship, and within days were talking of marriage.

Gloria was young, beautiful, uninhibited, and a comedienne. She was relaxed and easygoing, unlike the domineering Lowney Handy. Jones returned to Illinois, and Gloria soon followed him; but she did not meet Lowney, who had gone to Florida, where Jones was to meet her for a skin-diving trip to one of the Caribbean islands. Gloria and Jones then drove to Florida, but he did not allow her to see Lowney. Gloria had no idea that Lowney was anything more than her fiancé's foster mother. For many years Jones had stuck to that story.

Gloria flew back to New York from Florida, and Jones was left to break the news to Lowney of his impending marriage. Lowney battled to keep her young, now famous protégé. She suggested a marriage contract which would protect his assets should there be a divorce. When Jones telephoned Gloria to suggest a marriage contract, she rejected it unequivocally. Jones then told her to come to Florida. Soon after she arrived, they left for Haiti and the Hotel Oloffson, where Gloria had stayed several times previously. They were married at the hotel on February 27, 1957. Gloria still had no idea that Jones and Lowney had been lovers.

They spent a three-month honeymoon in Haiti and then returned briefly to New York before going on to Marshall, Illinois. Lowney was friendly the first few times they met, and Harry was a perfect gentleman. Friends came out from New York, and Gloria worked making improvements in the bachelor house Jones had built for himself. Nothing unusual happened until the Fourth of July holiday.

Gloria's young niece Kate Mosolino had come for a visit, and the two of them were downstairs when an agitated Lowney came crashing through the screen door, screaming at Gloria. Gloria sent her niece out of the room, and the agitated Lowney then attacked Gloria with a Bowie knife. The two women fought until Jones came in and separated them. Neither was injured, but it was to affect all the participants traumatically: Lowney had lost Jones to a young and glamorous woman, Jones at long last was going to be forced to speak openly and truthfully about his relationship with Lowney, and Gloria was to learn about an affair previously kept secret from her. Many years afterward Gloria can view those events dispassionately, but at the time she was badly frightened. James and Gloria Jones packed up and left Illinois, never to return. As they drove southward, Gloria learned for the first time the true nature of the Jones-Handy relationship. She felt betrayed, and they fought for days. She would get out of the car and walk alone down the side of the road. Finally, they decided they would never again talk about Lowney, and they did not.

Their marriage was saved, and it was to be for life. It was, as

Willie Morris observed in James Jones: A Friendship, *"the most exceptional marriage that I've ever observed. It was a life they shared of enormous fun and zest, of hard work and creativity. Marriages in the literary world have often been so fused with doom, tragedy and suffering, but this one was something to behold." Morris calls Gloria "one of the truly great women of America." An outgoing, gregarious person, she drew her husband into the social and literary life of New York and Europe, new and important experiences for him after his years of isolation in the Army and in Illinois during his early writing career. She read his work in progress, but she was a sounding board, not an editor. She did not attempt to control Jones's writing as Lowney had done. She became the mother of his children (Kaylie and Jamie) and his constant companion.*

Jones's philosophic outlook, however, remained pessimistic. Burroughs Mitchell gave an explanation: "The dark view of human probabilities that James Jones expressed in his fiction may seem out of accord with his personal life in the adult years—a vigorously enjoyed life, filled with family happiness and many friendships." Mitchell thought that a man holding such dark views as Jones did "will try exceptionally hard to make the most of every good thing he can find in his lifetime." Gloria Jones and the children were at the center of his good life.

The Joneses moved to New York after they left Marshall. Jones began work on The Pistol, *a short, symbolic novel. There were certain business details to be taken care of in Illinois, and Jones had a brief correspondence with the Handys.*

TO HARRY AND LOWNEY HANDY

NEW YORK 21 NEW YORK
MARCH 16, 1958

Dear Harry and Lowney,

Mainly, I am writing to find out whether you intend to reopen and keep running the Colony. Also, to fill you in on what's taken place with us.

First, I am selling the house.[1] Largely this is because Mos[2] and I have decided to live permanently in Europe. We leave for there April 12. And it is better not to keep property, or a residence, here since we don't intend to return. I am retaining the 7 acres of the Montgomery land, as a potential investment. I also expect to retain the Kannemacher lot—unless doing so would lose me a sale of the house. In that event, I shall sell but insist that whoever buys give you access to the Colony in the agreement. It is possible that at some time in future the Kannemacher land together with the strip of Montgomery land behind it may prove a valuable investment too, should there be development out that way. The reason I want to know if you plan to reopen the Colony and continue running it is because if you do, I will turn the jeep title over to the Colony as a donation. The boys will need it. Otherwise I'll sell it if I can.

I have decided also, since we do not intend to return, to sell the contents of the house. This has complexified the problems. Sylvia Millhouse, of course, since she has both mortgages, was the natural person to delegate the authority to sell.[3] I hardly could have done otherwise. But since I've decided to sell the contents, I have written Cas Bennett[4] to handle all legal matters for me and work with Sylvia. And since I am selling the

[1]*Life* on February 11, 1957, referred to the house as a "bizarre $85,000 four room bachelor palace." It was many years before it was sold.
[2]Gloria's nickname, at times spelled "Mos" but most often "Moss."
[3]A member of the Marshall Loan Company staff.
[4]A member of the Bennett & Bennett law firm.

contents, my friend Jay Landesman is going to handle this for me out of St. Louis. He's very bright, and a sharp dealer when it comes to auctions and antiques. The only things I am keeping are the books, which Sylvia has already had stored for me, and my guns which Dick Miller of Princeton is going to take care of for me. These both can be shipped to me in Europe once we are settled. I am keeping a few other things. Gloria wants the gold coffee set, and the silver, and these are being stored. Everything else goes. I shall probably never realize half of what I've put into it, but I guess that doesn't really matter. Andy [Turner] may buy the car if Sonny Daly,[5] who was down from Yale yesterday, does not buy it. Please let me know what you intend to do about the Colony so I can know what to do with the jeep. Having been in contact by phone with both Andy and Sylvia, because of this selling, I have heard rumors that you will reopen and that you will not and plan to go to Haiti to live.

Certainly from Doc's last letter, I don't imagine you ever expect to return to Robinson to live. That was a very interesting and intriguing comment you made, Doc, about people having resemblances to people in Robinson. I can understand that.

So much for the business part. As concerns ourselves, you'll be glad to know that *The Pistol* is now finished and in Mitch's hands as a short novel. It runs just under a hundred and fifty pages. Everyone who has seen it is very enthusiastic about it, and I feel satisfied with it myself. At present it looks like it won't be brought out until next year.

Running continues to remain on the bestseller list, though it has dropped a few notches the past two or three weeks. It will of course be some months before we know how much it is really going to sell. So far there have been no really substantial return of books from dealers, only scattered small ones, and

[5]Edwin "Sonny" Daly had been a member of the Colony. His second novel was *Legacy of Love.*

several of the medium-sized jobbers have reordered, although
none of the really big ones have yet. Tom's book has begun,
at Xmas time, to get back quite large returns from jobbers, and
may wind up as a loser. Tom himself is working hard on
another book, the Greek one, and should be finished soon, he
says. Sonny has finished a new book, his school project, and
Mitch is very pleased with it, says it is much better than the
first and shows real growth, both in content and in style. As
far as *Running* is concerned we won't know for some time its
final disposition, although of course it is not selling as well as
I had hoped. That doesn't matter, of course; it's a damned good
book. But I could use the loot. Its price, of course, is very
nearly prohibitive, but even at that—especially because of
that—it is doing very well, I think.

As for ourselves, we have been meeting lots of people, and
going lots of places, and picking up lots of material for my
New York novel. We plan to spend a month in London,
then live at least a year in Paris to pick up material for the
Django[6] novel. Then we will probably buy a house in Italy I
expect, though this is indefinite as yet. In any case we will
live there a while, no matter where we finally settle. At present, I expect to do the short combat novel next, while living
in Paris.

I read in the *Newsweek* piece that Harry is working on a
novel.[7] That's fine. There certainly is one in Robinson and the
Ohio Oil. And Doc has the organizational type of mind that
is a necessity to a really good novelist. Luck with it.

Oh, yes. One other thing. I believe that my share of stock
which Doc bought for me in the CC Country Club still reposes
in Doc's safety deposit box in Robinson. Is that not right? The

---

[6] Jones intended to write a novel about Django Reinhardt, the jazz guitarist.
The novel was not completed.

[7] *Newsweek* reported on January 13, 1958, that as proof of Lowney's contention
that she could teach anyone to write, Harry was spending four hours a day
at the typewriter working on a novel. Harry's novel was never published.

reason I ask is because, living permanently in Europe as we will be, I intend to cancel my membership. I have written the CCCC asking that my membership be cancelled, and asking if it is possible to sell the $100 share of stock. If it is possible, I would like to have it back along with the note, Doc, when you all get back to Illinois.

I have given Andy all the tools in the garage, and all the liquor, and all the canned goods that were left.

Please let me know what disposition you intend to make with the Colony, so I will know what to do with the jeep.

As I said, we leave on the *Liberté* of the French Line on April 12. After April 10 address all mail to me care of Scribner's. I have written the post office in Marshall to do the same.

Mos joins me in sending all our best to you both,

T/TL/C

After Jones moved to New York, he saw Mailer socially, and they also resumed their correspondence. Mailer had begun writing a column for the Village Voice, *and on April 25, 1956, had published a piece on the hipster:*

Hip is an American existentialism profoundly different from French Existentialism because Hip is based on a mysticism of the flesh, and its origins can be traced back into all the undercurrents and underworlds of American life, back into the instinctive apprehension and appreciation of existence which one finds in the Negro and the soldier, in the criminal psychopath and the dope addict and jazz musician, in the prostitute, in the actor, in the—if one can visualize such a possibility—in the marriage of the call-girl and the psychoanalyst.

He continued to write and think about hipsterism and finally published his creative essay "The White Negro" on that subject. Mailer probably sent the April 25, 1956, column to Jones.

Mailer had written Jones on February 25, 1958, objecting to what he considered the didactic presentation in The Pistol. *Mailer ended that letter on a friendly note, saying that Jones was the only person who had a chance of understanding him.*

TO NORMAN MAILER

NYC
3-18-58

Dear Norm,

Here's your article back. I enjoyed reading it. I can't agree with it—or, rather, let me say I can't agree with your quasi-religious-philosophical points you deduce from the material. I think Hipsterism is a good illustration of a swiftly accelerating decadence, like a good many other things. But I can't honestly see it as a new method of approach to "The full living" that intellectually guided revolution failed to achieve. But that's neither here nor there; you could very easily be right. In any case, you're pushing out and not drawing back in, and that can only help a writer's work.

I don't agree with you at all about *The Pistol.* First, I think it exists by itself solely on the level of being alive, real people and real events. Whether or not beyond that it exists as an accurate symbolization is something else again. But I think it does—if only because of the so many startlingly different reactions I've had from people who've read it. The pistol means something different to each—and means it with pretty strong effect. So much for that.

I was sorry about the other night. But as I said then, I still think Adele [Mailer] was pretty much out of line. Not only with Mos, but with a number of things she said to me which I ignored: trying to get my goat over this or that thing, telling me about a conversation (unflattering in the extreme) which she had heard in the hall about me, and did I want to know what people <u>really</u> thought about me? and when I said sure I'd like to know, suddenly getting coy and saying she had better not tell me after all, it might distress me too much. I just didn't feel like spending an evening which obviously was going to turn into some kind of belligerent hassle, possibly a great verbal fight. And as for me and you having a fist fight, that's something I never intend to engage in—for one reason because it's unimportant to me which of us could physically whip the other; and for another, as I said then, it would give Adele too great a happiness. All of this will probably alienate Adele completely, if not also yourself. If so, I'm sorry. Adele's a remarkably sweet gal when she's sober and I like her. So does Mos. We don't either one enjoy her much when she's had a few; too many underground things start coming out. I guess I'm the same way sometimes, as far as that goes. In any case, the evening we had after we left you sure wasn't any great shakes of an evening. But at least it was quiet and without any emotional sword-twirling.

I'll be calling you in a couple days, but I guess I'd better let you get, and read, this first. If you'd still like to come in town and spend an afternoon hoisting a few beers and talking cheap writing shit, I'd like to do it before we leave.

Rose [Styron], as you probably already know by now, has had her new offspring, another girl. We went up to visit a couple times, and saw it, and I must say I'm never very much moved by new infants. When they get old enough to be people and have a head, I can enjoy them—for short periods, but I sure have no desire to cuddle infants. Rosie is fine, and went through her "ordeal" with no more trouble or fanfare than a siege of constipation. Billy was much more upset than she, and we sort of rode herd on him for a few days, father-sitting we call it. And I can understand it myself, I think. There's something obscene about the way once he's knocked his wife up, a husband is sort of shunted off into the dim background, while wife and doctor have the baby together. I don't know why our society should make such taboos. I'm sure most wives are not especially for such a way of doing it. After all, the kid is partly the father's; although it's come to appear any more that in the end the doctor owns a bigger piece of the offspring than the old man.

As I said, I'll be calling you in a few days. And if you feel like writing me back a letter and calling me a no-good son of a bitch, please do so. I guess I'm just getting too old and too slowed down for that kind of perpetual hassling. If that's what you call living out at the furthest edges of danger, then I'm not for it, and will never make a hipster. I think sometimes maybe you romanticize these people a little bit—the way Hemingway did his "young eagles" he used to go on pass with in Italy.

Give our best to Adele, if she wants it, and keep some for yourself.

Best,

T/TL/C

The Joneses decided to move to Europe. There were tax benefits to be claimed by those living abroad, they could more easily use his foreign royalties, and living expenses were cheaper than in New York. Too, Jones was thinking of writing a novel about Django Reinhardt who lived in France. He had, however, begun work on The Thin Red Line. *The Joneses lived in London for a time before settling in Paris.*

TO BURROUGHS MITCHELL

LONDON S.W. I

ENGLAND

JUNE 10, 1958

Dear Mitch,

Nothing much new to report here, so this will really only be a garbled note. We ran into Synatra [*sic*] here at the Caprice, a more-or-less-ritzy nightclub-supper joint, and he had already told us that he had signed to be Dave Hirsh.[1] That's good from the movie point of view, because he's the hottest thing around now, I guess. It might conceivably mean me and Moss might even make a little off the picture. But I doubt it.

The past two weeks I've been doing a heartbreaking job, but have stood up very well under it. I mentioned it to Horace today in a letter, but only you can really grasp it I think. I've been going through in detail the German cuts on *Running*. I turned it over to Collins' head editor Milton Waldman yesterday. I'm glad I did it, for the British version anyway. I don't know what they had in mind, but at the end of the book they had cut completely the chapter where Dawnie seduces Shotridge into marriage, and then the later chapter on Dawnie and Shotridge at the U. of Illinois. To do that, at least to me, destroys the meaning and structure of the entire Dawn and

[1] The central character in *Some Came Running*.

Wally story. I put it back, pruning it unmercifully as I did, but there's still a lot of pages put back. I found that the German editor had assiduously cut every mention of the "end of the Roman Empire" business, which I also put back. Likewise the "mind froze" business of Mrs Hirsh and Vic Herschmidt. I also found a number of other places where open editing was done, and will write Fischer about this. I don't care what they do with their German edition, but intend to warn them that I feel they've seriously hurt the book by the Dawnie cuts. I've allowed the whole "driving lesson" and Civil War sequence including the fight in the cabin to come out of the British edition, although this cut was not actually made by the German editor, though he suggested it as a possibility.

You mentioned in one letter to Moss that you'll have to take some copies back from the stores but hope to sell them at reduced price when the movie comes out. But that was all you said, and I'm wondering just what the situation is regarding sales? I hope the book hasn't been a loss for you. Write me the details, will you?

. . . .

Anyway, I'm now working on *Red Line*. At present I have only four pages, the very beginning scene, which is quite catching and good. . . .

Yours,

P/TL

TO BURROUGHS MITCHELL

LONDON, ENGLAND

AUGUST 1, 1958

Dear Mitch,

. . . .

I now have 73 1/2 pages of the first chapter of *Line* finished. I expect it to run another ten pages or so. And I hope to finish it up, and copy it up also, before leaving here for Paris, which will pretty definitely be the 11th (August) as we see it now.

I don't remember just what I've written you about it: I don't think anything, since first starting out on it. I've not been keeping letter carbons since coming abroad. Anyway, here is about the way it lines itself up to me now:

The actual novel itself, which is the story of an infantry company followed through its initial combat (Guadalcanal) and its changes and reactions, and how it is different afterwards. The book will end with the outfit leaving for yet another island, with the idea that there is a pretty nearly infinite number of islands still ahead. This part will be handled in very long chapters, actually sections really, but I prefer labeling them chapters, which will run upwards of 70 to 100 pages, without any breaks or stopping points or reliefs in them, one long continuous section, skipping from viewpoint to viewpoint as occasion warrants. This first section is on the disembarkation from the transport, and the others will be on various events or conditions of the life, such as the bivouac, the first real fight, the first relief, second fight, etc., without ever so labeling them though. They will just be "Chapter I," "Chapter II," etc.

Then, in between these long unrelieved sections I intend to insert short italicized sections of three to five or more pages, never more than ten, all done in the first person by a man who is older and looking back at that war from the world of today, and the ghastly state it is in.[1] These interchapters will carry pretty much the same tone as the short story "A Bottle of Cream," and the character of the I person will be quite similar to the man in "Bottle of Cream." I have his personality all figured out, but have not yet attempted one of the sketches. He is a man of thirty-eight who after the war went to college on the GI bill and became a professor of English in a small mid-

[1]Jones eventually abandoned the plan to use interchapters in *The Thin Red Line.*

west town; he became involved in the loyalty oath business, and now no longer teaches; instead, he runs a tavern like the man in "Bottle of Cream"; however, he was not kicked out of college over the loyalty oath but because of drinking; that was when he started the tavern. He believes in drinking. It may even be the salvation of the world, he thinks. At least it is a very necessary palliative. This man thinks about writing a novel about his war, and attempting to explain it, if not to the world, at least to himself. However, this man and his short interchapters have no relation to the rest of the book at all. You do not know if this is his novel he is thinking of writing, or whether he is one of the characters in the novel itself, or whether he was even in that theater of war. Structurally, of course, and "philosophically," he is tied to these young men, though. In his interchapters, I want to get that peculiar haunting quality which stands out so much in "Bottle of Cream" and is really its best quality. It's a hard thing to describe, but I think you'll know what I mean if you remember the story, or re-read it.

The style—the tone, rather—the modal quality—of the other part, the long sections (chapters) of the novel itself will be highly contrasted to the hauntingness of the interchapters. I've already accomplished it, in this first section; and when I finish and go back to copy up, will heighten it even more. It too is very hard to describe in words, but you'll see when you read it. It's a very taut, cold-blooded style, not reportorial exactly, but something like that—provided a reporter could comment on the insides of the people as well as the outside, if, of course, the reporter was smart enough! There's absolutely no sentimentality in it; almost no sentiment, even. So far the humor that I used to speak of isn't there, or at least it's that very subtle type of humor, not the belly-laugh kind. Every time I try to inject that kind of humor it somehow becomes too glib, too slick, too easy—or something. So I haven't tried to force it upon the material. That kind of humor, I find increasingly, must come from an individual character, such as Maggio, rather than from the material itself, if it is not to be merely pert.

Well, there you are. I hope to be able to send you a copy of
the first long section before we leave here, and possibly a copy
of the first interchapter, if I have time enough to write it <u>right</u>.
If not, will send that from Paris. . . .

Yours,

Jim

p/TLS

Jones was faced with complicated tax laws, and he needed to negotiate foreign rights for his novels. He employed a Swiss firm to help with these European problems.

TO BURROUGHS MITCHELL

17, QUAI AUX FLEURS
PARIS IV
JANUARY 24, 1959

Dear Mitch:

First off, so you won't be shocked into a coronary, this one is being written through a secretary, a friend of ours here who needs the money and whose work I need. I finally had to succumb to the pressure of business letters, especially since this Swiss deal with Horace, and I must say it's a helluva relief—should have done it ages ago.

Thanks for your comments on the Interchapter. I'm still not satisfied with it. Somehow it doesn't quite get the emotional flavor of the bartender in "Bottle of Cream." Essentially that man is not as intelligent and as intellectual as I want this man to be. Whether I can even fuse the two is a question. At present I'm going on with Chapter 2 and the next long sequence of the acclimatization period before the combat. I think now I'll try to finish all the combat parts first and then do all the Interchapters in a bunch. For instance, the current Russian trend against vodka will have shown more shape one way or another by the time I finish the book proper.

Moss and I are both very glad of course about the reviews of *The Pistol*. I think it was very magnanimous of [Orville] Prescott to even suppose the possibility that I might even be smart enough to, in my awkward way, attempt to use symbolic meaning. I feel rather like you in your last note of the 14th—I guess I have a mildly vindictive nature also. How big an edition of *The Pistol* did you print? I don't think you've ever mentioned? I think you said advance sale was 17,000. I've received also the "Book-of-the-Month-Club" folder advertising *The Pistol* in the number-one spot. That should help some.

If you want to call Horace he can fill you in on the present status of *The Pistol* moviewise. I wrote him a long letter about it. I'm not satisfied with Irving Allen's approach to it or his attitude. He seemed too determined to commercialize it with all the worst connotations of that term. If Horace so advises me that I can legally get out of the deal, I will then be faced with a problem of my own which is whether or not to withdraw and try to work on it with a director myself; or let it go and just take Allen's money and withhold my name from the script. My writing of the script has been advertised around in several clippings that we've seen. Another clipping (probably untrue) says that Allen has gotten our boy Frankie [Sinatra] to do it after he comes back from Burma and doing Tom's [Chamales] book. I rather doubt this. However, if it's true, it could make a good deal of difference to the whole situation.

Concerning the movie contract for *The Thin Red Line* or for "No Peace I Find,"[1] I will keep in mind what you've said about giving a hard-back edition time to run before the pocketbooks come out in conjunction with the film. At present Ned Brown has some wild highfalutin' scheme about selling the rights to "No Peace I Find" to a guy named Harold Mirisch for $300,000 plus all kinds of bonuses and extras, that money to be held in escrow until the novel is completed. It sounds wacky to me and I have explained that it may take four years to write the book. Mirisch is apparently undeterred by that. My experience in the past with Hollywood has been that they talk like kings, but are very hard to part from any money, and in any case, Moss raised the point as to where the interest of that $300,000 will go during those four years. If it doesn't go to me or if it goes to Mirisch, I say screw it any way.

I wish I could make up my mind what to do about *The Pistol*,

---

[1]The jazz novel Jones did not complete.

but at present I cannot decide until, first, I hear from Horace about the legal status and, secondly, until I hear from Irving Allen the results of his trip to Hollywood. I don't intend to sign the contracts until both of these results are in.

Regarding Presses de la Cité: after great machinations and labyrinthine political maneuvering, which included among other things, my telling them I thought they were full of shit in not getting good translators, I have been able to squeeze from them, as from a bone-dry sponge, one drop: a letter of permission for my friend Anselme[2] to translate *The Pistol*. Since his return I have been dealing with Monsieur Georges Roditi rather than the Nielsons père and fils. At least Roditi is interested in literature. He seems like a nice man, though terribly bourgeois and pedantic as only French literary men can be apparently. Nevertheless, I think he is an astute editor, so it looks like I won't we leaving them now after all.

. . . .

I guess that's about all for now. I keep plugging on the new chapter, but I find I'm having difficulty coordinating my late hour research on jazz and booze, together with three French lessons a week, with my working time. Paris has suddenly become very social for the Jones'. Let me know what happens with *The Pistol* or anything else for that matter, and you'll hear from me soon.

Yours,
Jim

p/TLS

[2]Jones met Daniel Anselme, the French writer, at Le Petit Pavé.

Jones stayed on good terms with several writers who had been members of the Colony, including Edwin Daly, whose second novel, Legacy of Love, *had recently been published.*

TO EDWIN DALY

PARIS

JANUARY 28, 1959

Dear Sonny:

. . . .

What you said about a "master-tutor" or a "father-son" relationship is true, I think. It has always made for a sort of reticence or awkwardness on my part too. I have never known quite how to get around it. I have felt a difficulty in our talking together as much as you have, but I've never known what to do about it. Certainly I haven't wanted any "master-tutor" relationship. On the other hand, just out of sheer accumulation of experience in writing, I have been able to help you a little bit now and then and I have known more about the technical aspects of writing than you have had. God knows I don't feel like any "master." You sound rather pissed-off and depressed and somewhat worried when you mention giving up graduate school work. I can't blame you for being irritated with the majority of asses which will be foisting themselves on the future as professors. On the other hand, I think anybody could tell you that the percentage of asses in any profession, even that of a novelist, remains pretty constant. In thinking about this this morning when your letter came, I wondered why you don't consider having a shot at Paris for a year or so. If you could finish the year at Stanford without too much vomiting, perhaps then you could arrange some sort of fellowship which would allow you to come to Paris for a year to study. I know Americans here who are doing this. If you do it this way, it will make you exempt from the Army (which is of the most importance too, of course) for the time that you are here. I know students who are working for Master's and who are given some credit for this work here, which work generally begins with a semester of French, so that you can take other courses in French at the Sorbonne.

This is just an idea, but I think you would really love it here. Where we hang out, the St-Germain section of the Left Bank, it is full of all kinds of artistic ferment—painters, writers, poets, playwrights, many of whom are Americans. Actually, the percentage of asses applies here as well as at Stanford. Just about every other store is a gallery and, having painted, you would love the quality of the Paris light. I don't know what makes it and I have never seen it adequately written about in English. I have actually watched the sunlight and shade on the same side of the same building all day long and have never seen it look quite the same twice. In talking to other people, I've learned that this peculiar lighting quality is indigenous to the Department of the Île de France and I'm sure that explains a lot of the reason why Paris is a painters' city. Moss and I have been buying a few pictures (you can't help it after you've been here a little while). Nothing expensive, but all of them things which we both like very much and which might one day be valuable. That actually is not important if we like the work and like looking at it.

(Moss is just yelling at me to tell you that she liked *Legacy of Love* very much.) You know Moss well enough to know that she wouldn't say such a thing unless she really meant it. As for me, I liked it too. I can't give you a blow-by-blow description as to what I felt about it just now because I loaned my copy to a young American here whom we happened to meet. His name is Jonathan Kozal (it's either "zal" or "sal").[1] Perhaps you know of him. At any rate, he knows of you. His first novel came out the same time as *Some Must Watch*, I think—perhaps

---

[1]Jonathan Kozol, author of *Death at an Early Age* and *Rachel and Her Children*.

it came out in conjunction with *Legacy*. At any rate, Kozal
(whose novel was called *The Fume of Poppies*) knows about you
and about your being in the Scholar of the House programme
at Yale. He himself graduated from Harvard (and didn't very
much like it there). After that he became a Rhodes Scholar at
Oxford, but after half-a-semester gave it up to come to Paris
and write. He said it was, if not completely phony, at least
largely phony. He has recently finished a second novel which
he has sent off to his girl at Radcliffe because she's going to type
it for him. He now lives in a very cheap hotel, is wearing a
beard and no haircut, is very consciously dirty as becomes an
artist and having himself a ball. Nevertheless, he is not a phony.
His girl is going to join him in the summer and I fear she may
be deeply shocked at the change in him. At any rate, if his
parents saw him now they would probably take the first jet to
Paris to manacle him and bring him home. In spite of all of that,
as I said, he is not a phony. I expect he'll grow out of the
beard-toting stage in another six months or so. At any rate, it's
a lot of pleasure to watch him having so much fun being dirty
for the first time he has been free to in his life. He, as well as
some others I've met, have probably influenced my thinking
about the fact that it might be good (as well as a good evasion
of the Army) for you to come here. But of course that's something you'll have to work out for yourself. Anyway, Kozal was
most eager to read *Legacy* and I broke my rule about loaning
books and let him borrow it. . . .

Sincerely,

T/TL/C

Jones first met Styron in 1952, and their friendship developed over the years. Their bantering correspondence had little of the edginess of the Jones-Mailer letters.

TO WILLIAM AND ROSE STYRON

17, QUAI AUX FLEURS
PARIS IV
FEBRUARY 3, 1959

Dear Billy and Rose,

It was great to get your letter. I've been silently cursing you for not writing also. Now that I got me a secretary (part-time), I'm trying to catch up on a lot of letters. Some of them go as far back as 1957. I want to thank you also for the clippings. It's good to find out that all is well with the world, but who the hell is J. J. Miller? Are you sure you don't mean Henry Miller?

You would love our apartment. I can stand in the window and piss in the Seine, but I don't do it. No kidding, the river is really beautiful.

I wish you hadn't invited Moss to come live with youall whenever she's mad. Three times now since we got your letter she has packed a bag and started off for Roxbury. The only thing that has stopped her is the fact that I'm smart enough never to give her any money.

We've been getting a lot of reviews from Romeike. A few of them accuse me of being an adolescent with one thumb up my ass, but in general they've been very laudatory—almost always for the wrong reasons. It's amusing, if not also the reason for biting chunks out of yourself, to see what various wrong things reviewers can ascribe to both you and your work. If we weren't so neurotic, it would almost be reason enough to stop writing altogether.

We were glad to hear about *The Long March* making it on TV even though it turned out exactly like the movies of both my books. For God's sake, don't go and see *Some Came Running*—(but tell all your friends to go and indeed write letters to the newspapers if they want to—good letters, I mean).

What is the news with you and Norman? Mickey Knox, whom I think you know, was here in Paris for several weeks and should now be back in New York. He had a hard time. His mother died and he was apparently very close to her. Perhaps almost too close. He hears from Norman all the time and told me Norman had finally made the move back to New York. Probably better for him.

We certainly would love to have you come to Paris. It's been a lovely half-year here. In actual fact, we've taken a villa in Portofino for next summer, July, August and September, and should you be coming then we'll have enough extra rooms to put you up for a little while. But we can coordinate all that long before you come.

I know what you mean by the way you feel about your book right now. That long stage of ending up when you can see everything in front of you clearly but can't quite get there is the worst of all. I myself have been working on the same eight pages for three fucking weeks now and it's still not right. It got so bad that finally I just abandoned it and slept for a few days. Now I'm girding my jock strap to go back to work. It's a miserable profession any way you look at it and nobody but goddam fools like you and me would ever want to have anything to do with it.

You will be most pleased to learn that I now have a goddamn liver condition from excessive drinking. It isn't as bad as your potential ulcer, I guess, but it's the next best thing. At any rate, it hasn't become sclerosis yet. I'm going to knock off drinking entirely for a month or six weeks and see if I can clear it up. I'll probably be a gibbering maniac by that time, because about the only time I can ever feel hopeful for the world is when I'm blind drunk and just falling drunkenly to sleep. Such a pretty world—people really ought to enjoy it more. Anyway, to be in Paris and not drink wine is worse than your getting postcards from us from Rapallo. (Did you notice the mistake I made—confusing Rapallo with Ravello?) We never did get to Ravello.

Please, now that we've started, let's don't wait six months or a year before writing again. Moss and I both send both our love to Rosie and the younguns. It looks like we may be living in Paris permanently and if so, we'll be getting a larger apartment. And if we do, just remember that the latchstring will always be out.

Always all our best to you yourself,

Yours,

T/TL/C

TO R. P. ADAMS

17, QUAI AUX FLEURS
PARIS IV
MAY 18, 1959

Dear Dick:

. . . .

I enjoyed our lunch with old Stallman[1] and particularly listening to you two died-in-the-wool academics get going on us poor writers. Out of it has come a new understanding of just how ex post facto literary criticism really is—a thing I had always believed before anyway, but not with such <u>physical</u> clarity.

As for noting the relation between individual and institution, I'm willing to agree with you that a powerful individual can act effectively—as in Warden, whom you mentioned. I mean, I do not believe, as Mailer did with Croft, that <u>all</u> action is futile. On the other hand, I'm coming increasingly to see, I

---

[1]Adams was teaching at the Université de Lyons that year. R. W. Stallman was the Stephen Crane scholar.

think, that whether or not a given individual can act effectively makes very little difference. This is Ironic. And is the result of this increasing separation between the individual himself and the institution of which he is a part. I myself see no way out of the fact that government acquires personality and must attempt to perpetuate itself like any individual personality. And the only answer I can see for the future is that thing of living "underground" in the heart, and mind, that we spoke about. If that makes me cynical, and thereby pushes me further from modern romanticism, I can't help it, even though I'm sorry. At any rate, I would like to get your ideas on just where such a point of view would fit in with modern romanticism and the Organic Metaphor.

It was fun seeing you again and I hope we can arrange to get together in the summer before you go. Gloria joins me in sending all the best to yourself and to your family.

Yours,

T/TL/C

TO BURROUGHS MITCHELL

IL CASTELETTO
PORTOFINO, ITALY
14 SEPTEMBER 1959

Dear Mitch,

It's been some time since I've written. We've been leading a pretty full life here, what with diving, swimming, sailing, etc. in the afternoons and writing in the mornings and then boozing at night.

In addition to that I've had a siege of—not ill health, it's not that bad; but of not feeling quite well and energetic. For some reason this summer seems to have been selected to point out to me that I am no longer really a "young" man. I find myself still staring in astonishment and wanting to say, "But see here, you don't understand. This is me!" Anyway, the upshot of it all is, when discarding the highflown scientific crap about toxicity of the blood and all that, I just have to cut down on the boozing, smoking, overeating. So I'm doing that.

As for *Line*, I am now about 85 pages into Chapter 3. At present rate, this is about ⅔ of the Chapter which means it's getting a little long. I think before I finish I shall go back over the whole thing, cutting as I go and then perhaps copy it up before going on and finishing. In connection with cutting, you mentioned to me that you thought some cutting might be good in what you've read; and I am curious as to just what type of cutting you refer to. It might help me with this part if you could give me page numbers of the type of thing you mean.

I find this a singularly strange book to write. Moss insists (after all, she took several psych courses at Syracuse) that my semi-illhealth is due to psychic reluctance to write this book— or at least is caused by the enormous mental effort I'm expending. Maybe she has something there; I don't know. I do know that Kay Kendall's death has affected both of us terribly strongly.[1] And then you know I had a crazy attack of "digestive vertigo," whatever the fuck that is; nothing serious, but for over an hour while we were getting a doctor up this fucking hill, I lay there believing I was on the way out—I was absolutely convinced of it.[2] Moss says she would never have known from the way I acted; but I believed it. I guess I still haven't gotten entirely over that. My own eventual death is much closer to me now than it has ever been, even during the war. Anyway, the book itself plus all of this other has made it difficult.

I've figured a way to avoid, I think, one of what I originally considered the six necessary chapters. I'll just leave the last one off, and perhaps include a little of the effect that I

[1] The actress who died of leukemia. Rex Harrison and his wife Kay were neighbors of the Joneses in Portofino.
[2] This was the beginning of his illness (congestive heart failure) but was misdiagnosed by an Italian doctor.

want in the end of Chapter 5. You know the structure: 1) Debarkation; 2) Pre-combat; 3) First Combat; 4) First Relief; 5) Second Combat (so different from the first); 6) Second Relief (End of Campaign; and also so different from First Relief). I'm hoping to be able [to] cut the Sixth Chapter out altogether. But if it injures the overall point, I of course can't do it. But in actual effect, what I want to get is a rather small, not consciously profound book, light perhaps even, but because of all this frightening, after one finishes it. I feel it is becoming too long—the whole book, not just this section. So much of military life can be implied without great detail, now; so much has been written of it. Also, I feel that in fact there is not as much humor, cynical humor in it as I wanted in the beginning. I can't seem to do it, and after it's all done may want to go back over it to inject more of this humor. In a way this book is a labor of love; one that I'm doing because I just want to. I don't expect it to sell. And as far as I'm concerned to hell with dramatic technique in this one. The other night in Rome (we went there for a week a few days ago) I was in my cups and trying to describe this book to some ass who asked me about it and I called it "a combat novel in a Proustian style." Well, in a way that's what I'm working toward in it. But I think that every ounce of cutting that can be done to it will be all to the good. About injecting the humor after, I'm not so positive; perhaps it just wasn't meant by my psyche to be written that way. But the cutting, while intensifying the effect will also add to the petite oeuvre effect I want to make with it.

As to the big book [*No Peace I Find*], it's rather hard to talk about coherently. Some things have clarified both philosophically and materially. For instance, the structure and shape. When I do it, I want to do it in three parts, like this/: each in varying length/:

1)---------

2)-----------------

3)----------------------------------

Part 1 to be the actual days of the liberation of Paris; and in which the principal characters all meet, all being in Paris for one reason or another. They all meet in bistro where fictional "Django" is playing; all are equal lovers of his work.

Part 2, longer as you see, to be the postwar Existential period in Paris; again the principal characters meet, but now after several years of Postwar all have changed; many conflicts arise where before there was only unalloyed joy at the Liberation; the fictional "Django" becomes the center of all this contention; there are battles, disagreements, perhaps a fight or two.

Part 3, by far and away the longest section, to be contemporary, during the period in which we ourselves are living there— which of course is the period I know best. Here the principal characters to be fully explored as older people; the conflicts (still centering around the fictional "Django") to be fully developed and resolved—largely in misunderstanding and hatred; perhaps even a killing; all of it, the whole work, obviously a parallel with what happened to the world itself in that period.

This is as you see all pretty general. Of course I do not want to write a political allegory. And the things which will make or break the book here are the principal characters. All of the characters will be modeled on people I've met of course, and to date I have only three. One myself, another a French writer, another an English critic and writer. The French writer is from Danny Anselme, about whom I've written you; the Englishman from Ken Tynan, whom you may have met in New York. Perhaps I won't draw the American from myself. Or if I do, will add another American (a chauvinist) to offset. The French writer will be an ardent Communist; the Englishman an ardent socialist—as those two are. Their women and their loves will come into it too. And over all of this the huge background of Paris nightlife and the world of Jazz. Did you read my interview in *Paris Review*?[3]

[3]The interview appeared in *The Paris Review*, no. 20 (1959), pp. 35-55.

As it stands right now, I want to have these people all fighting over the fictional "Django." Each wanting to claim him for "his" side. And at present my idea is to portray the fictional "Django" merely going his amoral way, smoking pot, playing the music he loves to soothe his inarticulate sorrow and hungers, paying no attention at all to these various philosophical idealists who want to claim him; while these others fight, argue and kill each other over him and their ideals, he by boozing and bad living lands himself in an early grave because of his own inarticulate hungers like a Tom Wolfe of Jazz.

All of this plan is the result of what "research" I've done on Django. Each man or woman has a so totally different picture of him that it is impossible to fit any two together as being even part of the same man. But in general he's considered stupid, not dependable, lazy, etc. or else he is over-heroized. But he never seemed to do or care about anything except drinking, fucking and playing. It's hard to make a subject out of just this, without sentimentalizing him, and this was what gave me the idea of making him an <u>object</u>.

Of course as I say, the whole damn thing will still hang on the characters themselves. There will also be all kinds of minor characters, some jazzmen, some not. But this is the essential plan and shape I've got so far.

I'd be glad to have any suggestions or thinks that you have. You can see how the original concept has changed from the original title-idea *No Peace I Find*,[4] though I still intend to use that title.

The jazz will be hardest to make authentic. Most of my personal jazz experience, in which I'm sure of myself, dates back to pre-modern, and I've got a lot to learn about the modern and hypermodern.

The whole philosophic concept is based in the belief that the only way individuality as we know it can and will survive in the future will be by going underground and living on the edge

[4]Jones did not complete his jazz novel.

of the law, while giving it lipservice, a try at resolving that paradox. This is my own thinking, which is an attempt to study integrity too, is also an attempt to carry Camus's self-destructive Rebel one step further.

Let us hear from you soon. We leave for Paris the end of September. Moss sends her love.

Yours,

Jim

PS—Why have you not sent us Tom Chamales' new book?
         "   "   "   "   "   " other books you deem interesting?
                   "   are you neglecting your moral duties?
What did Cecile Gray[5] mean by saying Tom had made "An inscription" to Moss & Marilyn Monroe?
Moss says tell you she wants *Gimpel the Fool.* [6]

Love,

Jim

p/TLS

---

[5] One of Gloria's closest friends.
[6] By Isaac Bashevis Singer.

Jones read Mailer's "The Mind of an Outlaw" in Esquire *(November 1959), a piece which appeared in* Advertisements for Myself. *The* Esquire *article dealt with the difficulties Mailer had in finding a publisher for* The Deer Park. *Jones had not yet acquired* Advertisements, *but when he did, he was enraged by the comments on himself and Styron and other writers of their generation. In the section "Evaluations—Quick and Expensive Comments on the Talent in the Room" Mailer began with praise: "The only one of my contemporaries who I felt had more talent than myself was James Jones. And he has also been the one writer of my time for whom I felt any love." He then declared that Jones had "sold out" and that he had lost his rebelliousness. He disliked* Some Came Running *and referred to* The Pistol *as "a dud." He concluded: "If Jones stops trying to be the first novelist to end as a multimillionaire; if he gives up the lust to measure his talent by the money he makes; if he dares not to castrate his hatred of society with a literary politician's assy cultivation of it, then I would have to root for him because he may have been born to write a great novel."*

Mailer called Lie Down in Darkness *"the prettiest novel of our generation" and charged that Styron "has spent years oiling every literary lever and power which could help him on his way."*

In Peter Manso's Mailer: His Life and Times, *Gloria Jones has described Jones's "hurt and anger": "One way Jim had of dealing with this was that he would have people sign the book and write marginalia. Someone would visit, and Jim would read the part about that person, and then they'd get mad and sign the book, write comments in the margin."*

Gloria went on to report that Mailer and Jones met for the last time in 1972 or 1973: "They were very polite with each other. I don't think Jim would've taken any shit from Norman, but he'd also grown out of all that . . . because he was facing a sure death. Wouldn't you have believed there was affection in spite of the breakup? I mean, these two men, they're probably the two best of what are really the six best of that generation. I think Norman knows Jim was really good, and Jim, I know, right to the end felt exactly the same about Norman." Jones's ambivalent feelings about Mailer can also be seen in the letter to Mickey Knox, April 24, 1972, quoted later in this book.

TO NORMAN MAILER

17, QUAI AUX FLEURS,
PARIS
NOVEMBER 18, 1959

Dear Norman:

I hope this letter reaches you at the address which Mickey Knox had on his letter of last spring. I am putting "Please Forward" on it in case it doesn't.

I just finished reading the piece in *Esquire* last night, the piece from the new book, and it made me very sad. I am not sure I can say exactly why. But there seems to be such a tremendous awareness of an immense expenditure of energy, perhaps never to be recovered in order to re-expend. I guess that's always sad. And the romantic theory that the prodigal expenditure of energy always renews with still greater energy to expend just doesn't work any more after a certain age. I was scared pretty bad myself this past summer with regard to health, so in a way I can understand somewhat.

A couple of weeks ago, or one week ago, I read the *Time* piece on *Advertisements* and was so incensed that I determined to write you right away.[1] As usual, I didn't do it, but now at last I am—or at least I am trying to—the impetus being the *Esquire* piece. I haven't yet tried to get a copy of *Advertisements*. It probably won't be here for a little while yet, but I'll buy one at Brentano's as soon as I can.

[1]The *Time* review of *Advertisements for Myself* appeared in the November 2, 1959, issue, p. 90. The reviewer wrote: "By the early 1950s the spare, controlled prose of *The Naked and the Dead* had turned sour and turgid, and the author was drifting in a haze of liquor, seconal and marijuana."

Mentioning Brentano's brings Paris to mind, which reminds me that I wanted to say I was very sorry you were not able to get here as you planned on your last trip. I was asked to Phil Brooks' (a very nice man, in our sense of the word) cocktail [party] for you, only to find that Richard Wright was there and you were not.

I liked the article in *Esquire* and thought it very honest. I must say, it infuriated me that American letters can be in such a state that a man of your caliber should feel required to write it. That American letters is in such a state, I know only too goddamned well. Perhaps the piece, and the book itself, can shake some sense or balls or both back into some of those people. But I doubt it.

I assume that the book, in its main tenor at any rate, is pretty much in the same vein and viewpoint. Anyway, I can only talk about the piece I read. But if I were to say anything critical about it, it would be that perhaps in a way it is too honest, or an attempt to be too honest. Honesty is a funny thing. At least in my case. It seems to me that the more I search for honesty, the harder I analyze, the more I try to prove to myself my honesty's honesty, to understand fully my own motives, the further I get away from all honesty. And yet sometimes when being most dishonest, and yet at the same time the most spontaneous, I find myself capable of being more honest than when I am earnestly trying. Big mish-mash of words. I tried to say something I can smell, and failed to say it. This is the story of my fucking life.

Anyway, there was something I had in my head that I wanted to try to say to you.

I read the prologue of the novel in *Partisan*.[2] Knowing nothing about it of course, except your own hint, I neverthe-

---

[2]"Advertisements for Myself on the Way Out" appeared first in *Partisan Review* (Fall 1958) and was then reprinted in *Advertisements for Myself*. This was one section of an epic novel, never completed, using two characters from *The Deer Park*—Marion Faye and Sergius O'Shaugnessy—as major figures. Mailer published in *Advertisements* one other part of that novel, "The Time of Her Time."

less recognized Marian, and Sergius as the narrator. It's a terribly exciting idea. If anything bothered me, I think it was the style; although I think I understand what you were trying to do with it, it seemed to me to get lost in its own machinations. But then nobody could judge well in a piece that short. And anyway, who the hell am I to judge in any case? If I can only get done half the amount of my own work that I'd like to, I won't have time for judging anything of anybody's.

I seem to have rambled all over the fucking place, straining my ass to say something and saying absolutely nothing. The only thing I can wind up with is to say fuck all those bastards. They should suffocate in their own dry rot. I still think it's better to ignore them completely. Gloria joins me in sending both our love to you. If you need it at all, you have it, for what it's worth. If I say anything more, I'll become maudlin, and sentimental, and probably insincere to boot. If you ever feel like writing, do.

Yours,

T/TL/C

TO BURROUGHS MITCHELL

17, QUAI AUX FLEURS
PARIS 4E FRANCE
DECEMBER 2, 1959

Dear Mitch:

Judy Mullen[1] is sending off today the first part of Chapter 3. Naturally I'll be anxious to hear what you think of it. In a way, I suppose this Chapter 3 is the whole crux of the book. What you're getting now runs 133 pages and I seriously doubt if it can be cut very much. It may be possible to cut it yet again some more, but even if we do, such cuts must necessarily be stylistic, I think; they would not be sufficient to shorten the

---

[1] Jones's secretary.

length. As you know, I originally planned to do the book in five, possibly six, chapters, each dealing with one phase of the company's progression through the campaign. I still like that idea, and because of this I have decided to split Chapter 3 into two parts—I and II. The point at which I've made the break is a good one, I think. I expect the second part will run almost as long as the first, which means Chapter 3 will run somewhere in the neighborhood of 230 pages. There will be no Interchapter between I and II of Chapter 3. Chapter 4 I do not expect to be as long as the others, even shorter than Chapter 1, which to date is the shortest. That's the way it stands now. In any case, let me know what you think of this section as soon as you can. Yet once again I am finding a book growing on me in such a way that I cannot contain it to the original length I anticipated. This book, however, certainly won't run much over 600 typescript pages.

I don't know if you know the work of James Baldwin, a young American Negro writer. Novels: *Go Tell It on the Mountain,* and *Giovanni's Room;* essays: *Notes of a Native Son.* I first met Jimmy in New York before we left and subsequently have spent a good deal of time with him off and on when he is here. He is not happy with his present publisher, which is Dial, I think. He is leaving for New York in a couple of weeks and I suggested he call you up and go see you when he gets back. He has read us some portions of his new novel (which is being done in any case by Dial, per contract) and I think some of it is truly magnificent writing. He might be a good man for you to have should you and he hit it off and should he continue his decision to change. He is also getting rid of Helen Strauss as his agent, a very mature decision from my point of view.

Nothing much new here. Gloria is pregnant at present and we're hoping she'll be able to keep this one. Other than that there isn't much new to say.

Please let me hear as soon as you can.

Yours,
Jim

P.S. I'm giving this P.S. to Judy over the phone. It's one of the most important things I wanted to say in the letter but forgot. A friend here who read the manuscript made the complimentary comment that Fife is emerging as a fine major character. I don't want this. Because of that, I intend to change the scene where the Japanese is killed from Fife to Bead. This can be done simply by changing the name alone, with the addition of perhaps a single sentence at the very end of the chapter where they are climbing down into the basin. Also, which was the main reason for the phone call anyway, I forgot to add a sentence on page 22, which I have had Judy put in for me so she can mail the manuscript today. When you read this scene you will note the added sentence. I think it very important, because having read the scene to several people it was unclear to almost everyone whether Fife and Bead were committing pederasty or fellatio. I think this a very important point because if they're having fellatio it places Fife in as equally guilty a position in his own mind as Bead. If, however, it were pederasty Fife could escape guilt by rationalizing to himself that he was committing only a male action. This changes the whole scene. And that is why I feel it very necessary that in some way the specific act be made apparent to an adult reader. We may have a big fight about this later, but I consider it of truly prime importance. (And I don't intend to give in this time.)

Jim

p/TLS

TO BURROUGHS MITCHELL

10, QUAI D'ORLÉANS, PARIS
SEPTEMBER 17, 1960

Dear Mitch:

I've not felt up to writing before, what with the baby, the work on the apartment and everything else. Actually, I couldn't begin to give you a full report without writing at least half a novel on it. Suffice it to say that the baby [Kaylie] is in fine health and so is the mother and we now seem to be settling down to some kind of a reasonable life in the new apartment. She is a pretty kid and if I can't find one to include in this letter, I will be sending a couple pictures of her before very long. Incidentally, with your permission, I intend making you her official legal guardian in my will in the event that Moss and I should die together. You and Horace of course will be the administrators of my estate. What we intend, should such miserable tragedy befall us all, is that Gloria's cousin Florrie in Palisades, New Jersey, raise the child. She's a marvelous warm woman and great with children; but I would like for you to be the moreorless official, administrative guardian.

The new apartment, to describe it well, would require much more time and space than I can give it at the moment. I don't know how well you remember Paris, but there are two islands in the center of the river. Île St. Louis is the smaller one. The larger one, which we used to live on, has Notre Dame and a lot of the administrative offices of the city on it. This one here is much more like a tiny village set down in the heart of Paris all by itself. The people who live here feel that way about it. Our apartment faces on the river, as did the old one on the other island, but this time we are on the south, or sunny, side, so that we will be getting sun through our two windows on the river all through the winter. Living-room, dining-room and kitchen are in a 1920's building built on the Quai itself, while nursery, bedroom and my office are in a much older building circa 1680, connected by an interior staircase and corridor about half a floor high. When I feel up to it one day, I'll take some pictures and send you some snapshots of it.

As for the book, I went right back into it as soon as we moved in here, a new experience for me because usually it takes me several weeks to get back into writing. At the moment, I am just finishing up the second long half of Chapter Three (which at the moment I'm pretty sure I will subdivide into two chapters, making Chapter Three the one that you have, Chapter Four the one I'm about to send you). I have about 10 to 12 more pages to write on it. It covers the first full day of actual combat fighting of C-for-Charlie company. In length it is about 176 pages long and should go 10 to 15 more pages. I don't remember if I wrote you the growing concept of the structure of this book, but at present the way I see it is somewhat like a graph-line, starting low at the left-hand side, rising slowly and then more swiftly into the center of the page, then swiftly and then more slowly dropping away to the righthand corner, so that the intensity of the book itself is rather like a hill.

This means that the climax emotionally is reached in the center of the book. After this intense time of their first battle, the men themselves slowly become insensitive and inured to the whole thing so the tone of the end is rather like it is at the first—a low key feeling. In any case, I will send this on to you as so on as it is done. It should be done in a week or two.

As for finishing up the book, I don't really expect to be done by December as I had hoped. The apartment and the baby, plus the writing of the screen treatment[1] to pay for part of the apartment, have taken close to four months off of my working time. But now that I'm settled in here and back at work, I think it will go fairly fast. Once all of this actual combat writing stuff is finished, I shall address myself to the Interchapters.

[1] To meet his pressing financial needs, Jones often worked on film scripts during his years in Paris. He worked on Zanuck's *The Longest Day* to help pay for the new apartment. His film experience was not an altogether pleasant one. He wrote Darryl F. Zanuck that he was *"morally shocked"* by the Johnson Office expressing "concern" because of the "excessive slaughter" in the script. "What did they think Omaha was, if not a 'bloodbath'?" he wrote on October 23, 1961. He also prepared several scripts never produced.

I'm sorry to hear that you won't be making it over this year, but if you're coming next spring, it really won't make too terribly much difference. We certainly look forward to seeing you. Also, I've no intention of coming to New York while you're on a European trip, so our own trip (when the manuscript is finished) will have to come after your trip to Europe.

With regard to your letter of July 18th about the French royalties being paid direct, I don't really care whether they're paid direct or not as long as I have the information ahead of time for the French accountant. If Scribner's could let me know around the 1st of December exactly what my French royalty payments have been for that year, I will be able to turn it over to my accountant in plenty of time to do the tax statement in early January.

We too have heard from Childs,[2] and of his magnificent treatment at the hands of the Japanese. So far I have not done anything seriously about writing the little pieces to go along with his engravings. He tells me a Japanese firm is very interested in doing these as a book, my pieces and his engravings. I may take a few days off after I finish Chapter Four and see what I can come up with before beginning the next chapter of the novel.

I must say I feel very good about the novel as it now stands and as I hope it will be when finished. I read several passages from it to Bill Styron and his wife when they were here recently, and both of them were very excited and impressed with it. I think it's actually the best writing that I have ever done to date, true to the way people are (rather than as they like to think they are), cleaner in style, more mature and less romantic, and consequently more humorous in its approach to human existence.

With regard to Norman Podhoretz, now editor of *Commentary* or any other goddam thing, I deny ever having gotten drunk with him. In the first place, he couldn't drink long

---

[2]Bernard Childs, the painter.

enough to get drunk with me—not that that's any compliment to me. In the second place, he's sort of a shitty little guy and while I was pleasant enough to him, I didn't like him at all. Incidentally, did you receive a carbon copy of the letter I sent to Rust Hills of *Esquire* about *The Thin Red Line*? They had written me, you know, wanting to see it. Perhaps I went a little too far in calling Gingrich[3] "a shrivelled asshole," but after that shitty speech he made here that's what he really is called. I'm getting more and more tired of all these fucking fools who inhabit the literary life like some kind of soft creatures turned up from under a rock. No wonder there are so few good writers around. If these guys had their way, there wouldn't be any.

The girls send you their love and so do I. Let me hear from you when you can.

Yours,
Jim

P.S. If Jack Wheelock still comes into the office from time to time, will you please give him my best and tell him I will write him some time soon.

. . . .

p/TLS

---

[3]Arnold Gingrich, publisher of *Esquire*.

The strained relations with Mailer continued. After Mailer stabbed his wife Adele, Jones wrote Mitch on December 19, 1960: "I think a lot of it has to do with the fact that he has a lousy wife. . . . Several of our mutual friends here have sent Norman notes of sympathy, but I didn't really know what to say except to tell him what I really thought, which would only make him angry, so I haven't bothered to write anything since the last insulting letter I got from him a year ago. . . ."

Mailer's comments about Jones, Styron, and others continued to rankle. Jones wrote Mitchell on April 4, 1962, that he and Gloria had seen Mailer at the Club Rive Gauche: "Moss and I came in and he was sitting there with a group we knew. I said hello to one of the people who was looking right at me, and went on to the bar, where I sat me down . . . (as did Moss) and then we left. One by one, the people all came over (loving it all, of course) and asked me if we wouldn't like to join them, and I said no thank you. There was some laughter from the table. Norman went to the john right past us and did not say anything to me and I didn't say anything to him. He did, I found out much later, say something to Moss. This I didn't know at the time. (Moss didn't tell me for fear I'd be mad.) What he said was: 'I'll see you later, Gloria.' Whatever the fuck that was supposed to mean."

TO BURROUGHS MITCHELL

10, QUAI D'ORLÉANS
PARIS 4ÈME FRANCE
27 APRIL 1962

Dear Mitch,

I saw Hope Leresche[1] a few days ago here, and have some questions to ask you about foreign rights etc., but first I want to copy off for you what I received in the mail today, totally unexpectedly:

[1] Jones's agent in London who worked with translations of his works.

April 22nd 1962

My Dear Jimmy,

Just to prove that I mean it, to whom it may concern:

The Thin Red Line, the line between man and beast, so easily crossed, is a realistic fable, symbolic without symbols, mythological and yet completely factual, a sort of *Moby Dick* without the white whale, deeply philosophical without any philosophizing whatsoever. Touched by a weird, resigned and yet light-hearted, ironic, and even optimistic acceptance of our animal nature, with constant flashes of a sly, dark, peculiar humour, written with a deceptive facility that is the mark of truly great writing, this extraordinary novel achieves epic proportions through the magic of a joyful love of life and humanity, absolutely unique in contemporary literature. The book belongs to that vein of poetical realism which is the rarest and to me the most precious thing in the whole history of the novel; it is essentially an epic love poem about the human predicament and like all great books it leaves one with a feeling of wonder and hope.

ROMAIN GARY

I don't have to tell you what this made me feel. I was sitting on the bed laughing and crying like an idiot. I tried to call Romain but got no answer. He said Monday that he was leaving for Rome for a couple of weeks, so he must have written this just before he left. Naturally, I would not want this used for publicity without first getting Romain's permission, although by the way he wrote it he may have meant I was free to use it. However, I value it too much to let it be used for publicity without his permission specifically. Should he say okay, it might be a good thing to put on the original jacket before reviews.

. . . .

Yours,
Jim

P/TLS

After The Thin Red Line *was published—it received enthusiastic critical reception and sold well—the Joneses went to Jamaica
for an extended stay. Jones's skin diving experiences there were
incorporated into* Go to the Widow-Maker; *the central characters
in that novel were based on James and Gloria Jones and Harry and
Lowney Handy.*

TO ROMAIN GARY

MONTEGO BAY, [JAMAICA]
OCT. 21, 1962

Dear Romain,

· · · ·

I imagine you have now somewhat come to terms with that
miserable agony you were passing through when we left, having to do with getting a new book started. I myself am in that
phase now. Keep saying all day: I <u>have</u> written! I <u>have</u>! I <u>have</u>!
But it's always as if one had never done anything but talk about
art, as one did in one's youth without knowing a fucking damn
thing about it. Ah, well.

We've decided to stay on here until the end or middle of
Feb, before returning to Paris. I have several diving trips still
to make both on the island and to other keys and island groups
nearby. Actually, where we live here on the north coast both
the spearfishing and the bottom formations are dull, not exciting enough for the material I need.

· · · ·

Yours,

T/TL/C

Although Jones had a sizable annual income from royalties, with additional funds from his articles for journals and his film work, the Joneses had heavy expenses in Paris, their travels were costly, and he was generous to friends and fellow writers. His business letters indicate that he was constantly short of funds. He did not have an American agent and dealt directly with Scribner's, a firm which was conservative in its policies concerning advances. The Scott Meredith Agency then approached Jones; a Mr. Morrison from that organization informed him that a publisher would guarantee Jones $300,000 for his next two books.

TO BURROUGHS MITCHELL

PARIS 4 ÈME
10 JUNE 1963

Dear Mitch

I don't think you're any more of a businessman than I am. Anyway, your letter seems to me to be a bit vague about this thing in a couple of ways. The whole point of this sneaky offer, or so it seems to me, is the guarantee by a publisher to pay me $300,000. for the delivery of two books. Call it advance, call it whatever, the main point is that this here publisher promises me that he will guarantee me $150,000. profit each for two novels. Now I know that, usually, a novel doesn't make for its author $100,000.—let alon[e] $150,000.— from its original edition. I doubt if *Line* will make me that much. So that what this publisher is saying to me is that he, in order to have my illustrious self, will guarantee me that much whatever the book makes. If the book makes more, he's ahead, and if it doesn't he's out of pocket whatever the difference is.

That's a very different thing from the kind of advance you and I used to talk about. Which, namely, was an advance of money which eventually—whether for this book or another—would be paid back to the publisher out of royalties. See what I mean?

The reason you and I didn't talk about an advance was because I was thinking in terms only of a sort of loan—but this kind of a deal is a guarantee to the author of such and such a sum.

You know as well as I that I don't want to leave Scribner's at all. So why don't we do this? (Since I aint scared of bein indentured) Why don't you and Horace draw up some kind of a letter agreement, or something—a new contract if Horace thinks that is the proper way—which says that you guys (Scribner) will advance me $150,000. each for my next two novels, to be taken out of royalties (if royalties should reach that figure) and not to be repaid by me should royalties not reach that figure. Then I am guaranteed that amount of loot, no matter what the books make. I will sign it, and you can sign it. That way, everybody's safe for at least two books. And these other people can all go fuck themselves.

That seems reasonable to me. Does it to you? And when Mr Morrison calls again, (He called again last Friday.) I'll just tell him that Scribner matched that particular offer, and there's no 10% that's needed to be paid to an agent.

What's wrong with that?

Since I don't mind at all to be indentured for that kind of money, all that I can see wrong with it is that I now have to go and write two goddamned books before I can collect.

But as far as limiting my yearly income goes, all this money can by contract be paid to me at X number of dollars a year—which is what these other people suggested anyway.

Now that all that business crap is over, I'd like to be able to go on and tell you some news, gossip, etc. However, there isn't any to tell; I've had a bad throat infection for the past three weeks, which has forced me to cut down drinking and smoking which is probably damned good for me. It isn't all cleared up yet, but it's better and should be totally gone in another week or so.

Both the girls send their love, as do I.

Yours,
Jim

p/TLS

Mitchell responded to Jones's letter by explaining that Scribner's had a policy against multibook contracts and offered a $150,000 guarantee for the next book, with no agent's fee involved. Jones answered that he wished a guarantee of $300,000 for his next two books, and on June 14 Mitchell agreed and sent the necessary contracts.

TO BURROUGHS MITCHELL

PARIS 4 ÈME
19 JUNE 1963

Dear Mitch,

Herewith the signed contracts. Please give my copy to Horace to hold for me.

I was glad it worked out as it did. I was also pleased to tell Mr Morrison of Scott Meredith that I was rejecting the offer. I did not tell him anything else; only that I had a lot of loyalty problems with Scribner because of Max Perkins and yourself, and the house itself, so I was turning the offer down. It was a very short transatlantic conversation.

Things are hectic here. We're beginning now the modifications necessary to enlarge the apartment with the ground floor one we bought a month ago. They will be tearing a hole in the livingroom floor soon to make a staircase. Merde! However, I will be moving all of my office upstairs in a week, as soon as Addie Herder[1] moves out and into her new apartment. Then I will have three small rooms away from everything to work in—including the wild indian kids who live on our street.

Right now, as soon as I get a final draft of Chapter 1,[2] I intend to lay it aside and tackle some of those four or five remaining childhood stories I've wanted to do. In view of that,

[1]The painter who had long been a friend of Gloria's.
[2]*Go to the Widow-Maker.*

maybe you would like to think about bringing out that book of childhood stories first? It's something to think about, anyway. Four more ought to be enough, shouldn't it? I don't even know how many I have. I've already got the 1st line for "The Ice-Cream Headache," the one about adolescent incest: "There was nothing Faulknerian about the town, but there was something Faulknerian about the family." Good, hunh?[3]

All of us send our love.

Yours
Jim

. . . .

p/TLS

---

[3]The Faulknerian family in the story was based on the Jones family.

*The Joneses met Mary McCarthy and her husband James West
soon after arriving in Paris. The two couples often visited each
other. Jones sent McCarthy the manuscript of "Sons of Hemingway," which was to appear in the December 1963 issue of* Esquire.

TO MARY MCCARTHY

10, QUAI D'ORLÉANS
PARIS 4 ÈME
26 JULY 1963

Dear Mary,

Thanks for returning the piece, and for your criticism.
You're right, I hadn't meant for you to criticize it; and naturally, I don't agree with your criticism at all or I wouldn't have
written the piece that way. And I'm not at all sure that your
reaction will be the same as that of another good reader.

My whole point with the Pamplona piece was that it was our
first time, that we allowed ourselves to be taken in hand by this
bunch of guys, "writers," (deliberately, to see what would
happen) and that this was what happened. A whole generation
of guys limping through life because they believed what one
dirty old man told them about "life" and "manliness." Dirty
old liar, rather. A sort of gentle spoof of the whole syndrome.
What you call wobbly diction was a deliberate juxtaposition:
"highclass" words against "lowclass" words; "literary" words
against "tough guy" words; "intellectual" words against
"nonintellectual" words. You might also note that there are
actual Hemingway-type phrases scattered (unobtrusively, it is
true) all the way through it: "<u>the</u> hands high up over <u>the</u>
head"—"<u>the</u> career to think about," etc.—the old Hemingway
falsely symbolizing definite article. I am puzzled by your reference to "in-references"; I thought it selfevident that they referred to the group who had us in tow. The only one I find
I myself might be guilty of was the conversation with the Yale
boy in the seats, and that was absolutely factual.

However, if one needs to explain these things, they havent gotten across obviously. Of course, it is possible that with your own particular approach you either over-read into it, or else under-read into it.

I myself thought the "Lovely War" part was the least good and least interesting, largely because it was so predictable from me. (And if you'd known those English ladies, you'd have said lady too; even Gloria was being a lady, they were so ladylike).

. . .

Love,

T/TL/C

TO BURROUGHS MITCHELL

PARIS 4 ÈME

16 AUGUST 1963

Dear Mitch,

Here is the new first chapter, begun since our return to France. The old first chapter (never right) will (considerably rewritten) now become the 2nd Chapter which will deal [with] Ron Grant's period in NY just before going to Jamaica, his love affair, and if it works, a sufficient résumé of his long affair with Carol Abernathy (the mistress) in Indianapolis. However, that may require inserted small flashbacks all through. I'm not decided yet. As I'm not even decided what the fucking book is all about. Maybe I'll learn as I write it?

I think it's all pretty good. The length does not bother. It moves well, it hooks the reader well. What do you think? Make you want to read more? You will note the explicitness about sex. It's going to get worse—or better(?); we talked about that. I don't know how I can write it without being a great deal more explicit than up to now.

I've held off writing you until I could send this. But it's dragged on and on. We took a week in Pamplona, which you may read about in next Dec *Esquire* in a "European Letter" by me. Call Harold Hayes for tear sheets if you don't want to wait.

I now have my "office" finished in the 2nd floor back, above our bedroom. Most extra money we had since coming back has gone into that, and I'm now moved in. It makes working much much better and easier now. I spend almost the whole day up here. However, we are not doing any remodeling on the other part (the rez-de-chaussée) which we bought under our living room. We haven't the money to do anything at the moment. I'm hoping Bernheim[1] will arrange a film job for me doing a Western with a guy named Nicholas Ray: this will probably take a couple of months, but the money is needed. We really overextended ourselves by buying the downstairs. However, when it's finally finished, we'll have almost a mansion where we can live forever on practically nothing.

. . . .

Love from all of us.
Jim

P/TLS

[1]Alain Bernheim, the agent who represented Jones in film work.

In "Some Children of the Goddess" published in the July 1963 issue of Esquire, *Mailer mentioned Styron's reading aloud "absurd passages of Jones' worst prose," and Styron wrote to explain that he had been envious of Jones for having broken the barrier of the second novel. The Jones-Styron friendship was not disturbed by Mailer's article.*

TO WILLIAM STYRON

10, QUAI D'ORLÉANS, PARIS

1 AUGUST 1963

Dear Bill,

In going through some mail that had accumulated too high, I found your letter of June 6 which I never answered. But I did send you a drunken card from Spain, I think?

The whole thing of Norman's piece is a sort of tempest teapot hardly worth pissing in to put the fire out. John Crosby, who is straining hard to find stories for his column, came over and talked to me about it, saying he thought he might write a column on Norman, and must he foul the nest so. I don't know if John has yet done it. Anyway, it won't matter if he doesn't.

Anyway, this is a note to tell you that I've just had accepted my first *Esquire* Paris Letter. It consists of three short pieces: one about Pamplona entitled "Sons of Hemingway, or Cigars, Fried Food and Red Wine"; one about *Oh What a Lovely War* entitled "Oh, What a Lousy Race"; and one about Norman Mailer the critic entitled "Small Comment from a Penitent Novelist." If you're interested, call Hayes or Byron Dobell[1] and have them send you tear sheets. They should be printing right away.

I thought it was about time some one of us said a word or two about Norman's monopolizing the generation.

[1] An editor at *Esquire*.

What's new with you guys? We will stay in Paris through August and probably all fall. I am working hard and achieving little. But it moves a little. Are you and Rosie, the wife, planning to come over here at all this year?

After I finish final draft of chapter 1, I'm going to knock off and do four or five childhood stories that I've got cooking, hoping to bring out a book of just childhood stories, between now and the next novel. My editor Mitch says it might be nice for a change to see a novelist who uses his childhood for a collection of stories instead of the inevitable childhood novel. Love to One, Two, Three, Four, and Pup. From us all.

T/TL/C

Irwin Shaw, author of The Young Lions, *was one of Jones's closest friends. They saw each other often, and as a consequence there were few letters between them.*

TO IRWIN SHAW

Dear Irwin,

    . . . .

I'm sorry to hear about your appendix, but a big strong man like you ought to be able to take that in stride without missing more than two or three days skiing. I remember I had mine out in Hawaii in 1940, largely because I was bored with garrison straight duty in the Infantry. I remember the first day they let me out on pass, they told me to take it easy; I immediately headed straight for a whorehouse, where the girl looked at me when I undressed, shaved belly, Mercurochrome, an 11 inch band of tape, and all, and said: "My God! What happened to you? You have an abortion?"

    . . . .

Best,

T/TL/C

TO BURROUGHS MITCHELL

Dear Mitch,

Esquire is interested in the possibility of printing Chapter I of the new book.[1] I have therefore told Byron Dobell to call

---

[1] *Go to the Widow-Maker.*

you and ask to read your copy. I don't want to send him mine because I am constantly referring to it here. Chapter III is now finished. I finished copying it up today. I now find I will need still a third chapter to wind up the New York love affair flash back. I'm very pleased with it. I will be starting Chapter IV tomorrow and when I have finished it, and have a finished sequence of the New York flash back, I will send it on to you.

Line has been doing very well in France. All I know about Germany is that the Fischers[2] tell me it is doing well. They seem rather strange the last few years, withdrawn. Although they keep inviting us to their place in Italy.

I wondered did Don Sackrider mention whether Willy was with Lowney Handy.[3] I had a letter from her via Horace saying she had bought a house in Florida, meant to stay there till she died and wanted to give me the Handy Colony grounds. I wrote her some time back asking that she will the *Eternity* manuscript to Kaylie. She informed me forcefully that the manuscript would go to her relatives when she died.[4] Incidentally, do you ever remember either she or Harry stating in your presence that the *Eternity* manuscript was to be left to me in both their wills? That was the understanding I had with them when I gave it to them. At one time it <u>was</u> written in their wills. I can not think of any way of proving this, though. As a matter of fact, I don't know what has happened to the original manuscripts of *The Pistol* and of *Line*. Did I leave them with you to be boxed? I think you have the boxed manuscript of *Running*.

You may be interested to hear that old Tom [Chamales] may turn up as a character in this new book.

Moss joins me in sending all love.

Yours,
Jim

p/TLS

[2]The Fischers were his German publishers.
[3]Don Sackrider and Willard "Willie" Lindsay had been students of Lowney's.
[4]Lowney's heirs are still in possession of the manuscript of *Eternity*.

TO BURROUGHS MITCHELL

10, QUAI D'ORLÉANS, PARIS
SEPTEMBER 30, 1964

Dear Mitch,

I made notes some time back to ask you if you could send me a copy of the book on Hemingway by his brother Leicster. Also if you could check with the head of the book store to put me on to a permanent rare book dealer. My old man John Loos must be long dead by now.

I was 39 pages into Chapter X when I realized that it wasn't working. I have now begun to revamp it, and it's a miserable chore. So far I've cut a great deal out of it, but at present I'm at a total loss as to how it ought to go. I've been trying to tighten and condense this book as much as totally possible, and this may be that crucial point at which it will become a "long" book, or a "short" one (à la Jones). I've really been hung up, and the advent of Ambrose[1] (thanks much for your wire) has not helped. I'm struggling very hard with this; I want to make this a "short" (à la Jones) book. I have a hunch this is the point at which that decision must be made. The last few days I've done much more thinking than writing, though I put in my regular hours. The form has not yet crystallized, but I'm still hoping that it will. If it doesn't, I guess it will be a "long" (à la Jones) book. If I don't cut off my ear in the next few weeks, I will let you know what happened.

Everyone sends love.

Yours,
James Jones

P/TLS

---

[1]The Joneses' son, Jamie.

Jones's money problems were not completely solved. His new contractual agreement with Scribner's guaranteed him $150,000 for each of next two novels, but he did not receive advances. He had been reading about Scott Fitzgerald's having to plead for money from Scribner's, and the conservative fiscal policies of his publisher continued to bother Jones. During this time of his discontent, Irwin Shaw told Jones about his advantageous contract with Delacorte Press. Minor problems with Scribner's continued—his publishers initially refused to pay for Jones to attend a literary celebration at the World's Fair in New York—and Jones's dissatisfaction grew. He considered signing a contract with Trident Press. Before he could do so, Donald Fine, who was in charge at Delacorte, contacted him, but Jones was not interested. Fine would not take no for an answer and flew to Paris to see Jones. Fine agreed to match the Trident offer. The Delacorte agreement called for $725,000 for three novels, plus perks that substantially increased that figure.

It was especially painful for Jones to leave Burroughs Mitchell, for they had worked closely together on all the novels Jones had published, they shared many of the same ideas, and they had become personal friends.

After Jones left Scribner's in 1965, Mitchell wrote in The Education of an Editor: *"I saw little of him. Both of us had some feeling of strain, I suppose, which gradually wore off." Whenever the Joneses came to New York, they made certain that Mitchell was invited to the parties they attended. The two continued to correspond, though not with the regularity of earlier times. After Jones's death Gloria asked Mitchell, then retired from Scribner's, to edit* Whistle, *and he agreed to do so.*

TO BURROUGHS MITCHELL

10, QUAI D'ORLÉANS, PARIS
NOVEMBER 19, 1964

Dear Mitch,

While Alain Bernheim was in the States he became affiliated officially with another agency which is called Ashley Famous. This agency has a literary department, something Bernheim never had, and totally unbeknown to me on Bernheim's authority they began making inquiries around as to just how good a deal they could make me with a publisher. I want to make it plain to you that I knew nothing about all this, and I did not learn about it until Bernheim returned to Paris. At that time, when he told me, it was all very vague and indecisive, and I said forget it and went on working. However, at the other end, they went ahead—without any letter or authorization from me. At that time what they had come up with was not spectacularly different from the contract I have with you. However, in the last few days they have come up with such a stupendous offer that I simply do not see how I can avoid looking into it further and, if it checks out with all that Bernheim has told me, accepting it.

Therefore, I want to ask you if Scribner's would be willing to release me from the contract for this book.

As you know, there has been quite a revolution going on in publishing in America. Because of it certain publishers, usually affiliated with soft covers in one way or another, are able to make offers that the old-line houses simply are unable to match. This is something I had nothing to do with creating, and is something that I'm not at all sure I like, but it's something I simply cannot ignore. Not with a family, which if I drop dead tomorrow would be in serious straits simply through tax problems. A lot of this has to do with tax benefits which apparently the old-line houses cannot, or are unwilling to, match.

I have never had any complaint, or not any very serious

ones, about the way I have been treated by Scribner's. If I have ever criticized Scribner's, it has always been because they have not modernized the house in ways which would allow them to take advantage of these modern ways by which overtaxation of authors can be avoided. I have said this to you several times I think. Last year, when this $300,000 deal came through, I turned it down out of loyalty and affection for the house, and because of my close friendship and excellent working relationship with yourself. In all honesty I think had you not been my editor at Scribner's I would have taken it. But this new offer is so much bigger than that one that I simply don't see how I can avoid accepting it.

The only problem remaining, now that I've struggled it out with myself on this matter, is the current contract I have with you. Bernheim wanted to know about the possibility of my "buying it back." I pointed out that due to the terms I don't owe Scribner's anything on this book, that moreover I have an equity of $60,000-something. Therefore, I would be free to change provided you people will release me.

This is probably the hardest letter I've ever had to write. I think of you and Harry [Brague], and Cathie, and Wallace and old Whitney [Darrow] and all the lunches and the hours hanging around on the fifth floor and I don't really know if I can do it. On the other hand, this is an offer that will give me total financial security for the entire rest of my life, plus the important fact that Gloria and the kids would be totally taken care of no matter when I died.

Can I please hear from you soonest about the release?

Gloria joins me in sending all our love.

Yours,
James Jones

P/TLS

Jones's first novel for Delacorte was Go to the Widow-Maker,
*a critical failure. After reading it, Styron wrote Jones a long letter
praising the narrative drive and the believable characters, especially
Lucky, based on Gloria Jones. He liked the underwater scenes, but
he especially commended Jones's depiction of the anguish men have
over their maleness. Styron did find faults in the novel: its repeti-
tiveness and the presentation of certain aspects of the Grant-Lucky-
Carol (Jones-Gloria-Lowney) relationship.*

*Styron's comments, astute as they were, aroused Jones, and he
defended his novel against Styron's critical objections.*

TO WILLIAM STYRON

10 QUAI D'ORLÉANS, PARIS
NOVEMBER 24, 1966

Dear Bill,

I never heard anybody so full of shit in my life, though from
your letter you should have been empty at the time! Even so,
it's not a bad letter to get from a noncompeting confrère.

Material things first, literary things second. Your friend and
mine Don Fine was here in Paris and read your letter, and
would like to quote certain lines from it. Would you give your
permission for him to do this? If so you might drop him a line
at Delacorte Press, 750 Third Avenue, saying it's okay. Second
material thing: the copy of my book which you have is in fact
my own second carbon, not a copy or a [X]erox. Now, this
particular copy was given to Paul Jenkins[1] some time back
before the book was even finished, when he did me a favor
which in a round-about way was connected with Gloria's mink
coat. I just wrote him a note today telling him to call you about
it, and could you see that he gets it? His address is 831 Broadway, New York City.

Now, the literary matters. First let me thank you kindly for

[1]The painter friend of James and Gloria Jones.

bragging up the book as much as you did. The bare truth is that Don Fine thought your letter was great, but I was a little pissed-off myself. I shall try to explain why but before I do I wish once again to thank you for your compliments on it.

Probably my most serious criticism of your criticism is that I don't understand how a man of your sensibilities could read this book and not "get" two of the "substantive" (your quote) things about it. Mainly, that Lucky's long range pre-occupation with Mrs. Abernathy is in fact subjective and has to do with her secret feeling that she is in fact a whore; that is clearly explained in the chapters from her viewpoint, it is eminently Catholic and if I went any further into explaining it it would be so overly obvious as to damage the book. This of course is not to say that she is a whore; she obviously is not; but she herself thinks she is or might be and this is what triggers her response to the knowledge of Mrs. Abernathy and Grant. Second, Grant, and this is even more obvious, is of course afraid of cuckoldry because of having himself cuckolded his friend Hunt Abernathy lo these many years. (Even Don Fine got that.) Both are all in there, clearly developed, perfectly feasible to both characters, and whether you personally like this or not has nothing at all to do with the book as a job of work. Therefore, Grant's (your quote) "insane jealousy over the possibility not the fact" is perfectly understandable; and Lucky's (your quote) "bitter and antagonistic feelings toward Ron for so long" is really subjective and was perfectly understandable. As to the technical points you raise, you must be off your nut to say and/or believe that I could cut 200 pages out of the book by (your quote) "cutting the maneuverings of people around hotel lobbies and knocking transitional paragraphs down to laconic sentences."

Just between us turkeys (today is Thanksgiving) what you are probably referring to here is the method I used (deliberately, and consciously) of having various characters describe their own various actions to themselves in the second place, thus giving them a reflective viewpoint of their own actions which if described by me or them in the present would have been impossible. If you want to know, it's a method which I did not create but which was used to great effect by Ford Madox Ford in *Parade's End*. Whether Ford created it or not, I do not know, but that is where I got it. And for this kind of book I think it is, and was, a great advantage.

Naturally, as you said yourself I probably would not listen to you, and I haven't. Particularly I haven't because all of this was deliberately and consciously calculated a long time before. It didn't just happen. And I assumed you knew that. If you are so naive as to term my "lapses" lapses, I am shocked. It's okay to criticize my method, but please don't call it a lapse.

Like I said, the good things you say about it are very pleasing!

Please tell my pal Rosie that it wasn't at all autobiographical; but Bonham is now somewhere on Long Island and Grointon is in Kingston, Jamaica flying small commercial airplanes and no longer a diver. But none of that is really true, since the whole damn thing was all made up. And Cathie Finer has no prototype in real life at all. And as a matter of fact, Ben and Irma were never on any cruise that I know of and certainly not with any prototypes of Ron and Lucky.

Belated congratulations for the new infant, incidentally. Poor little thing, she looks exactly like her daddy; but maybe she'll grow out of that. Kaylie did.

Bill, should you not wish Don Fine to use any quotes from your letter, I will perfectly understand that and won't be angry. Myself, my only personal reason for wanting to use a quote of yours is simply to piss off "Norman Failure."

Enough of this mishmash. It's almost seven and The Moss and I are going to our French dentist's Thanksgiving party of all things. We have to go, since it was us who paid for it. And in ♠s. We will see there your friends Peter and Deborah [Kerr] Viertel.

All our love.

Yours,

T/TL/C

Jones was on good terms with several critics and book reviewers and consistently wrote thoughtful letters to them. Maxwell Geismar was especially perceptive in his review of The Thin Red Line *and praised* Go to the Widow-Maker.

TO MAXWELL GEISMAR

10, QUAI D'ORLÉANS, PARIS
JANUARY 21, 1967

Dear Max,

Your letter of the 29th came while Gloria and I were in Switzerland for the children's Christmas vacation. I've since heard from Don Fine who was quite pleased with your statement about *Widow-Maker* and on myself. I too am pleased with it and wish to thank you for it.

That novel took an awful lot out of me, and I'm just now getting over it though I finished it last June. If you're interested, I wrote about 700 pages of that book between October '65 and June '66. Up to that time I had spent about three years writing the first 600 pages. I think, personally, that this book gets a lot deeper into a lot of things than any of my other work except possibly *Some Came Running.* I am now working on a couple of stories, further to the group of childhood stories I would like to publish in a separate book, and am fiddling around with the beginning of another novel which will wind up the pentology of *Eternity, Pistol, Line,* and *Running*: this one, tentatively titled *The Believers,* [1] will fall between *Line* and *Running* and will concern itself with combat veterans returning to an affluent wildly living home-front wartime society. I would of course hope to make it symbolically applicable by extension to the society of today and the current "conflict."

I did of course realize that you were attacking our literary

---

[1] Published as *Whistle.*

Establishment in the book on James[2] which I enjoyed reading very much. I think you got a bit sticky in it perhaps, here and there and that you are inclined to be a little self-righteous now and then but I certainly wouldn't fault you for that. God knows, good as he is, James needs to be knocked off the God-head pedestal those cats have tried to put him on.

Incidentally, about the nicest compliment I've ever had is where you call me a black-hearted anarchist at the end of your letter!

I have no idea what kind of reception *Widow-Maker* will receive but I'm reasonably sure it will be bad. But then I thought that about *Line,* and look what happened with it—largely due to yourself.

Gloria joins me in sending all our best to you and Ann, and please let me hear from you.

Always yours,
Jim

B/TLS

TO WILLIAM STYRON

10, QUAI D'ORLÉANS, PARIS
FEBRUARY 9, 1967

Dear Bill,
. . . .

Don Fine sent a copy of *Widow-Maker* to Mr. Vance Bourjaily and I received back a strange, turgid, muddy kind of grudgingly praising letter about it from Vance. Most of the letter was taken up with how he was a "hand-tool man himself" and would not like to work with "bulldozers and giant cranes" the way I do as this detracts too much from the subtlety and nuance of his writing. I didn't answer the letter

[2]*Henry James and the Jacobites* (1963).

because I didn't know quite how to. Don Fine had sent us earlier bound galleys of *The Man Who Knew Kennedy,* and although I tried several times I found I could not read it. Gloria did and found it pretty worthless, but I see where it got a good review in *Time* this week. Since I couldn't write all this back to Vance, I decided it was better not to answer his letter at all.

What gives with you? It must seem strange not to have to work every day. Will you and Rosie be coming to Europe now that the book [*The Confessions of Nat Turner*] is finished? I now have a new office one floor above where my old one used to be, and there is a double bed in it now. So we could always put you up.

We ourselves are going to drive down to Florence and stay there for the three weeks of the kids' Easter vacation. We've never been able to spend as much time in Florence as we've wanted. This summer we think we might drive to Greece and take a look at that Skiathos property which you once loaned me the money to buy. There's a whole group of villas there now which one can rent by the month, apparently quite close to our property.

I myself just finished up a 45-page story[1] just yesterday which I think may be pretty good, but I'm pretty sure no magazine will want to publish it since one of its main handles is a brother and sister incest. Still, I can always publish it in the collection of stories when they come out.

Gloria joins me in sending all our love. Kiss Rosie for me. And once again congratulations on the completion of *Nat Turner.*

Yours,

t/tl/c

---

[1]"The Ice-Cream Headache."

When Jones was in the Army and during the years when he was writing Laughter *and* Eternity, *he was lonely and wrote often to his brother, Jeff. After* Eternity *was published, Jones had a wider circle of friends. The interests of the two brothers diverged, and their correspondence was less frequent.*

TO JEFF JONES

10 QUAI D' ORLÉANS, PARIS
JUNE 17, 1967

Dear Jeff,

Thanks for your letter about the book. The reviews have been much worse, in general, than you seem to have realized, back in April. The book seems to have triggered some nerve in most of the reviewers. The three good ones you mentioned are the only ones except for a good review that was in, of all places, the *Chicago Tribune.* In spite of all of that, in spite of the accusation by most of these rabid sons of bitches that the book is dull, it continues to struggle along in the lower regions of the best seller lists. I understand now, just today, that it will go back into eighth place on the *New York Times* list next Sunday. There is still some slight chance that it might really catch on, that happened to *The Caine Mutiny* almost a year after it was published with *Eternity* in the spring of '51, but if *W-M* does it will be a very lucky event. I had expected a great deal of venom but mostly anticipated it from the hinterlands. But I didn't expect the magnitude of it. This of course has to do with the language, and you might read John Thompson in the *New York Review of Books* on this, still another good review which I forgot to mention above.

Strangely enough I had a very nice letter from Kent Lewis[1] about the book and in which he enclosed a piece, with picture,

[1] A newspaper editor from Robinson, Illinois.

about grandfather's house being torn down. Also, Aunt Sadie sent me a review Kent wrote about the book. A praising one.

I think you've got a marvelous subject for a book about the Red Cross. It sounds like a great vehicle to show what is really happening to the technocratic-bureaucratic complex that is America today. God knows what will finally become of it all and I think you really ought to write that book, coldly, objectively.

There is nothing much new to report about us. Kaylie is now finishing 2nd grade, Jamie 1st grade. Our lives are pretty much geared to their school terms now, so that whenever we leave Paris it is during one of their vacations. In a few days we're off to spend a month on a Greek Island, the first time any of us have been around that area. I am in the process of beginning yet another book, one which will complete a trilogy of the war together with *Eternity* and *Line.* Of course if it is any good it will by extension symbolize what is happening today with the current war in Viet-Nam. It will be about the home-front war-economy society and about its impact on a bunch of busted-up vets all of whom come back deeply guilty because they feel they have not done enough. It is in fact the material which I used in that first book before *Eternity,* which I subsequently threw away.

I was glad to hear all the news about the boys, I'm sorry that Dave is getting separated. But as you say, if that's what they want let them have it.

I would like to hear from you when you have the time. We should be back here in a month or so.

Always all my best to everybody.

Yours,

T/TLC

After he was no longer involved with the Colony, Jones went on helping young writers, recommending their novels and stories in dozens of letters to publishers. This one to Mitchell about Daniel Spicehandler, who had previously published Let My Right Hand Wither *and* Burnt Offering, *is typical of those generous letters he sent during his Paris years.*

TO BURROUGHS MITCHELL

10, QUAI D'ORLÉANS, PARIS
SEPTEMBER 21, 1967

Dear Mitch,

A friend of mine here in Paris whose name is Daniel Spicehandler is a pretty damned good writer, I think, and he has a novel which has been turned down several places in America. I have read it and think it strangely brilliant, brilliantly strange. At my suggestion he is sending it to you in a week or so. I am writing to ask you if you will please give it a good reading.

Incidentally, your signed copy of *Widow-Maker* is going off under separate cover today to Tappan. The reason I have not sent it sooner is that the additional books I ordered did not come in until just before we left on vacation June 15. We returned September 17 to find them here.

Everything is pretty much the same with us. The book of course has not done as well as I had hoped, but it's still selling quite well even so. I am now at work on a new one, which is, curiously enough, about the same material I used in that first book—subsequently abandoned, which I brought to Max [Perkins] and Jack [Wheelock]. Incidentally, Gloria told me that she ran into old Jack on the beach at East Hampton last summer and that he would hardly speak to her. I am sorry about that. We both still love him very much, and have a very fond feeling for him. In any case the new book, while using that old material, will be vastly changed in concept, theme, structure and meaning.

I would like to hear from you what you think about *Widow-Maker*, now that all the junk written about it (both pro and con) has been written.

I am sending the book to your home address.

Please do give Danny's book a special reading.

Gloria sends her love.

Always yours,

P.S. Danny tells me he was also once recommended to you by Caroline Gordon. His book is called *The Mossgatherers*.

T/TL/C

Jones's collection of short stories, The Ice-Cream Headache, *was not part of the lucrative three-novel contract with Delacorte. Such collections traditionally do not sell well. Jones's stories, however, received excellent reviews. The* Chicago Sun-Times Book Review, *for instance, noted: "We feel the impact of James Jones's vitality. He is masculine, uninhibited, not abashed by whatever he uncovers of human weakness and sexuality, caring a great deal about getting the main thing right." The Nation wrote that most of the stories had been written early in Jones's career, but "they are anything but dated, and the variety of experiences they convey results not only in very moving fiction but, cumulatively, in a compact social history of what it was like for Mr. Jones's generation to grow up, go to war, marry, and generally, to become people in America." Jones reacted to the laudatory reviews of his short story collection in a letter to his publisher.*

TO DON FINE

10, QUAI D'ORLÉANS, PARIS
OCTOBER 26, 1967

Dear Don,

. . . .

I myself am not too terribly excited about those reviewers treating the story collection well. After the beating I took, I don't give a fuck what they do; I'm sure it will be much easier for them to laud my stories since the volume has no chance at all of becoming a best seller anyway. That's the kind of people they are. The only other comment in that area is the one Mailer keeps sending on to me via various mutual friends, a sanctimonious pronouncement in any case: "When they've knocked you on the last one, they have a tendency to be nice on the next one." As I keep telling these mutual friends, there ain't going to be all that many more for any of us.

   . . . .

Yours,

T/TL/C

Charles, James, and Jeff Jones feuded for several years with Kent V. Lewis, editor of the Robinson Daily News, *after Dr. Jones's death, for Lewis took photographs of the dentist's body after his suicide. However, Lewis wrote a favorable review of* Go to the Widow-Maker *and also sent Jones an article about the tearing down of the Jones mansion. Jones put aside his earlier animosity toward Lewis.*

TO KENT LEWIS

10, QUAI D'ORLÉANS, PARIS
MARCH 18, 1968

Dear Kent,

In going down through a stack of correspondence yea-deep I came across your letter of January 3, which I meant to answer a long time ago—but didn't, mainly because I am damned lazy. In any case, I certainly enjoyed getting it. It may be, as you say, that time and distance lend enchantment to certain views; this is almost certainly true; but I think one's old home town, coupled as it is with one's childhood and childhood memories, holds a special place in this kind of cerebral cheating that we all do to ourselves as time encroaches on our time. I certainly feel that way about Robinson; and it's both strange and hard to think that there is a whole generation of youngsters in Robinson who might be curious about me because I've been away so long. After all, it's only a little over ten years really.

One of the particular reasons I wanted to answer your very pleasurable letter has to do with the fact that a book of my short stories, called *The Ice-Cream Headache*, will be coming out some time this month—if it isn't already out. In this book, which covers stories of mine written from 1947 to 1967, there is one called "Just Like the Girl," of which—in an introductory paragraph—I mentioned having shown it to a newspaper editor in Robinson, and the rather disrupting effect it had on him. In case your memory is as inaccurate as mine, I wanted to make plain to you—personally—that the editor in question was in fact Vic Smith, of the old *Robinson Argus.* Several years ago I wrote Vic asking to subscribe to the *Argus,* just to have, periodically, local news about "the old home town," but I never had an answer. I do not even know if the *Argus* is still extant. In any case the comment was not a personal one at Vic, so much as a statement about our whole way of life in America. If Vic is not dead, and even notices the remark, I hope he won't take it personally.

I noticed in your letter that you mention "Norm Brown's newsstand"; the last time I was there Sy Seligman was still running the newsstand, which was then located on East Main Street just off the Square next-door to Woolworth's. That led me to think, almost automatically of Gordon's Drug Store, which was in the center of the East side of the Square; in my day Bob Gordon the son, who was about my own age, was expected to take it over and continue it. I am wondering if he did, and if he and it are still there?

Also you mention your third wife. This must therefore mean that you and Mary Fran must have parted ways, as they say in the 19th Century English novels. This leads me to think of Tinks Howe, and his marvelous mother, and that farm they had out in the country in the flat land over toward the river. I remember that it was Tinks's mother, taking me over North of Palestine to visit some old great-uncle of hers who was nearly blind and played a fiddle, who first taught me the words of "Plant Your Sweet Potatoes on Sandy Land." The old man sang it for us.

All these things keep coming back. Most particularly I was pleased to have the photograph and piece on granddaddy's old "mansion." In my study here I've got on one wall a bunch of things I value, for serious or for funny—such as my Bronze Star and Purple Heart citations and the *Holiday* Magazine Worst Book of the Year award for 1967; and among these is the picture and article on grandfather's house hanging right up there with all the rest.

. . . .

It's hard to envision the Country Club with an 18-hole course. Where did they put in the other nine holes? If I remember right, it could only be up on the North alongside the County Road, where there used to be a hog wallow we kids used to go swimming in.

It all seems so long ago—and I guess it is. All the fights, and back-biting, the murderous feuds, and now hardly anybody remembers what they were all about. It seems to be some kind of profound comment on the world we live in, but I don't know what it means.

Anyway, I hope I hear from you again, and if Vic Smith is still around tell him I'd like to subscribe to the *Argus.* I would subscribe to the *Daily News,* your paper, except that it's the old-fashioned country stuff I'm really interested in.

Always all my personal best,

Sincerely yours,

T/TL/C

Jones and Mitchell kept in touch. Mitchell wrote that two days before Josephine Herbst's death she said to her doctor: "Tell my friends I do not repent."

TO BURROUGHS MITCHELL

10, QUAI D'ORLÉANS, PARIS
APRIL 22, 1969

Dear Mitch,

I was sorry to hear about Josie Herbst dying. She was a great girl and I always loved her. Her remark to her doctor is characteristically marvelous of her.

The copies of *The Thin Red Line* arrived safely.[1]

Mainly, I am writing about *From Here to Eternity* in the French edition. I would like to have any information Scribner's can give me about whether or not the Presse de la Cité edition is still in print and being sold; also I would like a copy of the contract between Scribner's Foreign Department and Presse de la Cité concerning *Eternity*. Privately, and just between us two so that I hope you won't mention this anywhere, my new publisher wants very badly to get the rights to *Eternity*, so that he can do a new translation and bring out an entirely new edition of it. He says it is badly translated, and in addition that it was cut badly enough to damage the book. He would like to do a better newer translation and leave everything in. Any information you can give me about whether or not and how I can get those rights back from Presse de la Cité would be most appreciated.[2]

Gloria joins me in sending our love. We were at a dinner the other night for Ken MacCormick of Doubleday, whom I took a great liking to, and who promised he would give you our best

[1] Jones had ordered a dozen copies of his novel.
[2] A new French translation was not published.

at your next editorial dinner. I understand Gloria put on quite a show for him, by talking to Janet Flanner[3] about how strange it must be for lesbians to go down on each other. Janet Flanner apparently totally agreed.

Always all best.

Yours,

T/TL/C

---

[3] *The New Yorker*'s Paris correspondent.

Jones's second novel for Delacorte was The Merry Month of May, *set in Paris during the student rebellion and riots of 1968. The novel received a large number of unfavorable reviews.*

Irwin Shaw invited the Joneses to join him in Madrid in October for Luis Dominguin's comeback in the ring.

TO IRWIN SHAW

10, QUAI D'ORLÉANS, PARIS
SEPTEMBER 23, 1970

Dear Irwin,

That is a mighty enticing offer, but I don't see just how we can do it at this time. We are only just back a week and I'm still up to my ears in summer correspondence. In spite of that I've already started in work on a new version of the novel I put aside[1] to do the one about the May Revolution. I guess I've had my vacation during the summer, though it doesn't seem like one, anyway my Protestant guilts are telling me it's time to get back to work.

I too thought *Rich Man, Poor Man* was coming out the 17th. That was the last I heard. Ross gave us one of the first copies of it and we both read it on the ship coming back. Both of us liked it a great deal. Incidentally, I'm enclosing a copy of a comment on it which I've just sent off to Ross Claiborne.[2]

In any case I guess we'll see you here in Paris. I wouldn't worry too much about the reviews. Fuck them. I suppose you already know that we fell into the shithouse and came up with some luck. BOM is taking *May* as an alternate. Also *Esquire* is printing 34,000 words of it in their January issue December 15. Willie Morris is printing another 35,000 words in *Harper's*

---

[1]*A Touch of Danger* began as a script for a film, but after it was not produced, Jones reworked the script into a novel.
[2]Jones's editor at Delacorte.

in either his February or March issue. I'm hoping all this might give it somewhat of a send-off. Certainly none of this would have happened if we had not been back there this summer. It's a sorry comment on our Race that while everybody including reviewers have their integrity, they have more integrity for you if they get to know you and like you.

Gloria joins me in sending all our love. Say hello to Bodie.[3]

Yours,

James Jones

T/TL/C

---

[3]Bodil Nielsen, Shaw's companion.

Helen Meyer, president of Dell Publishing Company, sent Jones a packet of reviews of The Merry Month of May.

TO HELEN MEYER

10, QUAI D'ORLÉANS, PARIS

MARCH 19, 1971

Dear Helen,

. . . .

There surely must be something about me that just naturally rubs reviewers the wrong way. Well. It is interesting to note that Hemingway, who was head-kicked, ball-kicked and rib-kicked by almost all the reviewers who could reach him has now drifted quietly over into being the monolithic symbol by which these same reviewers now try to measure everybody else. I don't fully understand the process, but I think it must have something to do with the inability of these people to relate any new book to the entire growth and body of a man's whole work.

In any case, I simply do not believe that reviews of a book taken as a whole make or break the book. At best, they can only hurt it a little or help it a fair amount. And I am personally of the opinion that, whatever else irate critics or anyone else may say about it, true or false, this book is so readable that it will continue to grow in readership in the coming months.

There was a slightly encouraging note among the stuff that Ross sent, in that *May* has been picked for the Doubleday Book Shop best seller list of March 4. I really think if we just keep plugging away, and pushing it, it will continue to move up.[1]

. . . .

Yours,

T/TL/C

[1]Many reviewers attacked *The Merry Month of May.* The review in *Newsweek* (February 15, 1971) was typical: "Jones writes so badly that his offenses

TO JEFF JONES

10, QUAI D'ORLÉANS, PARIS
JUNE 22, 1971

Dear Jeff,

I'm sorry not to have gotten to your letter sooner. But I am back hard at work, as usual, this time on the book[1] I laid aside to do *The Merry Month of May*. I had about 270 pages done on it when I quit to do the other, and now am starting it over with a whole new approach; working from the old drafts. That is always very slow, and I hate it. But the new approach is a very good one—garnered from my re-reading the whole of Conrad two winters ago when I was in the stretch with *May*. I would explain it to you, it has to do with the approach used in the "Marlowe" books, but I haven't got time here, trying as I am to get things squared away before we leave on July 1 for Greece. We'll be staying a month on one of the Greek islands (Spetsai), and I've rented a 35-foot sailing boat for the month. This ought to be great fun but I never know any more. I hope it is.

. . . .

Yours,

T/TL/C

---

constitute as great a crime against nature as against literature. A book written this badly shouldn't be called a book. It should be called a reading instrument, or a money maker, or a thing." George Garrett in *James Jone* is more sympathetic: ". . . the realization of Paris as an exciting, *living* force in the novel is extraordinary and shows another dimension of Jones's sensibility."
[1]*A Touch of Danger.*

Jones attended a conference at Blérancourt, where he met again the scholar R. W. Stallman.

TO R. W. STALLMAN

10, QUAI D'ORLÉANS, PARIS
JANUARY 19, 1972

Dear Robert,

This may seem to be a long time to be answering your kind letter of February 14, 1971, and it is hardly more than a quick note written in haste. But I wanted simply to write to you and tell you that I do think of you. I too remember with a lot of fondness those days at Blérancourt. In re of which you might be amused to know that our handsome friend of that period, John Aldridge, gave *The Merry Month of May*—and my career—a hell of a shellacking in *The Saturday Review* of some time last year.[1]

I still stubbornly continue to think of *The Merry Month of May* as quite a good book. It may interest you to know that it was written deliberately in the genre of *The Sun Also Rises* and *The Great Gatsby*, a deliberate attempt to try to use the virtues of that form and update it. Some literary historian may some day rub his hands together over that fact.

. . . .

Sincerely,

T/TL/C

---

[1]Aldridge's review appeared in *The Saturday Review* (February 13, 1971).

Yevgeny Yevtushenko (Evgeny) and Jones met when Yevtu-shenko was on a reading tour in the United States. Jones did not visit the Soviet Union.

TO YEVGENY YEVTUSHENKO

10, QUAI D'ORLÉANS
PARIS 4°
MARCH 21, 1972

Dear Evgeny,

I feel I may call you that after our great evening together in New York. I was very interested in what you told me about the publication of *From Here to Eternity* in Russian. Also about the royalties that have accrued there for me! (You said "enough to live on for four months"). I certainly am not planning any trip there soon, not in this year. But maybe next year we could plan to come and see your great country.

I was also very interested in your desire to have all my other works to take back with you. To that end I have asked my publisher to accumulate all of these and have them delivered to you at the Doubleday address you gave me. Naturally, I hope others of my books will be translated and published in your country.

I am sending a copy of this letter to your Doubleday address, on the chance it might reach you before you leave America. The original is being sent to Moscow.

I hope our encounter will be the beginning of a fruitful correspondence. And friendship. Certainly knowing you, and having you at the other end to facilitate matters, is a big induce-ment for me to think about coming to Russia.

Again, I enjoyed our evening very much, particularly your

comments on English language poetry and those English language poets which are popular in Russia. Bill and Rose Styron asked me to send you their best. My wife joins me in sending you our personal best wishes.

Sincerely,

T/TL/C

Switching editors was difficult for Jones, but he made efforts to work with Don Fine and then Ross Claiborne, who was also at Delacorte. Jones was writing a mystery, A Touch of Danger, *which began as a script and was not part of his contractual agreement with his new publisher.*

TO ROSS CLAIBORNE

10, QUAI D'ORLÉANS, PARIS
MARCH 21, 1972

Dear Ross,

I am writing mainly to remind you about my request to send copies of all my works to Evtushenko in care of Doubleday at 277 Park Avenue. That last afternoon we talked was pretty hectic because of all the things I had to finish up. You remember I said I did not want an abridged paperback copy of *Some Came Running* to go to Evtushenko, and asked you to try and secure one of the original edition. You said you would try to get one, but I'm wondering if you were able. If you were not, please let me know right away and I'll send one to Doubleday from here as I still have about twenty of the first edition left. Other good news is that after meeting with Frankenheimer here, E. Lewis-J. Frankenheimer Productions has agreed to postpone setting up production on the mystery film [*A Touch of Danger*] until spring or early summer of 1973. This will thus give me time to finish the novel and get it in your hands for something like the proper period of exploitation. I expect to have it finished by the 1st of September. As of today I have finished and copied up final draft chapters 9, 10, and 11, a total of 35 pages; and as yet I have not quite gotten into full stride. Bill and Rose Styron have been here for ten days, and that has hampered me somewhat. They are gone now and I am moving into a higher gear.

But the postponement of the EL-JF PROD film production

has raised rather forcefully another problem. Naturally, Lewis is less positive of getting the initial monies, now, when the shooting date is postponed almost a year. Production money people do not like to lay out large sums that far ahead because of interest payments mounting. As a result, I will probably soon be facing a cash flow shortage which I expected to be covered by the EL-JF PROD initial payment.[1] As a result of that, I want to ask you and Helen [Meyer] to think about the possibility of making me an advance on this novel some time between now and, say, the middle of June. I will be writing Helen about this also.

I have been giving serious thought to the "personality cult" business which we talked about at our last meeting. With this film and book in the forefront for the next year, I don't know how much I can do about it in the coming year. But I am still fiddling and writing letters to various academic friends about spending that year at a university. I am toying with them for a lecture and making notes on it, one which could be used on a kind of lecture tour we talked about. Could you and Helen get me more detailed information through your sources about what such a lecture tour would entail and how much it would pay?

I enjoyed the time we spent together although it wasn't much, and although I fear I caused you some distress over the prospect of me writing a "mystery story." We never seem to be there long enough, when we come. Perhaps next time we will be able to stay longer. I enjoyed seeing Ellis.[2] I think he had a good time at Cecile's[3] party. Please give him my best. Gloria joins me in sending our best to you.

Sincerely,

T/TL/C

---

[1]The film of *A Touch of Danger* was not made.
[2]Ellis Amburn, an editor at Delacorte.
[3]Cecile Gray Bazelon, the painter, a close friend of the Joneses.

TO MICKEY KNOX

10, QUAI D'ORLÉANS, PARIS
APRIL 24, 1972

Dear Mick,

It was pleasant to get your letter from Budapest. Styron was here with Rose for a few days, then came back and spent a few days after Rose returned to America. We had some pleasant talks, but like with most other people of literary bent whom I know, we seem to be moving apart in slightly different directions, largely due to the fact that our lives through our wives and children and various other commitments tend to have less common rubbing space than when we were younger.

I saw Norman that same evening while we were in New York and as usual he managed to wind up attacking me with some totally gratuitous insult or other. This time he was charging me with being a George Wallace advocate. My being a WASP seems to be about the only thing left that Norman the Yid can honestly attack me for. Certainly he couldn't attack me for my writing, not if he ever looked at his own.

Anyway, I've had about a bellyful of all that shit over the years.

. . . .

Yours,

T/TL/C

Helen Meyer was not enthusiastic about A Touch of Danger *and offered fifty thousand dollars plus a twenty-five-thousand-dollar film bonus. Jones wanted more and rejected the Delacorte offer.*

TO HELEN MEYER

23.8.72

Dear Helen,

There was an awful delay in the delivery of your letter.

I have thought your letter over carefully, and I cannot accept it.

I am willing to admit I was perhaps a bit over-enthusiastic when I spoke to you by phone right after finishing, and asked too much, but the price you offer—$50,000.-, and a $25,000.- film bonus—isn't enough.

Let's get two things straight. One is literary merit, and the other is saleability. I think when you say "major novel" you really mean "big, long, naturalistic novel." Such as Jones is "noted for." I think you would be making a big mistake to present this book as a mystery novel, interesting only to "mystery" fans.

It is perfectly possible to write a book of high literary merit within the "mystery" form. This is what I have done, whether you can see it or not. Some of my best and most poetic prose to date is in it. Whether you can hear it or not. You were brutally frank, so I will be, too. I think you have "mystery" stuck on your brain like a rubber stamp, and can't see past it.

In any case, a "mystery novel" by Jim Jones is not a mystery novel by Joe Blow.

I am not saying we should try to sell this book as a "major novel." We should not. But we should not offer it simply as a "mystery." That will pigeonhole it, and kill it, for any wider audience. Call it a "thriller," a "murder story," call it a "departure," a "diversion," call it any other euphemism you prefer and come up with; but leave the door open for it to be evaluated on another level by those reviewers who wish to do so. Leave it open to be evaluated on another level by the really large readership you know I have.

I am not talking about the book's value now, but how to sell it. It should have a modest launching, and a modest price. I don't want a huge launching. The only thing that bothers me is that you may not be able to reprint fast enough if it should take off. But it shouldn't be a huge bally-hoo printing. The other thing that bothers me is a lack of faith on the part of the editorial dept., a lack of imagination.

As to what it really is as a novel, it's a symbolic novel couched in a "mystery" form. One big symbol of the crisis in ethics of America today. Because it's done in a tight, realistic style doesn't take away from the symbols, which are all there. It simply hides them more. But I don't want to try to sell it as that.

As to cutting, I agree it needs some cutting and am willing to cut it. But not so much it will hurt the literary merit. I think the cutting you will want is probably more than that. Any case, from about Ch. 9 to Ch. 19, it can stand some pruning—which I am doing and will send you when I am back in Paris.

But as to price I think we must talk more in the neighborhood of $125,000.-,—with a $25,000.- film bonus, "if you want to throw me that bone."

I don't think you understand what's a major book, Helen. It doesn't have to be 500,000 words.

Glory joins me in sending our love.

Yours,
Jim [1]

T/ALS

[1]The text reproduced here is a draft, and Jones may have made minor changes in the final version.

Lee Barker of Doubleday offered $250,000 for A Touch of Danger, *and Jones obtained a release from Delacorte. George Garrett, Jones's most appreciative critic, wrote of that novel: "As entertainment, as a genre piece, it holds up with the best of them and proves (if it needed proving) that Jones had the craft and the capacity to write economically and well within the strict limits of the thriller, that he was a more versatile writer than at least some of the critics had imagined."*

TO LEE BARKER

10, QUAI D'ORLÉANS, PARIS
OCTOBER 16, 1972

Dear Lee,

Under separate cover post haste I am sending the manuscript which you read as revised by me, using your various suggestions.

First, I have changed the name of Jacques to Girgis throughout. Not only you, but Bob Knittel[1] and others have commented adversely on the use of the French name Jacques. Girgis was the name Knittel suggested.

I have changed the name Tsatsos to Phalena (Greek for whale) throughout. I did this mainly because it turns out Tsatsos is a family name which belongs to a current Greek minister, as I found out this summer; but Dell and others have commented on the name adversely because of its being a tongue-twister. Now my wife tells me she likes Tsatsos better.[2]

. . . .

Sincerely,

T/TL/C

---

[1]Robert Knittel was Jones's editor at Collins.
[2]Tsatsos was not changed to Phalena in the published version.

Jones collected knives for many years, and his war fiction makes effective use of knives and stabbings. His assignment from The New York Times *to cover the last days of the war in Vietnam possibly spurred Jones on to attempt to acquire a Bowie No. 11 from Robert Abels, who sold fine knives.*

TO ROBERT ABELS

10, QUAI D'ORLÉANS, PARIS
FEBRUARY 1, 1973

Dear Bob,

I am hoping you will remember me by name. In any case I am the novelist, the author of *From Here to Eternity,* who last year bought your Bowie engraved THE HUNTERS KNIFE, while I was in the shop with a white-bearded painter called Paul Jenkins. At that time you gave me the name and address of D. E. Henry, with whom I have since been in correspondence and from whom I have ordered a knife. The one he calls "Old Grizzly." I just had a letter from him and in it he mentioned that you have closed up the New York shop and moved out to Hopewell Junction. You told me at the time that you were going to do that. You may remember at the time I asked you about a particular knife I wanted badly and it turned out to be the N° 11 pictured in your new edition of your Bowie collection. Now Ed Henry tells me you are selling some of the knives from the collection and I am wondering if you are selling the N° 11. And if not, I am wondering if you would sell it to me privately anyway. You may not remember but I was in your basement shop on Lexington with that same Paul Jenkins the day after you received the N° 11 knife from somewhere in Wisconsin or Minnesota. At that time I offered you the first edition manuscript copy, the only manuscript of my book *The Pistol,* in exchange for it. I remember you said that was nice, but that you were not a book collector. I still think you made a mistake. On the other hand, I still would very much like to have that N° ɪɪ.

Right now I am on my way to Vietnam for *The New York Times*. To do a series of articles for the *New York Times Magazine* on the end of the war. I should be back in three weeks or a month. May I hope to hear from you by then? I am hoping desperately you have not already sold the N° ɪɪ knife to someone else. With all personal best wishes.

Sincerely yours,

T/TL/C

After their marriage, James and Gloria Jones were almost never apart. The only letters of his to her were written when he was in Vietnam early in 1973. The following "farewell" letter was not mailed but kept in his personal papers.

TO GLORIA JONES

SAIGON
MARCH 4, 1973
1:00AM

Dear Moss,

You will only get this if something bad has happened to me. There isn't much chance of it. About 10,000,000 to one. But it is possible.

. . . .

I feel sort of silly even writing this. I've always loved you an awful lot. More than I've ever loved anything or anybody. Maybe my work I've loved as much. I could never have loved anybody else, under any circumstances. Well, so long.

I feel stupid. It's only in case of some accident. I'm not expecting any, and then you will never see this.

I love you all, you, Kaylie, Jamie.

Yours,
Jim

T/TLS

Henry Hyde, Jones's New York attorney, was concerned about the financial problems of his client, but Jones was optimistic, in this love letter, about the future of the Joneses.

TO GLORIA JONES

[PLEIKU-KONTUM, VIETNAM]
MARCH 7, 1973

My Dearest Darling

I just got your 1st ltr. Been carrying your wire in my wallet. The ltr was so great. You wrote it bfr you called Henry I think.

Don't worry about Henry. Or our situation. I'm so full of love for you I can do anything. I got us out of a bad thing once. I'll do it again.

I'm in Pleiku-Kontum. There has been a lot of fighting over the road btwn Pleiku & Kontum. The VC keep trying to cut it. It's the only rd we have into Kontum. Supplies to Army & civil. have to be flown in, mostly helicopter. But a lot of convoys get thru.

They flew me to Kontum several times by 'copter. I stayed last nite at the Bishop's "Palace." There is an Amer. Vol. Hosp. rt next door for sick & wounded Montagnards. Mostly sick. Main problem is enuf rice. Could hear firing all nite. No danger. VC won't attack Kontum now, with cease-fire. But the r'd w'd be dangerous.

Tomorrow I fly to Nha Trang near sea. A day there. Then Hué & Danang. Then back to Saigon. Then a trip down into Delta & I'm done. Another week or ten days.

. . . .

I think Henry is being very gloomy. He did not know H. [Helen] Meyer had written me suggesting book on Vietnam.

He doesn't know Lee B.'s [Barker's] strategy is to wait till publicity comes out, to sell paperback. Any case, if it is bad we'll be able to handle it. Long as we're together. Your love letter was a great boost. Don't think it was "silly."

I have to go—apt to meet missionaries in a leprosarium in Pleiku.

I love you forever. You're so lovely, inside & out. I long to kiss you. Everywhere.

Your Own,
Jim

T/ALS

TO GLORIA JONES

[VIETNAM]
MARCH 8, 1973

My Darling—

Wrote nite bfr last. But gave it to Chaplain, who marked it "FREE" instead of putting on stamps, so am afraid it won't reach you & am writing again.

Hope it gets to you, because it had a mood. Wrote it rite after staying o/nite in surrounded Kontum at Cath. Bishop's residence, listening to out-going artillery & small arms fire, with flares going up now & then. No danger. VC won't attack it now with cease-fire. But they cut the road in with fire now & then. Convoys can't go so 'copters supply it. I went in in a US one.

Mainly I wrote you how I loved your love letter. Don't you think it "silly." I've read it I guess 50 times by now.

I wrote you not to worry. . . . I got us out of a tough spot last year. . . .

You & I will beat them all.

But mostly I wrote how much I adore you. I've never loved anything as much as you. Maybe my work.

  . . . .

Don't worry. Just love me.

  . . . .

All my everything,
Your
Jim

T/ALS

TO GLORIA JONES

[VIETNAM]
MARCH 15, 1973

My Darling Love,

  So much to tell. So little space. I'm back in Pleiku after 6 days in Da Nang, Hué & Quang Tri. Will prob. spend a day or 2 more here, then back to Saigon, 3 days in Delta.

  I wasn't so homesick for you over there. I think coming back here reminded me of how I missed you here before. It was very painful.

  . . . .

  I'm so worried about the damned money now. You said "OUR SITUATION SERIOUS" in your wire. From you that's a lot.

  Well, don't worry. I'll whip them yet. Some way. . . .

  All my love to all of you from all of me.

Your
Jim

T/ALS

Jones had an affinity for soldiers and did not wish to undermine them during the Vietnam conflict, which he wrote about in Viet Journal, *published in 1974. Many of Jones's friends were opposed to the war and chided Jones for his independent views. Maria Jolas, who had been a friend of James Joyce and who with her husband had published* transition, *took Jones to task for his Vietnam views.*

TO MARIA JOLAS

10, QUAI D'ORLÉANS, PARIS
MAY 17, 1973

Dear Maria,

I let myself cool off a couple of days before answering your letter. Your nasty insinuations about me being pro-Thieu are only a little more objectionable than your self-righteousness and constant assumption of moral superiority. Just for the record I will state to you again, as I have many times before, that I am not pro-Thieu, not pro-war. Not pro-political prisoners, not pro-political oppression, not pro-torture. And I am not pro any of these last four whether they are done by North Vietnam, South Vietnam, the US, China or Russia. Neither am I pro-Pham Van Dong, nor the North Vietnam Central Committee, nor pro the Provisional Revolutionary Government of South Vietnam. I was never pro-My Lai, nor was I pro the North Vietnamese Hué massacres in TET of 1968. Your attitude of "you must be for us, or you are against us" smacks to me of a totalitarian way of thinking which I dislike wherever.

Since you seem to want to make a historical record out of your letter, let me add to it that while Gloria signed petitions against the war, and "marched" on the Embassy against the war, and is still free to do so whenever she wishes, I myself did not feel free to do such things until I was assured of the existence of such petitions and such marches on the part of

North Vietnamese citizens against the North Vietnamese Embassy also. With regard to Dan Berrigan, it did not seem to me that he was either unhappy or uncomfortable in my house. You are insinuating when you say that after a "decent interval," "you and Dan" left. Berrigan came to my house partly to meet Tito Gerassi, and I understand from Tito that he and Berrigan went off and got loaded together after.[1] I don't think either of them left my place until at least two o'clock. That is not your insinuating "decent interval."

. . . .

I had intended to go into your other insinuations, about my coming to your meeting as some sort of spy, but I guess I had better not go into that. I'm beginning to get irritated again. If I don't watch out, I'll become as morally self-righteous as you are. And I don't like to do that.

Sincerely yours,

T/TL/C

[1]Father Daniel J. Berrigan was an antiwar activist. John Gerassi wrote a biography of Fidel Castro and other books such as *Towards Revolution* and *The Coming of the New International.*

Jones covered the last days of the war in Vietnam for The New York Times Magazine *during the spring of 1973 and published his* Viet Journal *the following year.*

On his way home from Vietnam, Jones stopped in Hawaii for his first visit since wartime days. That visit is memorialized in the final chapter of Viet Journal, *"Hawaiian Recall," one of the most evocative sections of that work. While he was in Hawaii, he met again one friend of those earlier days, Tsuneko Ogure (later known in her journalistic work as Scoops Kreger), who appeared as Violet Ogure in* Eternity.

TO SCOOPS KREGER

10, QUAI D'ORLÉANS, PARIS
JULY 3, 1973

Dear Scoops,

—I really do find I dislike that nickname intensely, so if you don't mind I am going to go back to calling you Tsuneko. I have been working so hard on these articles for the *Times* that I haven't had a chance to answer your note. But now they're all finished, the Hawaiian piece having gone off to them a week ago. I don't really know what they will think of it, since it is not a reportorial piece at all.

The ring arrived in fine shape, and you can tell the people at the University that I am wearing it right now, if they are interested. . . .

It was a strange experience coming back to Hawaii, and seeing you again added a whole other dimension to it. I am glad we were able to get together. All my best to you always.

Yours,

T/TL/C

Jones often responded to fan letters, especially when the comments in those letters were preceptive or provocative.

TO R. STANLEY HEGGE

IO, QUAI D'ORLÉANS, PARIS

JULY 14, 1973

Dear Mr. Hegge,

. . . .

I found your comments about *Eternity* and *Line* very interesting. Certainly they are very complimentary, and I thank you.

You are one of the few people who has caught the hidden connection—i.e., Warden becoming Welsh; Prewitt becoming Witt. In fact, both do survive at least the combat part of the War. Both will be re-appearing again in still another book, entitled *Whistle*. This is a book I have been working at for some five years, off and on. Warden/Welsh will become 1st Sgt. Martin Winch; Prewitt/Witt becoming a Private named Bobby Prell.[1] The book is about the same group of men, returning to the United States wounded, sick or damaged to find themselves at sea in an affluent war-time society. This is a project I am addressing myself to next, and I hope to have it finished in a year or so.

Thank you for calling my attention to the Jack Coggins book.[2] I am sending in an order for it.

Always all my personal best wishes.

Sincerely,

T/TL/C

---

[1] Jones in "A Note by the Author" in *Whistle* made these identifications for all his readers of his war trilogy.

[2] *The Campaign for Guadalcanal* (Doubleday, 1972).

Jones met General Healy in Vietnam and found him an impressive man. He wanted to make certain that the facts in Viet Journal *were correct and asked Healy to give the manuscript a professional reading. Jones was also helping Healy's son, an aspiring writer.*

TO BRIGADIER GENERAL MICHAEL D. HEALY

10, QUAI D'ORLÉANS, PARIS
OCTOBER 5, 1973

Dear Mike,

I guess you have heard from young Mike or seen him since he left here. By now. I should have written sooner, but I have been so wrapped up in this damn book that I didn't get around to it. When young Mike was here, I was just at the point of starting to write about our Dak Pek trip. And I finished up that sequence yesterday. Unfortunately Michael didn't get to read it, because he badly wanted to.

After his rights at the Youth Hostel ran out, he came and stayed with us for four or five days. Unfortunately we don't have much of a guest room, but he seemed happy enough in it. I let him read the entire manuscript of *Viet Journal,* which he was very eager to read, particularly I think the parts about you, and which he seemed to like a great deal. He had talked a good deal about wanting to go out to Vietnam himself, just to nose around, talk to people about you, etc., and after he read my book he said he thought he might not have to go, now. He is very protective of you, by the way, and seemed secretly a little worried that I might be trying to cut you down. I explained to him that my problems with you as a character were not so much how to build you up, but to keep myself and the book from <u>over</u>-heroizing you. This suited him fine, I guess.

He's really quite a boy, Mike, I think. His head is screwed on right, despite the semi-hippy exterior, and we talked about that some, too. He understood right away—in fact, had pretty much figured it out himself—that the counter-culture style in itself is equally as inhibiting a set of attitudes as the Establishment suit and tie. He appears to have just about worked his way through the whole counter-culture syndrome. He is highly intelligent and very sensitive. I think he could really make a good writer, but I warned him it was a lot of hard work and not just emotional fun-and-games playing.

He seems to have an excellent idea working on this book about his grandfather. The only way he can find out if he has it as a writer is to go and have a shot at it. He wants to go out to Chicago, to soak up the material, and I think you should help him. Apparently a little money is a factor. I have always had a saying that I found it peculiar that parents were willing to shell out for seven years or eight for a kid to become a doctor; but they weren't willing to shell out for the same period of time for a kid to become a writer. And it takes at least as long to become a writer as it does a doctor. I mentioned this to him, and he said I ought to tell you. So . . . I'm telling. I told him, and tell you, too, that I'll be glad to read and comment for him on anything he wants to send me on the Chicago stuff. But I warned him I wouldn't pull any punches and might be pretty hard. He said that was fine.

Actually, I have worked with a lot of young writers over the years. And having been one, I know pretty much their problems. It's a lonely business at best. One of the biggest of the problems is learning how to structure a novel, or a book, so that it has a comprehensible form, and at the same time has the kind of off-beat balance which keeps readers wanting to read more. Suspense, it is sometimes called inaccurately. Anyway, I liked him a lot, and I'll be glad to help him any way I can.

Mike, I might like to ask you to read through this manuscript for me, if you wouldn't mind. Mainly for technical inaccuracies about the Army out there. (For example, I do not know if the plane which was shoved off the Kontum runway and taken over as a home by Montagnards was a C147. Things like that.) I don't have at my finger tips all the nomenclatures and structures and tables of organization for this "new" Army like I had for our Army in World War II. Of course, you'll be reading somewhat about yourself, and that may embarrass you. But if you think of it as a book about other people, as I have to make myself do, you can avoid that. Anyway, I am planning to have several [X]erox copies made of the manuscript as soon as I finish it. Part of the problem is that I must get it in as soon as possible so that it can be brought out next spring. As it is, I'm already running five days over my deadline.

But, with the finishing of the Dak Pek sequence, I can go back to stuff already written for the *Times* (and not used) without having to write much more new stuff. I should be able to finish in ten days or two weeks.

Always all my personal best.

Sincerely,

t/tl/c

Jones believed that the expurgated paper editions of Some Came Running *gave readers a false impression of that novel. When he learned that Avon Books was bringing out editions of his first three long novels, he immediately wrote to Robert Wyatt.*

TO ROBERT WYATT

10, QUAI D'ORLEANS, PARIS
OCTOBER 15, 1973

Dear Mr. Wyatt,

I got your name and address from Burroughs Mitchell of Scribner's. I thought it might be worthwhile to get in touch with you about the forthcoming republication of *From Here to Eternity, Some Came Running,* and *The Thin Red Line*—the rights to which I understand Avon has now acquired.

One of the provisos, insisted on by me, was that *Some Came Running* be published in its entirety, and not in an expurgated edition as was done by New [American] Library many years ago. This is a long, sad, perhaps uninteresting tale. The crux of it was that they did not have the technological means then to produce in one volume a book as large as *Some Came Running.* This only came later, and was first used I think for *The Rise and Fall of the Third Reich.* By that time *Some Came Running* was already in print. I have been hoping ever since to get the rights back in order to bring out a true edition of the book.

I have always felt that the intent and meaning of *Running* was seriously damaged by the cutting job done on it by NAL. Particularly I felt this about the exclusion of the end of 'Bama Dillert's story.

When I learned from Scribner's that Avon had purchased the rights it occurred to me that it might be a good idea for me to write a foreword or a preface to the new edition for you. I think if the book were properly handled, in bringing out a new, unabridged edition, it might have a big resurgence in paperback.[1] It has been a much maligned book, by critics and reviewers, and only lately amongst college English teachers and students who write to me has there been a resurgence of interest and liking for the book. I personally feel that, all things considered, it is perhaps the best single novel I have written.

In any case, may I expect to hear from you your ideas about this matter?

Sincerely yours,

T/TL/C

---

[1]Avon did not republish an unexpurgated edition of *Some Came Running.*

After living in Paris for many years, James and Gloria Jones decided it was time to return to the United States, and Jones made contacts with several writers in his quest for a writer-in-residence position at a college or university.

TO JACK CADY

10, QUAI D'ORLÉANS, PARIS
OCTOBER 15, 1973

Dear Jack,

I did not expect such fast and enormous action. Thank you.

I am unsure as to just how to proceed with these matters, never having tried to do this sort of thing before.

Should I expect to get letters from the seven people whom you wrote? Or, am I expected to write to them myself?

I would have answered sooner, but I have been killing myself to finish this *Viet Journal* book of mine. It was finished up yesterday, and went off to New York this morning. I feel very very pleased about it. I think even the form itself is an innovation itself, in a way. It is also, in effect, an appeal to Americans to stop hating ourselves so much. We have plenty of friends in the world who can do that for us. Strangely enough, in spite of everything, or perhaps because of it, America is really where things are happening today. More so than anywhere else in the world, I think. And not just because of the kids. But we are threatening to deball ourselves with this mea culpa holdover from our ancient puritanism we thought we had got rid of. All this is one of the main reasons that I want to come home.

I know next to nothing about how to go about getting these various jobs. I don't even have any idea about how much I should ask for a year. A lot of course depends on the size of the school and how much they can budget. One would not expect as much from a small school, say, as from a large, rich one.

. . . .

If you can be of help to me in this university thing, I would certainly appreciate it. Actually, the University of Montana at Missoula is the place I had picked in my mind as the perfect place for what I want. That of course does not mean it will work out. In any case, can you let me know whether I should write to these people myself, or wait until I hear from them.

. . . .

Yours,

T/TL/C

TO SCOOPS KREGER

10, QUAI D'ORLÉANS, PARIS

DECEMBER 5, 1973

Dear Tsunie,

I'm sorry not to have answered sooner. I've been hard at work getting my Vietnam book finished up, and getting started into another novel. Enclosed you'll find my check for $69.00 for the U of H[1] ring. I wear it most of the time around here, and the stone gets quite a bit of comment. The whole idea tickles hell out of me. I know it's one of my private little jokes, but I have a lot of fun out of it.

. . . .

It appears that next year I may be coming back to the States as writer-in-residence at some university or other, for at least a year. Hopefully, this will be somewhere in the West, in the Rockies. I have a couple of modern novels about the West that I want to write and need to live there again for some background. Also I'm getting a little homesick for America over

[1]University of Hawaii.

here. After all these years I must say I have never learned to really like the French.

I don't think you ought to be so blue about being broke. And I can see that you're not. You've got two fine sons, and you've had a pretty damned good life there in Hawaii, so you're probably ahead of the game. I must say I enjoyed immensely coming back there, even though for so short a time. It's strange how a place like that where you've spent a couple of years in your youth can have such a long-lasting effect on your memory and emotion.

. . . .

Yours,

T/TL/C

Viet Journal *received excellent reviews;* Time, *which had often scorned Jones's work, wrote: "With a large talent for observation and characterization he is able to separate individuals from the moral horrors of the war. . . . He has a nose for those human quirks that override ideology."*

As Jones prepared to return to the United States, he reestablished contacts with old friends and acquaintances, including Dr. Frank H. McCloskey, who had been his writing instructor at New York University.

TO DR. FRANK H. MCCLOSKEY

10, QUAI D'ORLÉANS, PARIS
MAY 16, 1974

Dear Frank,

It was good to get your letter. Those old days at NYU seem so far away, for me, that it seems it must have been a different person who experienced them.

You may have garnered from my *Today* show interview, or from that piece in the various papers, that I'm going to be teaching myself this coming year. I'll be a sort of Writer-in-Residence at Florida International University in Miami. I'm looking forward to it a lot. For one thing, I feel more and more that it's about time I came home. At 53 you begin to hunger a little for home ground. And a writer moving into an American community is essentially outside of everything. I think being a teacher for a while is an excellent way for me to move back and become a genuine part of a community where I move. Actually, I lived in Florida quite a lot in my life, and I found a lot of memories coming back I had forgotten I had.

Meanwhile I am working my ass off on a big novel which will make a trilogy about World War II when put together with *From Here to Eternity* and *The Thin Red Line.* I flatter myself that the three together may well be an important work of the English language. If I can maintain the level of excellence I have achieved so far in *Whistle* (which is the third volume) it will be better even than either of the other two. And they are both good books.

In any case. My address in Florida will be 251 Island Drive, Key Biscayne, Florida. I expect to be there from September 1st. Most of this summer we will be in East Hampton and Martha's Vineyard visiting friends. Always all personal best. Gloria sends you her best also.

Yours,

T/TL/C

The Final Years,

1974-1977

Jones spent the 1974–1975 academic year as writer-in-residence at Florida International University in Miami. His writing workshops were highly successful, but because of financial problems at the university, it was not possible for him to stay the second year.

In addition to his teaching duties, Jones worked on a nonfiction book, WW II. *Arthur Weithas, formerly art editor of* Yank, *had approached Grosset & Dunlap about preparing a book on the art that came out of World War II. The publisher then approached Jones about his interest in writing the text, and Jones agreed to do it.*

The WW II *book contained some of Jones's best prose, and Weithas's selection of illustrations was superb. Jones took part in a promotion campaign that took him across the country, from New York to California, with many stops in between. The book was also a critical success and buoyed his spirits as he returned to work on* Whistle.

During the summer of 1975, the Joneses lived in a rented house in Sagaponack on Long Island. From there he wrote to Steven Carter, who had recently completed a doctoral dissertation on Jones.

TO STEVEN CARTER

JULY 21, 1975

Dear Steve:

Yes, I did receive the copy of your dissertation.[1] I haven't reread the entire work, but I did reread the preface which you sent under separate cover. As far as the criticisms go, don't worry your head about them. I think that they are valid

[1] "James Jones: An American Master. A Study of His Mystical, Philosophical, Social, and Artistic Views" (Ph.D. thesis, Ohio State University, 1975).

enough. Actually, I can understand your second reader's qualms about a novelist structuring a work "around a philosophy he chooses to believe." And in fact, I have never deliberately, concisely structured any of my novels in that way. Instead, it is more as though I were trying to examine various philosophies in contradistinction to each other. As I told you in the beginning, I have never been able fully to espouse a religious philosophy that embraces reincarnation and various mystical ESP, largely because I have never had any personal experiences which I could point to as valid in any of these realms. Still, the idea of reincarnation has always intrigued me and interested me.

In the end, I think every worthwhile novelist depends first upon his vision—his subjective vision—of the world he sees, and only attempts slowly to find a philosophy somewhere which will coincide with his physical vision.

I simply haven't the time to get to the dissertation itself in its entirety. We're living here for the summer, in a fine place, but camping out, in effect, while I try to get on with the business of *Whistle*. The camping out makes it more difficult, and work on the galleys and page proofs and art proofs of the World War II book makes it more difficult and takes up a lot of time. It looks as though the World War II book may do very well. I hope it does.

Let me hear from you occasionally.

Yours,

T/TL/C

The Joneses liked Sagaponack and decided to settle there. They bought and remodeled a farmhouse, and Jones worked in his attic study. He wrote almost no letters during the last few years of his life. He was suffering from congestive heart failure, and he had little energy for correspondence. His social life was somewhat restricted because of his health, but he did spend time with his family and with selected friends. His main writing task, after the publication of WW II, *was the completion of his novel* Whistle, *the final volume of his war trilogy.*

Willie Morris in James Jones: A Friendship *has written the definitive account of Jones's struggle to complete that novel: the stays in the hospital for treatment; the return to the farmhouse in Sagaponack for intense work on the manuscript. Even after Jones was taken to the hospital for the final time, he went on dictating sections for the concluding chapters. Just a few days before his death on May 9, 1977, he recorded the final scene in the novel, the suicide of Strange. Strange (Stark in* Eternity, *transformed into Storm in* Line) *on a troopship sailing to Europe couldn't "stand being a witness again to all the anguish and mayhem and blood and suffering." He slipped over the side of the ship into the cold Atlantic water:*

> *And then as he's treading water with his woolen GI gloves, he can feel the cold beginning to swell his hands. And from this, in a sort of semihallucination, all of him begins to swell and he gets bigger and bigger . . . and swelling and swelling until he's bigger than the ocean, bigger than the planet, bigger than the solar system, bigger than the galaxy out in the universe.*
>
> *And as he swells and grows this picture of a fully clothed soldier with his helmet, his boots, and his GI woolen gloves seems to be taking into himself all the pain and anguish and sorrow and misery that is the lot of all soldiers, taking it into himself and into the universe as well.*
>
> *And then still in the hallucination he begins to shrink back to normal, and shrinks down through the other stages—the galaxy, the solar system, the planet, the ocean—back to Strange in the water. And then continues shrinking until he seems to be only the size of a seahorse, and then an amoeba, then finally an atom.*
>
> *He did not know whether he would drown first or freeze.*

Strange, as he came to eternity, had participated in the vastness and the minuteness of the universe. Jones the author, the controller of the narrative, himself was facing death. Jones had put aside many of the Eastern religious and philosophical beliefs of his earlier years, but he had not given up speculating on the enigmatic questions of life and death. The poetic passage is mysterious, as were the mystic passages of Emerson, Thoreau, and Whitman. The young soldier Jones when he learned of the death of his father went to the beach in Hawaii, where it "almost seems as if you can look right on into eternity." As Jones came to his own death, he dictated a poetic prose piece ending with human sensations as Strange faces eternity: "He did not know whether he would drown first or freeze." Jones went from here to eternity in that passage and returned here, if only briefly. He, too, had taken "into himself all the pain and anguish and sorrow and misery that is the lot of all soldiers" and that had been one of his major strengths as a writer.

PUBLICATIONS OF JAMES JONES

BOOKS

From Here to Eternity. New York: Charles Scribner's Sons, 1951; London: Collins, 1952.

Some Came Running. New York: Charles Scribner's Sons, 1957; London: Collins, 1959.

The Pistol. New York: Charles Scribner's Sons, 1959; London: Collins, 1959.

The Thin Red Line. New York: Charles Scribner's Sons, 1962; London: Collins, 1963.

Go to the Widow-Maker. New York: Delacorte Press, 1967; London: Collins, 1967.

The Ice-Cream Headache and Other Stories. New York: Delacorte Press, 1968; London: Collins, 1968.

The Merry Month of May. New York: Delacorte Press, 1971; London: Collins, 1971.

A Touch of Danger. New York: Doubleday and Company, 1973; London: Collins, 1973.

Viet Journal. New York: Delacorte Press, 1974.

WW II. New York: Grosset & Dunlap, 1975.

Whistle. New York: Delacorte Press, 1978; London: Collins, 1978.

SELECTED ARTICLES

"Marshall, Illinois," *Ford Times* (March 1957).

"Phony War Films," *Saturday Evening Post* (March 30, 1963).

"Flippers! Gin! Weight Belt! Gin! Faceplate! Gin!" *Esquire* (June 1963).

"Letter Home: Sons of Hemingway," *Esquire* (December 1963).

"Letter Home," *Esquire* (March 1964).

"Letter Home," *Esquire* (December 1964).

"Why They Invade the Sea," *New York Times Magazine* (March 14, 1965).

INDEX

Jones's letters, indicated by italicized page numbers, are indexed after the names of their recipients.

ABOUT THE EDITOR

GEORGE HENDRICK is Professor of English at the University of Illinois at Urbana-Champaign. His recent publications include *Remembrances of Concord and the Thoreaus, Toward the Making of Thoreau's Modern Reputation* (with Fritz Oehlschlaeger), *Ever the Winds of Chance* (with Margaret Sandburg), *The Selected Letters of Mark Van Doren, Katherine Anne Porter,* revised edition (with Willene Hendrick), and *Fables, Foibles and Foobles.*